HEAVEN ON WHEELS

HEAVEN ON WHEELS

FIRDAUS KANGA

BLOOMSBURY

First published 1991
Copyright © 1991 by Firdaus Kanga

The moral right of the author has been asserted.
Bloomsbury Publishing Ltd, 2 Soho Square, London W1V 5DE

A CIP catalogue record for this book is
available from the British Library.

ISBN 0 7475 0972 7

10 9 8 7 6 5 4 3 2 1

Typeset by Hewer Text Composition Services, Edinburgh
Printed in Great Britain by Butler & Tanner Limited, Frome and London

ACKNOWLEDGEMENTS

My deepest gratitude to:
Fali Pavri, for so much love and a huge generosity;
Jasmine Bharucha, my laughing fellow rover;
Paul Bailey for his kindness, always;
Matthew Evans, who thought of this book;
Liz Calder, who had the good taste to publish it;
Mary Tomlinson, who was with me from the start;
Frances Musker, for a warm welcome that never faltered;
Michael Thomas, my agent, for good conversation and good advice;
Aban Mistry, for her brave typing;
Alison Mansbridge, editor and now friend;
Firoza and Farrokh Irani, so loved that I can put them last.

The author would like to thank the Society of Authors for its support.

To Siloo and Jamshed Kanga
for the keys to heaven

Contents

Beginnings

The shoppers in the supermarket were trying their best not to look at me. That should have told me I was doing something very curious. But it was my first morning in Britain and I hadn't learned that the natives look least when they want to most; even when you are four feet short, whizzing around in a green and chrome wheelchair, trying to remember what goes where so you can empty your trolley back on the shelves and reduce your bill to pocket-size.

No one could blame me. And I couldn't blame the Russians any more. For coming to Bombay, where I lived, and buying not silver jewellery and sandalwood statues, but toothpaste and towels and deodorant that made you stink worse than if you weren't using any. Because here I was at Tesco's feeling what I was supposed to feel only at Harrods. That swoonlike pleasure in a pair of sandwiches which cost me the price of a roast chicken back in Bombay. Then there was the fantasy-rich mousse, the English Cheddar which I would have bought even if it had dropped its surname, and After Eight mints which, I was soon to discover, bore the mark of Cain since they had the bad taste to sell too well.

Talking of food, as it was I had flown into London over-weight. Not my bags or body, which weighed about the same – 44 pounds – but the suitcases of my imagination, which were packed with preconceptions, hearsay, literary memories,

BBC voices, tabloid shrieks, throated Thatcherisms, Boadicea, Bosworth, the Blitz, oranges and lemons, Oscar Wilde and Robbie Ross, *Pygmalion*, Royal Ascot, Abdication, Windsor Castle and the Food Hall at Selfridges.

My parents belonged to that generation of Indian Parsees which considered Independence a culinary disaster. Almost any conversation my mother had with her contemporaries turned within minutes to Quaker Oats, Bovril, Marmite, Anchor butter, Nestlé's chocolates and, when it all got too much, kaolin mixture.

The evening I left for London they came, my parents' friends, uncles and aunts, to see me off. 'Have Blue Bird toffees for me,' said someone. 'They're so sweet in tiny-tiny pails.'

'Silly!' said someone else. 'Those are Sharp toffees – the pails have a parrot outside.'

'Remember me,' quavered an old neighbour, 'when you eat Huntley and Palmer's biscuits – little puffy squares, quoosh! they go in your mouth.'

And I thought how ironic it was that this is what the Empire had meant to its most loyal subjects – something to salivate over.

For me, Britain was something better than the brand-names novel they had turned it into. Those overflowing suitcases contained all the words that had been the leavening in my life, allowing it to rise into a book that was going to be published the following year. I had never been to school or university except to be examined for symptoms of knowledge, and my real learning had been the books I had known. What I saw there was real to me, made more vivid by the fact that I knew no ruddy-cheeked boys who could pale my book-world with their high colour.

And though I would never watch the full moon without seeing it 'large and luminous' over Thornfield, I did not live there. I could not afford to. Having a body that does not work as well as other people's, I knew that unreality was a luxury that belonged to the walking world. If I were to make anything of myself, I had to see life with my eyes thrown open, everything as it is; not as it might have been.

And that included Britain. Tempted, as I was, to wander endlessly through the streets of Iris Murdoch's London or Jane Austen's Bath, I resisted by reading voraciously – everything the British Council Library had to offer – about the new Britain. The ferocious politics battling through the rage and pride of Thatcherism, single parents and gay rights, Paki-bashing, AIDS, the Big Bang in the City – out of all these I made another world for myself. Whenever elections were announced I read every line of every Party manifesto; when the votes were counted I knew all the marginal constituencies and how they might fall.

Inside me I had kept a universe spinning (metaphors, often gloriously mixed, were like little planks I used to bridge the spaces in my understanding), and now, by visiting Britain, I was taking the risk of seeing it vanish into the vastness of things real.

Even as I wheeled out of the aeroplane at Heathrow and heard a voice speaking that long-loved accent – for the first time not from the wireless or stage or screen – I felt a window breaking in my mind, a depressurisation that was beginning to suck those suitcases out of my head.

Growing up in Bombay, my life had been unusual, so that when I wrote my fictional autobiography I had to leave out the strangest parts simply because they would have made the story unreal.

Being born with brittle bones meant I could never walk, though for many years there was a tantalising hope that doctors abroad could do something with my legs when I turned into a teenager and the worst aspect of my genetic disease – frequent fractures – burnt itself out. And that meant I grew up waiting for a future, much as so many people of that other, older generation seemed to be waiting for the past of Raj and Empire.

We lived in a tiny flat with no room for a wheelchair – one of those middle-class families trapped in third-world irony. I went out, carried in loving arms to the cinema and to other loving arms, relatives and friends. But these were outings carefully planned, increasingly rationed as I grew older and heavier.

The boy on two beds, as I grew to think of myself, had many friends – most of them older girls who knew his sisters – and more books.

The friends provided the fun, the warmth, the ordinariness without which I might have grown into a hedgehog, prickly and frightened. One of the bizarre consequences of my disability is that people tell me things about themselves and about their lives that they would not say to anyone else. It has to do partly, I know, with the fact that I am physically small, unthreatening, someone who puts vulnerabilities to sleep. I loved the stories that came to me, and as my fascination and understanding grew I became an almost magical figure, someone to whom 'one could talk'.

But I was a lonely boy. The books I read told me about the life I was missing, the conversations I didn't have; and the more I read the more different my mind became from those of my friends, the more I longed for other people, people who thought in a different way.

For I had attracted more than my share of Indian superstition, of the stigma attached to being disabled and, as time went on, to being gay, something I kept a secret, even from myself, as long as I could.

It was little wonder, then, that I wanted another life. What was strange was that I believed I would achieve it. When the prospect was laughable, I planned an independent existence in the West; when I was studying law – good Parsee boys of my class became good solicitors – I dreamt of becoming a writer; when I gave up law ('You've ruined your future'), I studied journalism and did better than anyone I was studying with. And when I began to write little pieces and reviews, it was books I was looking towards, the books that would wheel me into another country.

And it happened. With perfect timing. I had planned a holiday in London, and before I left Bloomsbury decided to publish my novel, *Trying to Grow*. It was at that moment – when I held the letter with the news in my hands – that the chrysalis burst. But I could never, indeed I dared not, forget that I would still be in darkness if I had not beaten my wings so fiercely, for so long.

Beginnings

I came to Britain with that one book, like a trophy in my arms; I left with two. My first weeks, in London and the Lake District, were spent without any thought that they might be part of a book. But talking about what I found won me a long journey through Britain about which I would write. I saw no reason to change the way I approached places – armed with what I knew of them from my reading in India, nothing more. I would not try to learn places before I saw them; I would let them talk to me – and as things were, the talking came in useful. And I would watch, as I had done, from one eye misted with anglophilia, the other clear and wide open.

The first time I met my publisher, we, in that awful phrase, hit it off (as Hanif Kureishi once wrote, in another, sexier context: 'my flags flew my trumpets blew'). And when I had left her, my publisher turned to her assistant and said, 'Isn't he heaven on wheels!' People find it easy to tell me things; and I could think of no more appropriate title for the book I was writing for her.

F. K.
Bombay, January 1991

I

HEAVEN

ONE

Coming to terms with Finchley

I had to be smuggled into the house in Finchley. We got there in the Saab; the cars on the street made me catch my breath like the men of Florence had. In Bombay the cars look like the men – out-worn, out-dated, outrageously boring. When I was a little boy there was a ditty that went:

What a pity
In Bombay city
The boys are ugly
And the girls are pretty

As for the cars on the streets, Bombayites see Fiats that are young but look old, like little girls in pinafores with hair plaited tight. The car models never change, and if they do they move from one part of the fifties to another. The rich manage to bring in a Ford or a Mercedes once in a long drive, and we watch them like my mother watches Jacob's Cream Crackers in a smuggler's shop. 'Oh, look at that!' I once said to a friend from Australia just as she said that to me. We looked at the Mercedes, slim and silver. Then she turned to me and said, 'That must be at least twenty-five years old.' When you are in Bombay a little glamour lasts a long time.

And there I was sitting in a Saab, a real Swedish car,

bright orange, with a marvellously pregnant bonnet. My friend
Freddy (a Parsee; the Parsees like British christian names as
much as British brand names) had bought it especially for my
visit. I wasn't good enough for the Underground. I phoned
them one morning and a woman, her voice soft as cheese
spread, said to me, 'I don't think it's a very good idea for
you, sir.'

When the British say that they mean, 'Just forget it, buster.'
I didn't know that, so I said, 'Oh, that's all right. I don't mind
a little inconvenience,' and many pounds saved.

'Actually,' she said, and the cheese spread was spreading
thinner, 'we actively discourage people in wheelchairs.' Even
an Indian could get that.

'Her name,' Freddy was saying, 'is Mrs Honoria Gaskell.'
I was glad; my imagination could not have borne a landlady
called Mary Smith. Honoria Gaskell was alarmed at the prospect
of having a lodger in a wheelchair. She protested, in English
terms, by wondering aloud how they would manage. Freddy,
all sweetness and moderation, told her they could try having
me for a week – if, after that, she thought I was a bad idea . . . I
would be sleeping under the bridges. No one from Bombay can
afford an hotel in London; exchange restrictions see to that.

So, said Freddy, we had to be very careful with Mrs Honoria
Gaskell. She was not to see him carry me upstairs in his arms;
that might upset her sensibilities – and she didn't even know
I was gay. Besides, the sight of my wheelchair scudding up
her carpeted stairs might be the last plank on my bed under
the bridge.

Freddy snatched me out of the Saab and ran – the only time
I've ever run.

I was in a room I could not believe. The ceiling above the
bed was papered with faces – mustachioed men, droopy hippies,
nests of Afro-hair in which I could spot eyes like eggs. The wall
opposite was red, the colour of freshly spilt blood. This is what
comes, I thought, of reading *Jane Eyre* once too often.

And the moon was large and luminous outside my window; I could see roofs and smell a garden sweet as a poem's
promise.

Behind me I heard a noise. Freddy was grinning, and with him was Mrs Honoria Gaskell, who looked like her name. Fiftyish, as tall as I was short, she had heavy flaxen hair coiled at the back of her head and pale freckled skin that had never tanned. She was big, and shopped at Forgotten Woman. Yet her face was delicate, quick to smile, easy to worry. And about her was an Edwardian air.

'Good evening,' she said, her voice deep, her accent first-rate. Later, I discovered I wasn't supposed to say that about an accent; still later, I discovered I wasn't supposed to say a lot of things.

We got on fabulously, Honoria Gaskell and I. She was an expert on eighteenth- and nineteenth-century costume, in which I was very interested, and that had nothing to do with the view from under the bridge. She and her children were playing Scrabble that Sunday evening I arrived. I marvelled at that. In Bombay there lives a rumour that walks in disguise as a fact: the British have no family life; they lead an existence of miserable loneliness. And how lucky that makes us, Indians, by compare. If ever I wanted to be by myself, I had, first, to face a deftly combined medical and psychological test: has a girl (no one thinks of boys) ditched you? do you have a pain in your body? your head? do you have gas? are you feeling down? something has annoyed you – what? By which time, of course, I could tell them what.

Not that British families didn't seem strange. The parents of a girl I knew couldn't rest till she had left their home, and now they were trying to get rid of her brother. They had a comfortable house, plenty of money – anyone like that in India would give one eye to have the children stay with them. It seemed to me a lack of feeling, something unnatural. Until I began to see their life, and understand. The husband and wife were friends; in India they would rarely be more than colleagues in the business of marriage. They were getting on but they had made a life for themselves – bridge evenings, drives around the countryside, holidays in France. They didn't need their children to bring the bigger world to them. In India self-fulfilment is short; people in their fifties live through the children, their talk, their careers, the excitement of a daughter's marriage, a son's first child. That is all they have and it isn't out of lethargy that they don't have more. In an old, tired, insular culture, life rarely reaches beyond the essentials into positive selfish pleasure.

When, towards the end of my stay at her house, Mrs Gaskell left for Florence, I was appalled that none of her grown-up sons was there to see her off. One was having a lie-in because it was a Sunday, another had taken himself off to Yorkshire for a weekend's vacation. Never, never, said Freddy and I to each other, as we kissed her goodbye, would we treat our parents like this. But our parents would need us, not only because it had always been so, but because things in India were not easy – taxi-drivers could cheat old people, the way to the airport was often unsafe, and a whimsical bureaucracy waited there. Besides, the British travelled abroad as often as we went to a hill-station to escape the heat. For our parents a trip abroad would be what it was for the British in the nineteenth century – a singular occasion; to be graced with farewell parties and fond noses pressed against the plate-glass walls of a departure lounge.

To comfort themselves over the impossibility of living in Britain, Indians have invented dark legends about the land that swirls in a dank grey fog. No matter how often you explain that the fogs, in London at least, went out with the coal fires, it does no good. 'There's rain, all the time, cold-cold wind, and zero sunshine. Oh! You won't be able to take it!' said everyone who envied my leaving India. Where it rains, *all the time*, three months in a year, as if there were no taps that work in the sky, where the sunshine is like a fire turned too high so that to step out of your house is to sweat, to scorch, to melt, but not to wilt. And sometimes to die, as hundreds do every summer, of heat exhaustion which has elbowed sunstroke aside.

'Oh, to be in England,' I muttered through clenched and clattering teeth, as the ice-sharp rain acupunctured my neck. We were looking for a house in Muswell Hill. Freddy, who believes amnesia to be the privilege of the pianist that he is, had

6

parked the Saab at number 46. A little later, the rain reminded him that we wanted number 64. It reminded me that I had a health insurance policy. Which wouldn't be much good if I died of a chill because my socks were wet. That is how Queen Victoria's father died. Lytton Strachey had told me that when I was ten; anglophilia, like muscular dystrophy, starts early and gets worse with time. My wheelchair's seat was a little pool in which I sat, an unwilling statue with a wet bum. I thought of my typist who on a visit here had been hospitalised for hypothermia and filled with Bovril and Marmite and Cadbury's Cocoa and –
'Sixty-four!' said Freddy.

'Warmth!' I murmured as Usha let us in, but did not feel any. 'You must be soaked, *yaar*,' said Usha, surprising me with an accent Indian as mangoes; she had lived in Britain ten years now.

I was cold. 'Is the heating on?' I asked. In a few weeks I would lose the ability to ask so direct a question. Into me would seep the other (I already had the one) English vice, politeness, and I'd probably say, 'It's very pleasant, in fact quite cool here, isn't it?'

'What heating?' said Usha. 'Winter is over, it's April.'

'But it's freezing,' I said, and Freddy gave my chair a little bump, front wheels only.

'I'm sorry,' she said. 'I know, I felt just like you when I first came from India – you learn to take it.'

To help was my first party in London. The drawing-room was wide and golden with light, remarkably like the drawing-rooms Parsees tried to reproduce in their Bombay flats. There was Usha wearing what Parsees called a Punjabi suit, loose trousers and tunic; her flatmate, Grace, almost as lovely as the Kelly, with hair even a gay guy would want to stroke. Lovelier was her fiancé, Alexander, with hazel eyes in which you could see the pupils – you've got to shine a torch into Bombay eyes for that – and an English Nose, which is Parsee for small, tilted, beautifully placed. Such noses are to us what round eyes are to the Japanese, blessed as we are with beaks out of the Old Testament.

Alexander was a solicitor and worked in the City, as did

Richard, bearded, small-eyed, I've forgotten his nose. But Richard wanted to become a Buddhist lama. I was as horrified as I had been when I had met an Oxford don at an ashram in Poona. To surrender life in Britain for a fictional spirituality was to me an act as insane as climbing the Berlin Wall from West to East.

Religion, in India, seemed to me an admission of defeat, a renunciation of reality. I was not speaking out of snobbery, for I had been religious, once. Living with brittle bones, I had sought a world in which bones did not exist, or, if they did, then only as shadows of the soul. For Hindu philosophy never tires of repeating that the body is but the apparel of *atma*, which changes clothes innumerable times in the course of its millennium-long life.

That comfort was a fierce temptation to those who lived in a world like India's, where so little was possible. The future was rarely brighter than the hard present or the hungry past. Only in another dimension could the future be what it is meant to – a bigger, more hoping space. Without which the present can only be a confinement, finite and claustrophobic.

But the escape had turned into a trap. Religion, which kept the future breathing, also rendered it unreal. The good life could belong only to that other realm of rebirth; here, now, there was little to do but drift and blame the current when you found yourself, or someone else, drowning. When my father killed himself there were any number of people who said his end was written into his destiny, or that it was a punishment for my own disbelief. There was no psychological effort to grasp his motives. Even the simpler, more solid facts that he was deaf, prone to hours of hiccoughs, crippled with arthritis, counted for nothing.

A young lawyer I knew had a desperately unhappy marriage. 'But it is my karma,' he said. 'I have to go through this means I have to go through this. Something I did in my past life must be paid for. In this life I have been such a good husband – you know, I've never beaten my wife, never lusted for other girls.' He could not connect the circumstances of his marriage to its disastrous state. He had wanted to renounce the world, become a *sanyasi*, a holy man, but his guru had declared him unfit for that exalted destiny. Broken-hearted, he had called a girl who he knew was keen on him and proposed marriage. Now all that was forgotten, rendered irrelevant. He had learned nothing – only that his life was not his to control. How could it be, when a debt from an unremembered, non-existent past could make its claim of pain at any moment?

Someone was talking of thermal underwear even as I ended my dissuading diatribe to the would-be lama. This, I was to discover, was a peculiarly English gift: the ability to keep the waters of conversation just right – never too cold, certainly never too hot. Perhaps it had something to do with their experience of bath-tubs, which almost never had a mixer, so that one was always fine-tuning the taps.

It wasn't easy for me, this conversational cool. How, I wondered, if you feel deeply about something, can you remain so detached, so ironic? Where I came from conversation was a sauna, the temperature of talk rising higher and higher until it plunged into frozen silence. In cultures where you cannot do very much, you argue.

Late one night, I watched the writer Tatyana Tolstaya on television. A man from the *Guardian* was saying how dull Washington was compared to Moscow, where he had had the most fascinating conversations deep into the night. Yes, said Tolstaya, if the Russians have to put a nail in the wall they will first discuss China, anything, and the nail will remain on the table. In Washington, they may not talk, but at least the nail will be in the wall. The English friends who were with me thought, how prosaic, how dreary, to care more about nails than about good conversation. But I understood; for I too came from a world where the nails are never in the wall.

My voice, however, was trained for those Indian conversations, so that a neighbour living three floors above me could say, 'I enjoyed what you said about the Prime Minister last night, but there's a point I want to make . . .' and we would talk our way into the sauna again.

But as time went on I learned to modulate my voice, control the colour of my face. There is some good in the British way.

Without all that steam you look at each other more clearly, you learn and, best of all, convince quite often, because there is none of that 'I'm on the front-line of my cause' business.

'Marks and Sparks,' Usha was saying. 'That's where they'll make him feel warmer.' I realised the discussion was about my underwear. I joined in, embarrassment fuelling my enthusiasm; Richard, I realised, had intended to be a lama about as much as I wanted to be a high-board diver in my off-moments. And there I was, sounding like one of those garrulous, perpetually explaining Indians from a Ruth Jhabvala novel. I had done something that did not exist in Bombay – gone over the top. 'A bit OTT': the greatest accusation that could slide through English lips.

The party stayed in underwear till dinner was done. It was as if having found a safe bay everyone wanted to keep the boat bobbing there. That was strange, because a consensus had been reached right at the start. 'Marks,' said they all, except Usha, who called it 'Marks and Sparks', her accent quite British, very different from what it had been in the hall when we came in. I wondered if Sparks was the right thing to say, whether I should use it or not – perhaps it was like the Cockney 'trouble and strife', perhaps it was non-U like water-closet.

'What should I see?' I asked Alexander. I had been watching his English Nose for a long time and I had to make an excuse for my interest. Not that it mattered. Because the gorgeous Grace was watching Freddy in the same way. Now Freddy has a Jewish nose, but he has dark curls and a mouth that can, and often does, launch a load of love letters. Living with him I felt like an alcoholic in a wine-shop with all the bottles locked up behind glass; Freddy was as straight as Queen Victoria's back, with a slight scoliosis.

'Lyme Regis,' Alexander was saying, one slender pink finger with a quarter-inch of nail indicating its place on a map that he held in his lap. But I was thinking of a black cape blowing with a sea breeze and a bearded old man writing, writing. I thought I might wheel where Sarah Woodruff walked.

'And then there is Lulworth Cove,' where a bright, steadfast star shines in the sky, I thought. Keats was beginning to make me maudlin. I had loved Britain for most of my twenty-nine years but I had never allowed myself to miss her. That way, I knew, lay madness, a hunger so powerful it could wash away my whole life in India under a tidal wave of wanting. Now, I was here, I could let myself feel. But it was pity that was swamping me, as if I was saying, look, I've been a brave man all this time now, let me cry. There are few things more moving than the memory of one's own courage.

To make matters worse, Alexander and Richard were singing 'And did those feet'; they had asked me if I had heard it sung, and when I said I hadn't they took their chance. The English love their country passionately but passion is not something to be exhibited in public. (Sex is all right, it does not involve emotional exposure.) Singing a hymn that links England to Heaven was not something these solicitors from the City could do without an excuse.

They sang breathing deep, their mouths arced with pleasure, as I often yearned to sing my national songs:

Till we have built Jerusalem,
In England's green and pleasant land.

I knew I was supposed to be thinking of Blake, but there was another echo sounding in my head. So that I was watching a despair of tramps at a Salvation Army Mission with Sergeant Marybeth at the piano. They came from Paul Bailey's *Old Soldiers*, and Sergeant Marybeth, like me, had been enticed to England by literature, even if she had found her vocation in Whitechapel among the poor. 'She saw through tears, the healthy bodies they might have had; that they would surely have in the Jerusalem their singing invoked.'

Soon the thermostat came on and the conversation turned to money, whether it was right for City solicitors to earn as much as they did when teachers and doctors could hardly make ends touch.

'Well,' said Usha, 'it's these times, you know. Social injustice is now the norm.' The solicitors looked appropriately guilty.

I looked away; I could afford another argument as much as luncheon at Claridge's.

Later, Richard left, and Freddy followed the women into the kitchen to help with the washing up. Alexander sat on the carpet next to my wheelchair. 'Things are not so bad,' he said softly.

'I don't think so either.'

'If she hadn't come in when she did . . . '

'Are you a Thatcherite?' I asked.

Alexander's eyes clouded; he looked like a Russian who had been asked his opinion of America. I thought I'd help him. 'I think she's doing a lot of good.'

'Yes,' he breathed, and smiled his relief. 'I am one. But it doesn't do to say it.' The love that dare not speak its name, I thought.

'Why ever not?' But I was thinking of something Freddy had said to me on the way from the airport: 'Don't tell anyone you are an admirer if you want to make friends here.' I had refused to believe that, but now, watching Alexander – handsome, rich, successful – sitting scared on the brown and orange carpet, I felt my determination wobble.

The next day, we went looking for thermal underwear. They shook their heads at Marks and said, 'Winter's over; it's April now.'

'Doesn't feel like it.'

'Let's go home,' said Freddy.

I couldn't believe my ears. We were at the Brent Cross Shopping Centre. Which was to me what the ocean is to a gawk from the Gobi desert – an endless sea of possibilities and never mind the pun. To be given a glimpse of those miles of John Lewis, W. H. Smith, Sock Shop, Tie Rack . . . then to be wheeled away, was so elegant a form of torture only a sensitive pianist could have dreamt it up.

'Tomorrow,' I said, 'I'm spending the day at Brent Cross.'

'It isn't just your day you'll spend – remember what happened at Tesco's? And anyway, there are millions of things to do in London. Why Brent Cross?'

I had never gone shopping on my own, in my life. And I was twenty-nine. But in India if you're in a wheelchair you are not supposed to shop, any more than if you are penniless. Since most people in wheelchairs are penniless, that isn't as strange as it sounds. Shops are small, the department stores are about half the size of a local Sainsbury's, with as many steps as a split-level stage set. When I did wheel into a shop, usually with friends, sometimes with a servant, people came closer, peered at me, shook their heads and quite forgot to ask what it was I wanted. When I asked, they giggled with astonishment as if they couldn't believe a man like me could talk. And even if I could, surely I wasn't serious. I mean, if Barbie doll strolled into Selfridges and asked for shoes, you'd smile indulgently and say, 'Next!' It wasn't cruelty; merely a lack of imagination. The same kind of thing that, magnified many times over, allows caste Hindus to roast Untouchables alive, or someone in Belfast to shoot the knee-caps out of a man's legs.

Here at Brent Cross I was about as conspicuous as a shopping trolley. Around me bloomed so many wheelchairs I actually had to swerve to avoid them. I saw young men whose fingers were doing their walking for them, by playing a switch; plump, middle-aged women riding little scooters roughshod over their arthritis; old ladies, fragile as my bones had once been, pushed along by sons and daughters. But nobody, said everybody in India, cares for their parents in Britain. They are left to die, slowly, like old animals. Unlike our old, who die rather faster, about twenty years before their British counterparts.

At the entrance to John Lewis they were selling perfume and I was mesmerised by the scent-kitchen smells. In Bombay there are no perfume shops. There are hundreds of shops selling attar, the essences of various substances; if you wear them you are sent to olfactory oblivion by anyone who has a nose. Real perfume – Dior, Coty, Jean Patou – has a romance that is unimaginable to anyone living in the West. Bottles are given as gifts to someone very special. Once received, they are exhibited to every visitor like a newly acquired Fragonard, kept as carefully, used only for an evening hung heavy with hope. Those who buy scent from the smugglers tear a hole in their purses that takes a long time to repair. Sometimes they find that their bottle of Diorissimo is nothing but attar with a film of the real thing floating on top – which is why there is a fortune to be made in selling your empty perfume bottles.

I found my way out of the enchanted goods to men's wear.

'Look,' said a black man, 'I'm not trying to be funny but . . . '

'Yes?'

'I'm not trying to be funny,' he said, but he was, anyway, looking at me and making faces, pushing his lips together, grinning, shrugging.

I began to laugh.

'Glad you take it this way,' he said. 'Maybe, maybe, look, this is just a suggestion, you can look in children's wear.'

I looked. The sales girls were very kind. They offered me sweatshirts from which masked men glowered and jumpers with shiny pictures of little boys winking salaciously.

'No, no,' I said. 'I'm conservative, you see.' I saw the horror on their faces and realised I'd almost said the T-word.

'Then it's time you changed, sir,' said a sales woman with steel-grey hair.

'I doubt it very much – ' and I fled.

To ladies' lingerie. Around me slithered the most exquisite pinks and greens, lace and satin, soft and stylish. I looked and thought of getting some for a neighbour I had. She always hung her undies out to dry. Everyone minded so much. 'Only because it isn't English, you know. Otherwise where is the shame? They have such pretty-pretty things, even for inside wear.'

I tried to find my way out of inside wear and retreated when I saw the steel wig again. Another foray took me to the changing rooms, and I stopped just in time. I couldn't see any other door. The sales women were beginning to not look at me. Maybe they thought I was a pervert; I was outraged at their misdirected suspicions. I mean, if I were lost in men's swimwear . . .

Finally I asked my way out, and while I was at it, into a

loo. My first disabled loo; in India the very idea was a laugh. Whoever thought of the disabled? Who ever thought?

Here I was, bitching my country even as my eyes whirled in wonder at the gleaming handrails, the button in the wall, the hand-dryer, the wash-basin which looked so different I decided to wash at once. There was a kind of slot into which you slipped your hands. I did. Nothing happened. I felt about in the slot. Nothing. This can't be, I thought. In Britain, everything works. It has to. Or I've been mad all these years. I saw the sign. It said 'Water Cooler'. I thought of Peter Sellers at *The Party*, the Indian making an ass of himself in a Hollywood mansion. I was glad. Because it meant this kind of thing didn't happen only to types who spoke Sellers Indian. I had loved the film and felt terribly guilty. Now it was all right. I had been laughing at myself.

It wasn't so easy when I tried to get to Marks for my lunch. The Food Hall was on another floor, and I had never used a lift on my own. Indian lifts usually stop high, like hitched-up skirts, and I have to be tipped in. But I knew it was different here. I pressed the call button and waited till there was a little queue behind me. I pressed it again, impatiently. A lady in a strawberry dress stepped up and said, 'I think it might be a better idea if you pressed the call button.'

'That's what I did,' I said, pressing it again.

'Um . . . no,' she said. 'That's the light.'

I didn't feel a thing; hopeless shame is passionless . . .

The Food Hall was a wheelchair's delight. I didn't have to move a finger or foot; the crowd rolled me along. But when we got to the sandwiches, I found myself in a wire-mesh cage made entirely of shopping trolleys. The good thing was, I was at everyone's crotch-level getting the best view of my life without having to worry about anyone catching me at it. After a time I began to feel hungry, and a bit breathless. The standers were getting all the oxygen before it could reach me. 'Excuse me,' I said in my Indian parliamentary voice, and an aisle began to clear in front of me. Through it walked a lad, golden-haired, sweet as the English summer I'd never seen.

'Let me help you, sir,' he said, handing me a basket. 'Tell

15

me where you want to go and I'll take you.' I was so surprised the basket fell from my hand – also because it felt as heavy as a baby in my arms. 'Will you carry this,' I said, 'while I wheel myself?'

'Of course,' he said. 'What would you like?'

I shopped till you couldn't see the wire for the food. 'Thank you so much,' I said to the golden lad.

He looked at me and smiled. 'Thank you,' he said. 'For getting me off my job – for a little while.'

I hadn't been mad all those years.

TWO

Class-speak

'Would you like to see a play?' Mrs Gaskell asked me soon after I arrived.

'Oh yes!' I bubbled. The West End rivalled the Royal Family for Parsee popularity. 'What is it?'

'It's an amateur production at a local hall. And my son is acting – it's Steven Berkoff's *West* – '

'I'd love that,' I said, wondering if I should have heard of *West* or Steven Berkoff.

The hall had appeared in the black-and-white films I loved; and so had the audience. In the interval they trooped into the tiny foyer in their little hats and belted frocks, the men in grey suits with hair to match. 'Have some wine,' offered a cheerful lady in canary pleats with a face like Mamie Eisenhower's. 'Or some orange juice and a biscuit?' The single biscuit sounded irresistible, and I bought it. A man with a goatee and glasses, just like Trotsky, limped up to me and asked, 'What do you think of it? I'm the reviewer for the local paper – wonder what I'm going to say about it.'

'Very interesting,' I said, talking about my dream. I had fallen asleep about twenty minutes after the start because the play was not in English.

'It's Cockney,' whispered Freddy, 'and don't be such a snob, you're disgusting.'

'I'm not. I just can't understand a single word,' except for the occasional line from Shakespeare which seemed to have been tucked in to tease me. And it wasn't as if I was the snoozy type. In Bombay, I saw every play that hit the boards, every amateur production; the socially relevant stuff replete with recorded screams of rape; Ionesco and Brecht; chopped-up Shakespeare – Romeo and Juliet on the balcony followed by Hamlet and Gertrude in her bedroom; faultless performances of *Agnes of God* and *Noises Off* and *The Diary of Anne Frank* four times, but that was because I'd taken a shine to the slender, jerky boy who played Peter. I would have been an actor; there was, to me, nothing more glorious than slipping into someone's heart and breaking the audience's. But knowing the way I moved, I knew I'd probably be condemned to a lifetime of playing Molière's Imaginary Invalid.

The next day, I asked Mrs Gaskell about her son's accent – he didn't have to change much to act in *West* – but I crept up on the topic crablike. 'Why is it,' I said, 'that so many children of parents who speak beautifully talk in this low-class way?'

'Oh dear! We don't refer to the lower classes any more,' she said, blinking and taking her lips in before shutting her face.

'But they do exist don't they – the lower classes?'

'The working class, you mean.'

'That's not very accurate – we all work, teachers, writers, doctors, solicitors . . .'

'Ye-es, but not the same way.'

'And a lot of the . . . working class don't work, do they.'

'Yes, poor things; it's all That Woman's fault.'

'I don't think so.'

'Well, I do – I can't stand her.'

'About accents – '

'Oh yes, I know what you mean. I think it has something to do with not sounding posh.'

'You mean they find it shameful that their parents are educated – an undeserved advantage?'

'I suppose so – and it's also a fashion; everyone talks that way, so why shouldn't we?'

No, I thought; accents said something more important. Talking badly, unintelligibly, was part of the levelling process.

And like most levellers, British society had taken the easy way out. Grasping that accents were no measure of moral worth, and that it was unfair to make some people feel inferior for the way they spoke, the cultural establishment had opted for an obliteration of standards. Instead of seeing that everyone, or most people, learned to speak precisely, they had declared that clear, pleasant speech which could be understood the world over was mere snobbery. It was easier to demolish the mountain than to help people climb it.

And the tragedy was that even this had not worked. British society remained fixated with accent. Only people did not talk about it any more, so that judgement was driven underground by moral intimidation. Almost every person I got to know, in turn, referred to somebody by saying, 'Not a very good accent, you know.' The redoubtable Mrs Gaskell, whose liberal credentials were impeccable, once told me I had been 'phoned by a man with an uncouth accent'. The egalitarian Blanche often spoke about people with awful accents; and no matter what the levellers said, people saw the mountain, because it existed. Standards like these are not artificial creations to keep people down but objective representations of reality; and like reality they cannot be wished away. I would not have been taller if tape-measures had been banished from the world.

I was always playing Monopoly in London. In Bombay, as a boy, I had played on a thirties board that had belonged to my mother. It had split in two, but if we didn't shake it the stations stayed in one piece. In London, going from Piccadilly to Oxford Street, snubbing Whitechapel, looking for Mayfair, which refused to humble itself into a road, managing to stay out of jail, Monopoly turned real.

There was Regent Street in my head, lined with shops, coloured green, costing £300. When I wheeled down the length of it I knew how much imagination can fail reality. I had never visualised its width, its curve, the stodgy splendour and the shy greyness that seemed to be London's second colour. (The first was green.) Finchley resembled nothing more than a cantonment town back home, except that the houses had a kind of uniformity that colonialists would scorn. One of the rewards of life for Englishmen in the humid hothouse of India must have been the freedom to let themselves go, without worrying about seeming over the top, so that their bungalows almost always had eccentric little features like a Juliet balcony sticking its tongue out at conformity.

But after a while, in Britain, I ceased to be surprised by the look-alike streets; I began to expect them, and actually frowned when I saw a house that was outraging the modesty of its neighbours.

Driving down from Finchley, I couldn't quite believe I was in the heart of a recent empire. For London seemed to me a sequence of sturdy, sometimes elegant villages standing in lush green countryside. Where I came from, grass and trees were like snow – almost never seen. Bombay's green spots were visual absurdities, little sprouts of grass like an old woman's beard. Sometimes I would discover a flower-bed small as a tablecloth outside someone's window. I'd stop and gasp and shake my head at the glory of it all.

Who is over the top now? I wanted to ask the astonishment of blooms wherever I happened to look in London. All those flowers that I didn't know by name or lovely face, so that I could only guess that these were a hundred tulips and that a single daffodil. I had arrived too late to catch ten thousand at a glance. In a way, I was glad. The poem could remain frozen in my imagination, inviolate as a childhood story.

I thought it strange that a part of London should be flaunting colour while another half remained grey and dowdy as an Indian government office. And this had little to do with poverty. The West End was nothing like I had expected it to be. I could hear no throb as I had in New York as a boy, no rhythm as I had in Rome earlier that spring. Houses seemed to look inwards, like the people in the street. The occasional attempt to draw attention was half-hearted, tentative and so embarrassed. Even the punks looked apologetic, as if they were saying, look, this is just a joke – don't think we're crazy.

The piazza at Covent Garden was enough to make you cry, with its forced gaiety and frantic performers, the boys break-dancing for an audience that stood swallowing, hands in pockets brought out for anaemic applause. Regency architecture, lovely, long-limbed, made Victorian buildings look like whiskered, portly men. The Barbican was a vicious joke, as if some non-human had poured a spaceship of grey filth over London's soul – it seemed to ask for abuse, for a fairy godmother (alas, I was one but not the other) who would wave a wand and cry, 'Be gone, darkness!' And the South Bank complex, with the pavements that sounded a death-rattle when you walked them, had the lifeless vulgarity of proletarianism; the garish light-sculpture I saw from there seemed a beacon of bleakness.

People were dressed as if they had picked their clothes in their sleep, not, as in America, in a fire-alarm. Perhaps I had never really divided the two cultures, much as China and Japan or Peru and Mexico are mixed up in the mind. Backward was a cruel word, not one I would have used to describe Britain, and yet it came to me again and again, stubborn as the imagined truth. What else, I thought, can describe a place in the West that hasn't caught up with the America that I had known seventeen years ago? What kinder word is there for the shops that say, yes, we sell, but we don't want to shout it, for the bloated black taxis, the drowsy cafés which make eating at home seem a lively treat?

In my imagination, the West was, well, the West, and I was surprised to find a distinctive British style which was really the absence of one. Perhaps the shops were to blame. Even while I loved them, their lack of anything beautiful in the way of clothes – except those terrifically expensive ones that make you long for a woman of your own to buy them for – depressed me.

The women I met – unless they were rich – dressed in lumpish jumpers, skirts that didn't quite manage to keep their end up, blouses that were twee or tatty so that the word casual took on a new, almost sinister, look. Back at home there is a style called Bombay Parsee. My mother, and many younger women, dress in it as stubbornly as Paloma Picasso wears *haute couture*. Bombay Parsee dresses in floral skirts, pleated frocks, low-waists and gathers. Now I knew; London was its birthplace, and because its origins were 'over there' nothing could argue against it.

The Italians, poorer than the British, dress about ten times more elegantly – perhaps that is why, because they are poorer. In Florence there was hardly a young woman who didn't stop and look at the show-window of a boutique as if it were stocked with good-looking men. In London, girls walked past dress-shops as if they were selling smokers' accessories.

In Bombay I could take the shabby, often dirty, clothes, the buildings standing on crutches, walls black and sodden with urine and grime, neon-lit rooms painted chutney-green so they could be ignored for years to come while the colour faded slowly. I knew it was the look of a city that had no choice. But for the genteel dreariness of London, I could find no excuse. In those first, and uncomprehending, days.

THREE

Bloomsbury and all that

In Bombay, as a boy, I used to spread the map of London on my pillow and stare till my eyes shut, like my contemporaries were doing with the *Playboy* magazines they bought from the smuggler with six months' pocket-money. And now, fifteen years later, the look of London had let me down. I felt like the Indian bride who sees only a photograph of her fiancé, if that, before she gets married. Only to find the object of the picture objectionable when it lands up in her bed.

And so it was that, in Britain, I was often disappointed in the places where I had rested my highest hopes, while unexpected, unthought-of pleasures peeped out like the mischievous badgers in my childhood picture-books.

I had never imagined the literary world would be so accessible, or so real. And yet here I was at the Bloomsbury headquarters, which weren't in Bloomsbury at all but in Soho Square, which was nothing like the Soho I was warned about ('I never step into Soho,' said Honoria Gaskell, making it sound like Sodom), but very staid, hands folded in its green lap.

Soon after I got there, splendid women descended on me. There was my publisher, Liz Calder, serene and silver with a laugh that made you want to stay with her for ever. (I sometimes tried. Until she said something like, 'Would you like me to call you a taxi?')

'Are you shy?' she asked.

'Of what?'

'Of appearing on television?'

'Tell me when!'

Freddy looked at me and lifted one side of his upper lip.

I asked Liz Calder about the mysterious Imogen Parker. This was someone I'd never met who had changed – and never mind the Hollywood sound – my whole life. She was a literary agent who had never been my agent but had read my manuscript, suggested improvements – all the while warning me not to change anything I didn't want to – and put me in touch with the agent who sold my novel to Bloomsbury.

Liz was telling me something when there was a soft rustle that announced Caroline Michel, with a wiggle of her padded shoulders and a toss of her auburn head. She had huge grey eyes which looked straight at you, raising your body temperature by two degrees, so that you immediately felt much loved. She was going to handle my publicity, and she wanted photographs. 'I'll send someone over,' she said. And I froze. Television was one thing – I knew I could talk the camera into forgetting my four feet nothingness – but photos, I knew, made me look like a demon. 'Don't worry,' said Caroline, 'I'll send Nigel Parry – he's very good. You're going to look wonderful.' She smiled and laid a gentle hand on my shoulder. Why don't they make men like her, I thought.

Other gorgeous women walked in, some tweeted a hello, others gulped it, still others sang it strong, and left.

One of them seemed quite apart from the glitzy others. There was something quiet about her, as if she had come back from a month's meditation. Her eyes were blue and wide, her generous lips were pursed in restrained disapproval. 'I've read your novel three times.' Mary Tomlinson spoke softly and perfectly and I could only think of that absurd and lovely word, gentlewoman. 'I'm going to edit it. With you, of course.' Later, she came to the house in Finchley. I asked Honoria Gaskell if I could use her drawing-room; I really couldn't invite my editor upstairs. Being English, she understood. Upstairs, Freddy and I, Parsee Indian princes, brought up on a ratio of one servant to two people, lived in a centrifuge of socks, shirts, letters, both English

24

and French, orange juice, crackers, books, music-sheets and tea-bags.

Back there in the Bloomsbury office, bright with the surprising sun, I was trying to be myself, dropping hints about my homosexuality, being enthusiastic about gay writing, Edmund White and Alan Hollinghurst and Paul Bailey. (Was he gay? There was that certain fine and emotional quality about his writing which told me so.) In Bombay my homosexuality was something I talked about only by writing tragic short stories. A happy ending was as unimaginable as it was for the fiction that screamed out of South Africa and Eastern Europe.

To be gay, in India, was to surrender your claim to be a man, to slide into a self-parody of make-up and earrings, neither of which quite tempted me. What else could it be when gay men saw themselves in a cultural looking-glass that turned them into hermaphrodites, cowards and molesters? Not to be married was tantamount to a confession of impotence or madness, a denial as inexplicable as disbelief in God. I, for one, was safe from that. The fact that I couldn't walk automatically disqualified me, in the Indian mind, from marriage – or, for that matter, any romantic relationship. Besides, I came from a Westernised community in which bachelorhood was only a personal failure, not a moral disaster.

Not that it did me much good. I was afraid. As it was I found it difficult to be taken seriously. Outside of the people who knew me well, I was a cute joke, 'just like a real-life walkie-talkie doll' someone had said to me, handing me a box of chocolate animals on my twenty-ninth birthday. 'Not even walkie,' I'd said, helpfully. To add to that terrifying erasure of myself by declaring my gayness was not something I wanted to do.

And then the gay world itself was so sad. Homosexuality was a crime in India. And the absence of prosecutions for many years had not meant the absence of harassment by police and blackmail by homophobes. Anonymous sex in public parks was not my idea of passion, any more than were the gay men who were doing their worst to fit into the masks and disguises allotted to them by an uncomprehending culture.

25

But Britain, I knew, was different, and I was not going to lie about myself. In Soho Square I had made a start. But it would be many months before I could talk about my homosexuality without making my ears go hot, without the feeling that I was dragging some poor fellow out of his priest's hole to face a firing-squad.

In India, wealth hangs high, and out of reach, for anyone without the ladders of influence or corruption. So the chief directions in which ambition can grow are mystical or intellectual. Any status achieved is held on to for dear life. Poets always come with a capital P and writers float majestically over the unwriterly world. My life had barely touched that inner circle, but the smugness, the pathetic vanity and emptiness of what I had seen, had frightened me. A professor of literature, who was a literary critic and had written books himself, talked to me endlessly about the radicalisation of writing. When I asked what he thought of Gordimer's latest novel, *A Sport of Nature*, and its vision of a post-revolutionary South Africa, he said, 'Oh! I don't know – what does he write? I think I've read one or two short stories.'

Poems often resemble a verbal accident, a twisted mass of imagery. The desperate words jump up and down waiting for someone to take notice and stop. At a seminar I once attended, the poet Tom Paulin read some of these efforts and said, 'I'm sure there must be so much to these poems that I am missing, not being Indian.' He looked up, and there wasn't the slightest recognition of irony in any of the faces.

I had heard from an English friend who taught literature at a comprehensive that most of her students were almost totally ignorant of romantic or modern verse. At the end of the seminar, I asked Paulin how awareness of English literature among the participants compared with British levels. Before he could say, 'Oh! Excellent – people here know so much,' a poet had pounced on me. 'Why,' she said angrily, 'do you want to know what the Englishman thinks of us?'

'Why not?' I said. 'I'm always being asked by visitors what we think of them.'

'Then you know all the wrong sort of people.' I quite failed to see the point of that. 'Typical neo-colonial attitude,' she snorted, and stamped away.

I didn't argue – I didn't say that I would have asked the same question of someone from Nigeria or Singapore – because I knew it would have made no difference. For those who live in a closed room, a window is something to be afraid of, a hole through which you might see too much.

I realised how innocent I had been and how little I knew about the book world when I discovered the truth about Liz Calder and Caroline Michel.

My surprise began in a small way when I left the Bloomsbury offices and Liz Calder came to see me to the taxi. She said, absolutely ordinarily, 'Can I lift you in?' I couldn't quite get that; someone like her, in Bombay, might call out a peon to give me a hand, but to offer to do it herself? That was as much to be expected as self-criticism.

Later, I was to see my publisher with a shopping-bag ('Is this really happening?'), and to eat scones she had spent an afternoon baking. Whenever I spoke of my astonishment to Londoners, their eyes would crinkle and their heads fall back with the effort of understanding. I'd try to tell them how most people who were someone in India didn't remain themselves. In a way, their status seized them so that they became what they had become. And that was not like something from Lewis Carroll, because men disappeared into their achievements until you could see only a Judge or a Literary Critic or a Professor or a Head Clerk.

My publisher, I gathered, was one of the most powerful women in British publishing; any book she was enthusiastic about was taken very seriously. Her power emerged not only from her ability to pick the right books, but from a personality that almost everyone I met said 'cast a spell' on them. Before I knew any of this, I had felt that spell in a peculiar, physical way. Being with her was like entering a room where strange powers were being tested – you felt a flow swirling around you and a sense of tremendous withheld energy.

I told myself I was being very silly and giving in to the kind of magical thinking I had always resisted in India. Talking about this sense of being in a Presence would have seemed absolutely ordinary in Bombay, where Great Souls were considered as real as great figures or well-developed muscles.

I tried to find an explanation for what I felt with Liz Calder. Of course, she was my saviour, the woman who had recognised my ability to write. Like many young men I wanted an older woman who would take charge, shape my career. And she did it with such joy – as if she were thrilled to have spotted my talent in far-away India. Her enthusiasm for my novel almost convinced me that it was going to be a best-seller. So that my agent, a sober Englishman, had to remind me that first novels rarely sold more than eight hundred copies in hardback.

And there was the fun – we had a running joke about money (I could never have enough) and about her son, whom I saw once and desperately desired. 'What's in it for me?' she asked, looking over the top of her reading specs. She presided over Bloomsbury so regally, I once gave her some roses with a card that said, 'To One Queen From Another'. Seeing me being lifted over a precarious staircase, she called out, 'Take care! You are handling one of Bloomsbury's major assets.' And I felt the sun on my face.

Then I discovered something else. Most of the people who loved her – and there was no other word for it – admitted that they were a bit afraid of her. None of them had a reason; they had never known her to be vindictive or even nasty. But they felt that if ever she became their enemy, they would find themselves in a very unpleasant position. I remembered a chill moment when she told me how she had refused to read A. N. Wilson since he had called a colleague of hers at Jonathan Cape a dreadful name. 'Even though I discovered he was right,' she said, laughing ruefully.

Her great friend and rival was Carmen Callil of Chatto & Windus. 'My very best friend,' said Liz. 'I never steal her authors.' A pause. 'Unless they come to me.' And she chuckled, rich with confidence. I felt goose-pimples on my arms and a huge exhilaration. '*That* is her power,' said one of her authors. 'You feel so lucky and strong in her camp – the prospect of falling out is unbearable.' I thought of that every time I went silly about her, keeping every little scribble she ever sent me.

About Caroline Michel, someone had said that her dress allowance surpassed the national deficit of Honduras. When I met her I knew she looked different – as if she had actually chosen what she was going to wear that morning. 'She has private means,' I was told with awe, something I didn't quite understand. In Bombay, if you don't have private means, you fall out of the comfortable classes quicker than a smuggler's wink. Private means, then, were rare among the British middle class. Most people lived well on what they earned and saved nothing. An unimaginable state of affairs for someone like me, who had learned early that when you don't save you live without a future. In India, we have to weave our own safety-nets.

No one was thinking of safety-nets when they were talking about Caroline Michel – her house in Belgravia, the soirées she held there, the suntan she could afford always to keep. That was one of the most delicious ironies of British life. People trying desperately to gain a colour they did not particularly admire in people who were born with it. In India people spend millions on creams and lotions trying to get rid of the darkness they have come with. The catastrophe of colour, there, is frightening. The shade of a girl's skin makes all the difference to her life – it can determine the dowry her parents have to pay, the class of husband she will get and, of course, the life-style that goes with it. Conversation is coloured with references to skin – swarthy, sallow, milky or wheatish! And this has nothing to do with the imperial past. Long before the British arrived, Indians had announced their colour preference in social choices and in their literature. It was only when the miserable absurdity of colour was turned against them all, as in South Africa, that Indians called it evil.

If the girls back home could only see her, I used to think, every time I was with Caroline Michel, brown as a Bombayite, attractive as well, herself. Her charm was ignited by people.

When she moved towards you she came alive; everything she did then was a message and a response to you.

I knew this was part of being a publicity person – and back home I was astonished to read one author's description of being with her. It was as if I had written those words myself, down to the fact that after she read my novel she said it had made her cry. Perhaps it hadn't; but I was convinced that she was the kind of person who was moved when she read, who did feel a great deal, who loved being with people, and since you were 'people' she loved being with you.

My agent, as English as understatement, once told me, 'Caroline is the best,' and I was shaken to think of my novel in those superlative hands. When I left London, she came to see me to my taxi. By then, I was blasé about these things. But I wasn't blasé when I read she had left Bloomsbury to become the managing director of another publishing house.

Sometimes I felt I was only a dream in the mind of John Irving. In his novel *The Hotel New Hampshire*, he had created Lilly, a girl who, like me, never grew tall. But she turned into a writer and produced a best-seller called *Trying to Grow*. I stole the name when I wrote my autobiographical novel. Then John wrote a novel called *A Prayer For Owen Meany*, about a boy who was tiny like I was, had a high-pitched voice just like mine, and like me was always being lifted high and passed around from one pair of arms into another. So that Freddy started calling me Meany.

I read the book before most people because my publishers had just become John's publishers as well. They were quite delirious, and were planning a book launch that was going to be a literary royal wedding, at Claridge's Hotel. There were rumours leaping around that they had asked Claridge's to redecorate its drawing-room in blue to match the book's jacket.

When I held the invitation in my hand, my head felt that weird lightness which came from yoga-breathing too enthusiastically. After all, there's only so much a boy from Bombay can take in on his fifth day in London.

Claridge's used to make me very angry. That was where Indira Gandhi stayed whenever she visited London. At the same time the foreign-exchange allowance for everyone else was eight American dollars. Later, in an act of heart-breaking generosity, it was raised to five hundred. Which still meant going to the black-market money-changer, looking over your shoulder all the time, buying pounds at air-filled rates, hiding them in the most unlikely, and often uncomfortable, places you could think of, praying that you would not be discovered. That last bit was, of course, very little trouble for most Indians, who prayed when times were rough, and when they were smooth as a kind of prophylactic.

Now here I was where the last Empress of India had put up tent. I saw a footman in stockings and knee breeches straight out of Cinderella (the Ladybird version). I thought that wasn't too inappropriate.

While I had always known that my disability was, in the most real sense, only as important as I allowed it to be, and that I could work my way into a life where it would be about as relevant as the colour of my hair, to most people, in Bombay, I was Cinderella. Transformed by some special blessing, bestowed in lieu of healthy bones, from 'pitiful handicapped' to 'London writer'. So that when I got back innumerable people said to me, 'How? How? I can't believe all this has happened to you.' So, doubtless, spoke the Ugly Sisters, in more grammatical idiom.

Now John Irving stood before me in that so-familiar-from-his-books wrestler's stance, legs apart. Liz had told him about my theft of his title, and he was writing something for me in a copy of his book:

> To Firdaus
> With my apppreciation
> from
> John

I found myself lapsing into superstition, trying to figure out if those three p's in appreciation had some secret significance.

After all, if I had not loved his writing as I had, if I had not gone away from his books a little braver about 'the things you want and cannot have', would I be shaking his hand just now? And asking him where Lilly had come from, and was Owen Meany a male version of her? No, he answered, Lilly was imaginary, but he had known a boy like Owen years and years ago and then he had heard of his death in Vietnam. He had created someone like Owen in *The Cider House Rules*; when he sat down to write his new book he kept feeling he had met this character in someone else's fiction, and he was terribly worried about this major theft. Until his agent said, 'You ass, you're borrowing from yourself.'

I liked the realness of the man, the way he had kept himself himself. Without that, I supposed, it was hardly possible to write anything substantial.

'But his literary reputation, in Britain, isn't very high,' I was told again and again, as if I were risking mine by saying how much I enjoyed his books. I was getting a bit tired of this social blackmail. I had not defended the West in lonely article after article in India only to fall silent when I got there. Thatcher, accents, After Eight, now John Irving – I made it a point after that, wherever I went, to recommend his books, and say how my novel was a distant relative.

At the party that evening I knew I had to be very careful about not appearing author-awed; rising stars are not dazzled by Orion.

But I was. I had to have a photograph with John Irving. My editor, Mary, succeeded in getting someone from the *Daily Express* to take a picture, which he promised to send me. There was John sitting on his haunches next to me, and the flash melding us together. I never got that photograph. Funnily enough, the sitting for it was enough; like buying a book and going home with the feeling that I had half-read it already.

'We haven't met,' said a woman with a surprised face, short hair and a soft smile. 'I'm Imogen Parker.'

I began to say the first of fifty-seven thank yous.

'I'm so glad it worked,' she said. 'You know, this is the first time I've recommended an agent to anybody.'

I had reached thirty-three.

'And soon after I wrote to you, I got a call from your agent, gloating, "We've sold his book."'

I held her hand and smiled my face into an ache till she was gone.

I began to feel I was in a book-shop asking for all the titles I wanted and could never get in Bombay. 'Is Iris Murdoch here?'

'No, but her publisher is. Carmen Callil, you know.'

At that time I didn't know – all I wanted to do was talk about Iris Murdoch. 'Oh, I must meet her – please introduce me.' My enthusiasm was fatal. 'They'll never let you meet her,' said Timothy Mo, much later. 'She is so charming, so good at attracting authors – '

'No more than Liz,' I said, thinking we were sounding like schoolboys talking teachers.

'And Ian McEwan? Is he here this evening?'

'He was supposed to be, but he's finishing his new novel – ' which he was to sell for a quarter of a million pounds. But having read his brilliant, invincible prose, I thought that cheap.

A man, brown and tall like a tree-trunk, came up to me. 'I was born in Bombay,' he said. 'I write.' I wasn't interested, and I was ashamed. But it was as if I was at Thornton's and somebody was offering me Indian sweetmeats. 'John's agent isn't here,' said the Indian, 'Deborah Rogers.'

I smiled. She had almost become my agent; hers was the other name Imogen Parker had sent me.

'Oh! So you know something about it,' he said.

'No, no – '

'Oh yes! Much more than I do.' He waited expectantly. I was inventing something outrageous involving a threat to wax off Liz Calder's silver hair, when I saw her watching me from a corner of her eye, and smile. Changing my mind, I began to look around. The tree-trunk stood up and left.

I saw a short, pink-cheeked man with a kindly, humorous face being escorted towards me. 'This is Paul Bailey.' But he can't be, I thought. He has to be dark, his eyes wide with the pain he writes so well. Something that always surprised me when I had read his books in Bombay was that I could get so much by paying a bit of money. The unhappy thing was, I knew no one who had read him. And I used to go around telling people, 'But Paul Bailey is so good – you can't go through life without reading what he has written.'

One of his early novels, *Trespasses*, had been difficult to read because I found myself in tears every ten pages or so, and that used to fog my specs. 'Yes,' he said, '*Trespasses* is my favourite, but it isn't my best.'

'Do you know where can I buy gay books?' I asked him. In Rome I had bought a gay magazine so ugly, with hard-faced men doing hard-hearted things, I had had to chuck it into the first dustbin I found. Now I wanted serious stuff, all the books I couldn't get in Bombay.

'Gay's The Word,' he said. 'In Marchmont Street.'

'And what about gay bars? You know, we don't have those – life is awful if you're gay in Bombay. It's as if you don't exist, people bury you sexually. It's horrible.' Paul Bailey nodded. He had grown up when things were that way in Britain. 'Oh! And this is Freddy – with whom I live.'

Someone switched on the lights in Paul Bailey's eyes – he stood up. Freddy smiled and I felt thirsty. I grabbed an orange juice.

Freddy was telling Paul about the gay life in Moscow where he had lived for eight years as a piano-student. Paul was laughing; he knew Moscow, he had been there with Sue Townsend and other writers recently. They had had an uproarious time. He was like a pocket-book of anecdotes – you could mention anyone who wrote and he had a story that would land you in a libel case if you put it in print. Sometimes he was just funny: 'Christopher Isherwood – oh! I interviewed him for television in California. And you know Americans – the technicians were all so friendly, they were calling us Chris and Paul. Then I asked Christopher, "Why did you go to Berlin in the twenties?" and he said, "For the boys." You should have seen their faces; after that, of course, we were Mr Isherwood and Mr Bailey.'

After the party, my head was floating around the top of the Telecom Tower. 'Let's go there,' I said, 'and have dinner.'

Freddy looked at me as if I'd suggested we have sex on the roof of the car. 'It's all right,' I said. 'I'm going to start earning soon.'

We walked around the Tower but we couldn't see an entrance. 'This is absurd,' snorted Freddy.

'Excuse me,' I said to a man in evening-dress. 'Can you tell us how we can get to the restaurant?'

He looked pained. 'That's been shut since three years,' he whispered.

I didn't care. Something had happened to me. Britain had not been what I had expected it to be. But compared with India it was like a huge globe of blown glass, and I was dancing on wheels in the space it afforded me.

At the strangest moments – watching the cold-blue lit steeple of St Martin-in-the-Fields, signing a petition against apartheid outside South Africa House, listening to a lieder recital at the Royal Academy of Music – I was seized by a ferocious prayer to myself: Let me stay, let me stay, let me stay for ever. This was wish-making of a dangerous sort, the kind that could not endure a refusal; something I might have killed for, if killing would have helped. It seemed to me a matter of my whole future, a choice between my life as it was meant to be or the kind of death that people, in India, called life. Perhaps I knew I was exaggerating, but with something as valuable as my happiness I could afford no moderation. This, I thought, is how revolutionaries feel: if they don't go over the top, they don't go at all.

For I was almost as terrified of staying in Britain as I was of returning to Bombay. There, I had everything shelled and weighed and bottled. Love abounding, my mother, adoring sisters, friends whom I had once said I wouldn't exchange for a place at Oxford, but now I wasn't so sure. And servants, to take me to concerts and the theatre, to cook and clean, so that I had washed my first plate in my twenty-ninth year. Oh yes! I had my thirty guineas and a room of my own. And the future was even better – my mother was an heiress and I was her heir; I wouldn't need to work at anything but my books in a few years' time; I would have a comfortable old age.

To leave this cocoon that I had wrapped around my brittle bones for the discomfort of strangers seemed to me sometimes nothing but an attempted slap at the face of a culture that would not even feel it. I had never let myself know my anger until one day, in the Lake District, a passing policeman looked at me and clicked his tongue and shook his head sadly in a gesture so familiar to me from India that I was deafened by the echo.

To the person who was with me I said I was used to it, it was all right, but it wasn't, because I was flooded with runnels of rage that I managed, somehow, to keep from breaching my eyes. For twenty-nine years I had been told, day after day, in the street and the cinema, at weddings and at exams, in shops and at restaurants, that I was not a person. 'To deny someone else their humanity is to diminish your own,' James Baldwin had written. But that was small consolation to me, who could be ambushed by a quiverful of questions and advice, then tied up with bandages of pity.

A taxi-driver in Bombay turned to me and asked, while I held hands in the back seat with someone wonderful, 'What is wrong with you?'

'Brittle bones.'

'From the beginning?'

'Yes.'

'Or from birth?'

'Yes.'

'You should apply tiger's fat – in my village also we had a pygmy like you. Every day his mother would apply tiger's fat – he could even walk then.'

'Really?'

'How did this happen to you?'

'Chance.'

'No-no, must be something you have done – before, in your past life. We all have to pay, some people little, some people like you, heavy payments. Are you married?'

'No.'

'Who will marry you also – you cannot have children?'

36

I didn't think that worth denying.

'But you can pray – some girl might take pity on you.'

The hand in my hand gripped me tighter; I turned and smiled. But nothing could be wonderful now.

To be robbed is rarely painful for what you lose; it's the thought of what has been done to you that keeps you trembling and awake into the night. To be open to a plundering of your personality at almost any time lends a subtle terror to your life that lies sulking beneath the surface of your smile. I could open my door and the salesman would say, 'Poor thing you, to be like this.' A passer-by would stop a friend who was wheeling me and exclaim, 'Well done! This is the true spirit of service!' A moustachioed man would block my way and stare in horrified fascination as they did at Victor Hugo's boy who laughed. Everything so insane that if it were not happening to me I should have said it was imagination, a disabled man's psyche ballooning into delusions of mockery and defeat.

Not that I was defeated, beyond the moment. I fought as if, and indeed, for my life. I fought with every weapon I could fashion, because I knew that the way people looked at me was a lie. And I was not going to become what they said I was – a little monument to sorrow.

I lived relentlessly, wrote and read, loved and melted, shared all those Oxford-unbartered friends, wept with poetry and at the movies, practised my accents, turned those highwaymen who stopped my laughter with their long faces into anecdotes. So, armoured with a self, I ventured into Bombay's world. More and more often I won the skirmishes; sometimes, with those for whom I was beginning to care, I lost. It was one thing to know what I was, another to convey it. And when I failed, I became the battlefield, leading a doomed revolt against my own body.

In Britain, I had found a world where I did not need to fight. Wherever I went there was safety – not only for me, but for everyone else who did not consider me a reproach and a reminder of another, unforgiving world.

In London, too, people were taken aback when they saw me, but how considerately, how quickly, they rearranged their faces. How wonderful it was to hear the woman whose child was pointing at me say, 'Yes, isn't he lucky to whizz around in his wheelchair.' And even that was the only time. Children never stared or said funny things; sometimes a tousled-haired little boy came up to me and lisped, 'Hello! I'm David. What's your name?' And we'd have a conversation from which I'd wheel away knowing I had succeeded in making him forget my legs. Lying at ease in a society so sensitive, so civilised, I wanted to tell all those long faces waiting for me, I wanted to tell them softly and politely, to fuck off; I wasn't going back.

That was only half the door I wanted to shut behind me. The other half was the good life in Bombay: the blue-and-white mornings of writing and the books at night, sandwiching hours of conversation, films, plays and piano recitals. But I was only twenty-nine, and the prospect of eating that sandwich for the next thirty years had me reaching for a bottle of anti-depressants. I wanted a big life, fat with people; I chewed them like calcium, and I came away from them flushed and renewed. How many people, in this world of strangers, might I meet and know and grow with?

Having stopped at four feet I knew I had stopped in more places than my body. Often when I shut my eyes I saw myself as a precocious fourteen-year-old, astonishing people with my brilliance, charming them with my pranks. This juvenile part of me suggested sandwiches made with Oil of Ulay; framed friends by slipping expensive watches into their handbags before ordering a search; asked questions like, 'Would you find sex more pleasurable with a lion or with a sea-lion?' And even while I found it enormous fun to act like this, I hated the silly streak in me, because I knew it slithered through my writing, detracting from its seriousness and its worth.

That most people refused to treat me as bigger than my size was an explanation, but no excuse. I could not stand in queues to buy tickets to the theatre; somehow, that inability was bloated to exempt me from visits to the bank or the stockbroker. There was always someone to do things for me. Very often that was easier than solving the logistics of flights of stairs, or encountering lifts that didn't work just on the day I happened to go somewhere. The less I did the more reluctant I was to attempt the doing; and the fact that I always had difficulty in being taken seriously ('Just like me – only I'm not in a wheelchair, I'm a woman,' said a friend to me once) made me avoid the risk of being reduced to a pair of legs that did not work.

That was what surprised me most about life in London – how the disabled were treated. With consideration – as you would treat someone whose leg was in a plaster cast – and nothing more. So that I never felt my body like a stain on my self, as I did in India, nor any desire to disown the way I looked. For the first time I knew what it was to be whole, in the world outside.

This meant I was ready, indeed eager, to live by myself, to do all the things (never mind if I was sounding like Julie Andrews in *The Sound of Music*) I'd never dared. To say I was looking forward to roasting a chicken and emptying my dustbin, talking to my bank manager and taking a train, was like saying that Neil Kinnock wouldn't mind becoming Prime Minister.

Freddy and I had ended up at a Dutch pancake restaurant. Watching me dig into a chicken pancake as long as my torso, Freddy said, 'Do you realise how much your appetite has increased since you came here?'

'Yes,' I said, 'I have noticed.'

FOUR

Sex-lives and stereotypes

When I met Blanche in Bombay, four years before I arrived in London, I decided she came from the under class that I was always reading about in the *Guardian*. Her hair was a mess of tangles that hung around her shoulders with nothing to do. Soon after she came to stay at Freddy's, his old *ayah* crept up on her with a comb and tried to find what she called a partition in her hair. I thought how hurtful it must have been for Blanche – first the tearing of the tangles, then the reminder of the hair stylist she could never afford. Her clothes were torn at the seams, the colours pale with age. Her accent was not something you would hear on the Beeb. I felt very sorry indeed.

I discovered that Blanche lived with her parents in a house in Surrey. Her father was a company director who made a great deal of money, for which Blanche despised him. She did not believe in capitalist exploitation; she voted as left as she could. She was a brilliant artist and had studied not just at the Royal Academy but in France as well. She lived on the dole, which at that time was a little over £29 a week. Her father didn't take any money from her, though she had offered him a slice of her small wedge. She wished he would take it, because this way he was always complaining about the bills and turning the heating off so that her fingers froze around her brush.

I suggested she take up a job so she could live on her own.

'But I can do that anyway,' she said. 'The state would pay my rent.'

'Oh,' I said. 'Then why don't you move out?'

'Oh, I couldn't,' she said. 'That would mean I would have to remain unemployed, to claim the free rent.'

'Why don't you start working then?'

'At what?'

'Teaching, perhaps.'

'Oh, I couldn't do that,' she said. 'I have to find a satisfying job.'

'Yes, but till you do – '

'I remain unemployed and the state has to support me, since it is keeping me unemployed.'

'But you could get a job.'

'Of course I could – but it's the state's duty to get me a job I enjoy. You don't understand, you don't live in a welfare state.' There, I thought, but for the grace of the unfair state, go I. It would be easy enough never to edit third-rate manuscripts again, or review books at £6 a review, or write pieces for £4, as I was doing then. I would be excused from something I was perfectly capable of doing. And not even because I was disabled.

'You must have a lot of time,' I had said to Blanche. 'Do you go to the theatre, see films often?'

'I can see films at home – my parents have a video.'

'Mine don't. What about plays?'

'Oh, they're terribly expensive – but if you're unemployed and there are unsold tickets you get them cheap. Sometimes you pay three pounds to sit next to someone who has paid fifteen.'

'Wow! That's wonderful!'

'Not at all. It means waiting in a queue and never being able to plan your evening.' Perhaps, I thought, it might be a good idea if the dole came with two free tickets every week.

Now, four years on, Blanche had a £40 perm, which she hated; she was trying to wash it out of her hair. The state had found her a satisfying job teaching, but it paid her about £18 an hour, and she was a home-owner with a flat in West London.

The pleasures of home-ownership had not altered her views.
She still voted as left as she could, which wasn't very far these
days, what with Labour losing its convictions to win votes.
She became almost asthmatic if she heard Thatcher speak.

One morning in the Buttery at Burgh House, where I had
to eat the name rather than the food, Blanche said suddenly,
'I could never live in Hampstead – it's so bourgeois.'

'What do you mean?'

'It's so comfortable, it makes you forget everyone who
isn't.'

I didn't see how Hampstead was more bourgeois than where
she lived, except that a taxi into town cost less from Hampstead.
But when I visited the house in Surrey where she grew up, I
understood.

Much later, Blanche asked to see the journal I was keeping
about my season in the West. I had said some rather nice things
about her so I let her have a look. Some three minutes later I
heard a shriek. She was reading out, 'Met Blanche's charmless
parents in their ugly house with their too huge furniture.'

And I wanted to ride my wheelchair straight into Honoria
Gaskell's gas oven.

One morning, in the park, Blanche revealed her sex-life
to me. I was insanely curious, and appalled. I thought she
might be a verbal exhibitionist. In Bombay, sex-lives are like
salaries – coyly touched upon, politely guessed. But never,
never to be talked about except in a jokey, pubescent way –
'What were you doing last night? We saw your lights on till
dawn,' in the same tone as 'Hey! You seem to be splurging –
bet you've got a rise.' Rarely, and then as a mark of the highest
friendship, did we confess our sex-lives to someone. For sex
outside of marriage, or uncontrollable love, was as shameful
as shop-lifting, and much more sinful. Those who enjoyed
it took extraordinary precautions to remain undiscovered. I
had a friend who never went out of town without leaving her
stock of condoms with me, in case her mother found them
while cleaning her cupboard. Of course, it was worse if you
were a woman; a man was supposed to be discreet purely out
of convenience – once he lost his reputation no girl worth hers

could be seen with him. That would mean narrowing the field into nothingness.

Blanche's life seemed to me, then, something like Fanny Hill's. Her experience was of many years, and wide. I was cunning enough not to show my astonishment, so that she might go on. She was telling me about one lover, Mark, who could go on and on 'Deep into the night,' she said, and laughed at her pun. She had a marvellous time with him until he became increasingly reluctant to go to bed with her. She was hurt, but not for long. She discovered that Mark was gay.

'I want to meet him.'

'You will,' she said, 'you will.' And went on to tell me about a Frenchman who was a fire-cracker, not in bed – that was so bourgeois – but in the snow, between the hedges.

'We'll commission you to write *The Gay Guide to Britain*,' Liz Calder said to me once, and laughed. I didn't tell her I had enough information to publish a mini sex-survey of Greater London. There was the woman who told me that nine times a week was just about average – for her, at least – and proceeded to give me a timetable; another girl who had seduced a Buddhist businessman, thereby considerably reducing his non-attachment to the material world; yet another who, because she couldn't stand her husband, wrapped herself in layers of underclothing and over-coats. ('Thank God for our dreadful weather,' she said), but the persistent devil still managed to find his way through.

As time went on, I began to see the sense of all this, the existence of sex as something louder than a whisper, disdainful of furtiveness. So much healthier, I thought, to keep it in perspective next to your mortgage than to hide it under the magnifying glass of secrecy. But I was also disturbed by the divorce of desire from feeling and what psychological somer-saults that must entail. Sometimes it seemed to me that doing things with your hands and mouth without the participation of your real self was as sad as the unmarried couples of Bombay holding hands even while their minds were taking the clothes off each other.

Blanche's Mark and I did meet, quite by chance, one night

43

in Leicester Square. Freddy and I were there because I was getting angry with Finchley for being so dull when it had everything going for it – a high sky that never seemed to go dark, parks where ducks had ducklings in green ponds, long quiet lanes that loved wheelchairs – and Margaret Thatcher as its MP. 'That is why Finchley is bloody boring,' said Blanche.

I had press-ganged Freddy into our own London By Night, but it was too vulgar for his taste, so we spent most of the tour in the Tower Records shop, which with its floors of captured concertos and cantatas was a sneer at my Rhythm House, back in Bombay, with its one large room and claustrophobic, graffiti-clad listening booths. Then we walked down to Leicester Square, and I loved it all.

'You have an American soul,' said Freddy, making me sound like a Hindi film-song to his ears.

'But this is the heart of the British capital.'

'Look around you – can you see anyone British? Everyone here is a tourist; this is a bit of London they've kept for people like you, who can't stand the real thing but can't stand not standing it. So you all come here and pretend.'

That, I insisted, was ridiculous – Leicester Square was special ages before the Americans got here. I could hear my grandfather, in jacket and tie with sola hat, tapping his fingers against his leg, singing, 'Goodbye Leicester Square!' in memory of his days as a teenage volunteer with the St John ambulance in the Great War.

One of the very few reasons I had for pitying people who lived in the West was that they would never have the joy of reaching it. Soon after I returned to Bombay, East Germans began that huge and wonderful escape via Hungary. Seeing the pictures, from which their joy seemed to lick your face, I thought, never, never, will any of my friends in Britain know this incandescent happiness. They would so easily misunderstand it for a new-found delight in sleek cars and smart clothes, bright lights and big money. What they wouldn't grasp was that this was true, but only as a symbol. What keeps the West flickering like a hard little flame in the slums of Calcutta or in Tiananmen Square is the place it gives men and women – right in the centre of their own lives.

Where I come from, there is no lack of gaiety, noisy celebrating or blazing lights. Weddings dance in the streets, festivals fling colour into faces or turn whole cities into giant candelabra. But it all ends in a god, in an idol with an elephant's head or a bloodstained mouth or a mischievous smile. The singing and the oil-lamps, the drums and fire-crackers, are for someone else, someone who has to be kept happy. So it is, too, in those other lands, where the idols lie embalmed in glass cases.

But in the West you roar in the streets or stand on one foot or have sex or get drunk or jump out of a window because you want to. As for those Westerners who growl that the dark gods inside us are no different, no less powerful or tyrannical than the ones in the coffins and the temples – they have never known the inside of an interrogation cell, nor been in the capricious hands of a godman.

Before I could explain the metaphysics of Leicester Square to Freddy, he was bounding across the road shouting, 'Maa-aa-rk!' who was tall, slim, blue-eyed and had dark hair shot with silver. 'Hello,' he said – his accent was all right – 'I've heard so much about you from Blanche. What is your name? I'm sorry, I didn't get it – '

'Firdaus, it's Persian, it's the root of the Greek word *paradisos*.' I'd heard that on BBC television, and had been delighted by my connections.

'Not *paradisos*,' said Mark, waving his palm in my face. 'Par-*aa*-disos. I should know, I'm half Greek.' How appropriate, I thought, remembering Achilles and Patroclus. 'Meet Edward,' he said, waving his hand at a limp-faced boy who was leaning against a wall. Watching him, I understood what Thatcher meant when she talked about Wets.

'Blanche and I are going to Oxford,' said Mark. 'I'm delivering her paintings.'

'You should go with them,' said Freddy to me. I ignored the leer in his voice and said I'd love to.

'I hope there's room in the car,' said Mark, and I thought we had come on too fast for the half-Englishman.

We said goodbye. 'Did you like him? Did you like him?' said Freddy before we were out of his shadow.

'How do I know?'

'Come on! He's handsome, he talks the way you like, he knows Greek – '

I grinned. I knew what Freddy was aiming at. I was talking about being a dipsomaniac in a wine-shop, living with him. I'd never stopped to think how the wine must feel.

The next day Honoria Gaskell's youngest son had a birthday party for about a hundred people. I was a bit surprised, though I shouldn't have been. When my sisters got married we had about a thousand guests, and that was only average. But a birthday was different, and Robert had not only invited his friends but had asked them to invite whoever they wanted.

Then there was the matter of gifts. The English were strangely casual when it came to giving presents. Flowers and wine were wonderful, but to me seemed insubstantial. In India, presents were as lavish as affordable, and sometimes more – heavy sarees, a quartet of books (never one), a couple of records, pounds of sweetmeats – and carefully reciprocated. The outrage of a friend of mine when her English sister-in-law gave her a set of toilet-soaps was something to be seen. 'Soaps!' she said. 'And to be used after going to the toilet?'

Freddy too, had been given a free hand. He had called Blanche and Mark and the Girls of Slender Means. Joy and Klara lived in the house next to ours. Joy was from Devon, tiny, with mousy hair and the face of a little boy that turned red with the sun or shame. She was nineteen, a pianist and a student, and London was to her what it had been for her provincial ancestors – a wicked, glamorous place where you could be yourself in spite of the dangers. Her parents were terribly conservative, they had punished her once for speaking with a working-class accent, she said, and I grinned. Terribly conservative obviously meant that it was all right for Joy to share a house with a man. In Bombay, that would be so liberal the parents would be liable to fall off the social scale.

Joy lived not only with Angus but with Klara too, and of course no one was sleeping with anyone. Klara was German, from Stuttgart – her mother was dead and her father remarried, with a little boy whom Klara loved but preferred to live without. She too was a piano-student, but as different from Joy as Riesling from Malvern water. She was large and sleepy with heavy gold hair and spectacles to match. While Joy wore white and red and yellow, Klara never dressed in anything but black. Joy twittered with things that mattered to her, Klara spoke ponderously about nothing at all.

Neither of them had much money – I was always appalled by how little money young people had: when they went to a cashpoint machine it was for £20. Slowly, I had grasped that in Bombay it is only the youngsters who have money that do things – eat out, hear concerts, have parties. In Britain, a little money went much further, and that meant so did little people. The Girls had a very good time on their Slender Means. At night we'd go looking for Death by Chocolate at Muswell's Café, which was so noisy I once sang the stirring Indian national anthem without making a head turn; on our way back we'd steal the unofficial roses that clung to walls like red velvet pin-cushions in the dark. Or we went tramping around London, and there was a perfect moment when I read, and revealed, the 'Ode on a Grecian Urn' to Joy, who was kneeling next to my chair before the Elgin Marbles. I was thinking of Macaulay and his desire to create a class of Indians English in taste, and how I was returning some of that, making his circle complete. Much later, Joy offered to marry me, purely out of love: my love for England. She knew how much I would have liked to stay and make my life in London, and if a marriage of convenience was the only way, she'd make it possible. I was undone by her ability to grasp my longing and her willingness to do something more than just feel. Then I thought of the terribly conservative parents and what they'd do to her, and I flew back instead, before my visa died on me.

At a party that evening, things were more cheerful. The

birthday boy had just received a Strip-o-Gram, much to the consternation of Mrs Gaskell, who was determined never to have anything that dated after 1914 in her drawing-room. I missed the modern invasion, since Freddy had insisted I stay upstairs; to enter the party proper was to court a crush worse than Marks at mealtimes. I didn't mind too much since I was waiting for Blanche and Mark. When they came in, Mark and I smiled at each other and shook hands with Freemasonic familiarity. Maybe, I thought, this is how dogs feel when they meet each other in a world of humans.

The party below was making peculiar sounds, grunts and groans mingled with the kind of music that Parsees said would tear the curtains in their ears. Freddy returned from one of his exploratory excursions to tell us that a couple was having it off in the room next to ours – with the door open. 'What fun!' I said, sounding as if I had said how ghastly.

The next morning, when we crept downstairs, sleeping people were everywhere, like clothes flung over sofas and chairs and on the carpets.

Freddy was not going with us to Oxford – he had a recital waiting a week later. That was a relief to me. Mark was there and I couldn't cope with a doubling of desire.

As it was, I couldn't see Oxford too well. It was as if somebody had taken me up in a spacecraft, landed somewhere, and said, 'Look! You are on the moon.' There was no way I could hold that in my mind; it was too huge.

At the exhibition, I went to sleep. Later, Blanche asked me if I had dozed off. 'Of course not!' I said, sounding as indignant as Neil Kinnock being asked if he were a unilateralist. 'The paintings were so sublime I was lost in a trance.' She nodded and smiled at my Indian sensitivity.

We went around the colleges with Blanche's friend, Anne, and her father, who had both studied at Oxford, at a college I hadn't heard of. Anne's husband, David, was sweet, and small enough for me, but his little daughter, whom he was carrying in a back-pack, made me feel guilty.

And anyway, there was Mark. Watching Mark all that time

against the skyline of Oxford reminded me of Proust, and how he had remembered nothing of his first visit to Venice because he had seen everything through the mist of his lust for the gondoliers.

Even closer to my imagination that afternoon was Philip Larkin's second and last novel, *A Girl in Winter*. A German girl spends a day with her English pen-friend at Oxford, feeling much as I did with Mark, only to discover that it wasn't even the boy's idea to invite her to visit him; it was his sister, who had wanted a diversion from her tedious life.

With me, too, was Margaret Drabble holding *A Summer Bird-cage* in her hand, saying, 'Oxford in the summer is so undergraduate and closed and nostalgic – ' and I was ambushed by envy. No matter what I made of myself, this would never be mine, I would never be eighteen again or an undergraduate here. An exclusion so painful I would willingly have left Oxford half seen.

But the shock of Evensong at Christ Church clicked my mind into focus again. I had expected something like the Sunday service I had wept through at Santa Maria Maggiore in Rome, the devotion soaring into song, flame and colour gathering into a gust of longing that blew the mind to nakedness. I never could understand why atheists were not supposed to enjoy religion. That was as idiotic as ignoring the Russian Revolution because you were a capitalist and did not think you would have joined in.

In Christ Church the emotion seemed to me false, a matter of routine, of going through the paces. Even worse, the choristers smirked and passed sidelong glances like obscene notes, and sang as if they were working out, a vocal Jane Fonda session with all the creativity you could expect from that.

The Cherwell after that felt like Virginia Woolf after an hour with Oscar Wilde. This grassy water and quiet, with the spires in the distance printed on the blue paper of the sky, was my England. We sat on a little bridge in silence.

When we left Oxford it was still light. 'That,' said Blanche, 'is St Hugh's.'

49

'The only thing they cook well there is mint sauce,' I said, and she looked at me and smiled, waiting. But I didn't remember how I knew that.

'You don't *meet* it. You *feel* it, you know it's there.'

In between sight-seeing trips, I was gathering information on life in London for the immigrant population. I wanted to know how it felt to live here and be an outsider. I had asked my taxi-driver, who was slim and black with a helmet of crew-cut curls, if he ever met racism.

'How? Do you mean the way you're treated in restaurants, in shops?'

'No – no one treats me bad; if they tried they'd be in trouble. Most white people are decent, you know.'

'Oh yes.'

'Very often it's the Asians who are the worst.'

'Really?'

'Oh yeah, sitting in my taxi and talking fancy – "As I was saying old chap" – trying to prove they are different from me.' He made a retching sound. 'I think they are the dregs.'

I squirmed; I had been practising my British accent on every new person I met. 'You know,' I said, 'some Asians don't put it on – they've been to school where they talk like that.'

'Sure,' he said, 'like I never thought *you* were putting it on.'

'Does it discourage you – this racism?'

'Can't afford to let it – I'm going to do my best. I'm going to apply for every job I can, I'm not going to be a taxi-driver all my life.'

'What are you planning to do?'

'I'm studying.'

'What?'

'Things.'

I was silent, chastised.

'I'm not going to fall for their stereotypes – you know, black people are good for nothing and all that rubbish.'

'Oh yes, that must be so hard to deal with.'

'Yeah, you probably know – people think if you're in a wheelchair you can't do a thing, don't they?'

50

'Yes, yes.'

'But I don't swallow any of that bullshit about black people. You know why? My parents took me back to Nigeria when I was twelve. I lived there seven years, I learned it was all right to be black. Because you see everyone black – teachers, doctors. They can do it and they prove white people wrong. Do you know what white people say to me now? They say – "Oh! You're different because you're from Africa. Not like these lazy West Indians." But I've grown wise to their ways. I'm not going to let anyone rubbish other black people.'

'Of course – only, why did you leave Nigeria?'

'Had to. It's no good there. You can't get ahead – too much corruption. Here I'm okay; I'm a taxi-driver, but I make money. It's better for small people in Britain, racism and all.' He got out to remove my wheelchair from the boot. 'You take care,' he said as I slid out. 'Talking to you felt good.'

Outsider was not a word I would have used to describe the Asians I saw; aliens was more like it. In Finchley, they stopped at Tesco's, the women in silky polyester sarees divided down the back by thick plaits of glistening oiled hair. They shopped single-mindedly, not noticing anything that wasn't on the shelves; and they wore the closed faces of the deaf. My sister is deaf, and I was reminded of how her lively, beautiful face can disappear into a smudge of nothingness when she is in a strange place.

Not once did I see these women or their men interact with anybody; not in Oxford Street, nor in Hampstead or Bayswater. If I saw them coming towards me I'd flick a smile and they'd return a sulk and a blink. In a lift at Selfridges an Asian woman pushed herself out as if she were making her way through furniture, not people, and I could have sworn she had moved back to Bombay inside herself. Or perhaps never left it at all. Even when I saw Asian people with other Asian people in the street, they wore a sullen, and – was I imagining it? – hunted look. As if they had known great danger and had managed barely to escape.

An overwhelming sadness crept over me – these people back home talked endlessly and loudly in the streets; the men laughed and scratched their heads, the women swung their plaits in annoyance; if you were in a train with them they'd offer you their *chappatis*, soft as linen handkerchiefs, and invite you to lunch with them during your stay in their town.

What had been done to them so that they had locked themselves into psychological space-suits? What injury or insecurity could alter a people's personality in this way? Who had rejected the other's culture? Or was it mutual incompatibility? I wished I could travel all over the country, to Bradford, to Leicester, and find out. But this book was still just a gleam in my publisher's eyes, the water was running out of my cash pool, and I could afford, only, to imagine the truth.

I was on my way to meet Helena, outsider. She came from Yugoslavia via the Soviet Union and was the third wife of a famous Soviet pianist. She hated her husband, who was a drunk and a womaniser – 'He would fuck a pig if he found one,' she said. She spoke like that: loudly, dramatically, over the top and beyond. But she was an inspiration to me.

She had come to Britain on a visit and worked as a waitress in a café where the owner made her open her mouth at any time to see if she had got tuna inside, which was expensive and forbidden to the staff. She had managed to save £500, which she had paid to her best friend's fiancé so that he would marry her and she would become a British resident. He did so with pleasure, and used the money to have a pre-marital honeymoon with his real girl.

How safe Helena felt now. And how much I envied her, and pitied her. I knew that after three years in Britain she still felt like a stranger, and, worse, that she always would. Her English was perfect and ridiculous. So that she said things like, 'It was raining cats and dogs today, but I didn't let that get me down. Just a storm in a tea-cup to me, my dear – I was used to being under the weather in Moscow.'

Her brother, who came to visit her, was even better. Listening to him was like hearing the soundtrack of a B-grade film. 'Go man, go!' he said to Freddy, who was driving. 'Let it rip. Anyone feel like a smoke? No, well, I'm gonna light up. Ooh! Think of me in London – you've come a long way, baby.' I was very sorry to see him get out of the car.

And all the while I was thinking how lucky I was to have grown up speaking English, so that Britain never felt foreign to me. The strangeness I felt was the kind I experienced when I spent a night at a rich friend's flat – the lights all shaded, the bed reluctant, the toothpaste and the jam at the breakfast table something I'd never tasted (because they came from the smuggler).

But language had disabled Helena and her brother. Access to this country was barred to them as surely as it was to me, on frustrating occasion after occasion, in India. 'I'm going to see *Lear*,' exulted Helena one morning. The next day she was despondent. 'Nothing, nothing, Shakespeare meant nothing to me.'

'That's all right,' I said. 'He means nothing to a lot of British people.'

'But that's different – don't you see? They can push him out of the way; I have no choice. That is why I came here – for freedom, for choice. And now I don't have it. It's true what they say, freedom is for the few in the West!' she said, remembering a safer time.

'How can you say that? Of course, there is no freedom from reality. I'm disabled, that can't vanish in the West; you are – you are new, your English needs time. That's a fact. Freedom doesn't offer you liberty from facts.'

'Wrong! Wrong! Wrong!' she said loudly. I was glad to see her becoming more Slavic, more genuine, never mind that we were in the foyer of the National Gallery. 'Freedom is only for the rich. Where is my freedom? Where is my credit card? The bank refused me a credit card because my bank account is off-balance. Where is my freedom? Harrods is not for me, Café Pelican I cannot eat at – '

'I have; it isn't very good. My agent took me,' I added as consolation.

'But the West has too little freedom – only it is worse in the East.'

I settled for that. I couldn't wait to get to the pictures. I have one of those gargantuan appetites for art which is a sure sign of vulgarity, or at best of deprivation. In Italy, my friends would slump into a sofa, shading their eyes, murmuring, 'No more, no more.' Having run out of push, I'd steer myself through mile-long corridors using the little bits of strength my legs had, which never seemed to run out.

'Velázquez!' said Helena, asking for directions. When we got there, she pushed me from picture to picture, as if we were inspecting clothes in a dress-shop. And she stopped level with the painting, which meant I had to turn around and look back in anger.

'Do you think we might see the pictures better if we separated?' I suggested.

'Absolutely not! Art must be shared.'

I had forgotten I wasn't talking to an Englishwoman.

'Anyway,' said Helena, 'let's go.'

'What!'

'Yes, let's go, scram, scoot. My eyes are tired; I can only watch pictures for fifteen minutes.'

'Oh . . . oh . . . I know what we'll do – you sit down on this sofa, and I'll go around a bit and get back to you.'

'Why should I sit on the sofa? My *eyes* are tired; not my feet.'

'Oh! Right.'

'But you have spent so much on the taxi – eight pounds, I think?'

'That's all right.'

'No. I must show you some more.' And off she went, whizzing through room after room, making me sick with unfulfilled desire.

According to Mark, I thought, listening to his life-story in Regent's Park. We had taken to meeting at Freddy's Academy in the Marylebone Road, where I loved waiting in the common room watching the boys, worrying and wondering if I were developing a fetish for music students. When Mark arrived, always late, as if he knew I wanted the waiting, we'd go to Thornton's.

Chocolate was as much a part of our friendship as homosexuality, so that Freddy added them up and produced the theory that gay guys like sweet things; he even asked Paul Bailey – who just made an impossibly good plum and rum preserve – if that was true. Poor Paul was quite taken aback, not quite sure if Freddy was propounding a new kind of sexist tastism.

Then Mark would wheel me and the apricot truffles, and the passion-fruit whirls, Rowntree's Fruit Pastilles and Aero bars, to Regent's Park, where we'd stop ourselves by a football game, if the players looked promising, and talk.

Recently, while waiting for a teacher's post, Mark had been washing dishes at a restaurant, which I felt was positively heroic for a middle-class man. Where I came from, a kitchen in a café would be seen as a way-station to beggarhood, a fall so steep nothing could enable the victim to climb back to social respectability. I remembered the fate of the Burger Boys. A couple of teenagers in my neighbourhood were making chicken rolls, hamburgers and money in their college vacations. Their stuff was good, their customers hungry, the boys themselves bursting with achievement. But not for long – the outcry from the neighbourhood was loud enough to be heard a street away. Why did these young boys have to work? And as cooks? Couldn't their parents look after them? Couldn't they provide them with pocket-money – everyone else did? And to let their children go from house to house asking people to buy their wares! Did they want to turn their boys into beggars? That the boys were moving in exactly the opposite direction was out of the vision of people whose attitudes, like stiff necks, allowed them to look one way only.

But I was a fine one to talk. When Liz Calder suggested that I might work, temporarily, as a means of gaining a work permit, as a telephone operator at the Bloomsbury office, I was shocked, as if she had proposed that I become her butler; and of course, there was nothing shocking about that either. I was, then, one of those Indians I met at the literary seminars of Bombay.

Heroic Mark was done out of his job – he was reading *The*

Trick of the Ga Bolga between sud sessions and the manager had caught him at it. He had been most polite about giving Mark his *congé* – 'I don't think you're quite suitable for this job,' he'd said.

Mark didn't mind. Being in Britain was enough, for him. He had been living in Greece for nine years, lured there by his ancestry and the need to get away from his parents. His half-Greek, highly anglicised father had married his mother, a great beauty, for her looks, though she spoke no English and came from a village near Athens. Unable to see her as his equal, the father had mistreated her for years, and as a child Mark couldn't bear to see his mother beaten. This sounded very Indian – wife-beating in Bombay is, for the poor, a matter of course, a safety-valve against social explosion. For the better-off things are more sophisticated, and sinister. Unmalleable daughters-in-law are burnt to death, caught in kitchen fires, to prove an accidental end. The widowers then marry again for a bigger dowry, like shoddy goods sold twice over.

But Mark's mother had survived; she was a talented and hardworking seamstress and she could make a small living for herself. Now, past sixty, she had gathered the courage to ask for a divorce. She had, behind her, Mark's brother and three sisters, who were her great support, as well as Mark's. He had not told his parents about his homosexuality – they wouldn't understand, he said. Beneath that, I felt, was a stronger emotion. To tell his father was, somehow, to lessen himself, to admit defeat before the old man. I knew how it was – I too had never told my father. Knowing what he would say and the full absurdity of it, I still could not bear to be called his sissy son.

Optimistic in their ignorance, Mark's parents looked on Blanche as his future bride. Whenever she visited them, his mother sent her home with a *baklava* and his father said he was waiting for a grandson. Blanche would look appropriately coy – she liked Greek food.

Mark had been to India, and also to Morocco. There he had found a tall, curly-headed Arab boy with a grin as cheerful as a slice of watermelon. Ali invited him to stay in his house, and

Mark went. There was a huge family, but Mark couldn't make much of them; Ali was the only one who spoke English. His mind was bright, like his smile, and he was desperate. There were no jobs for him in Morocco, his family was poor and he was the only one who could change that. With Mark's help, perhaps.

Certainly, said Mark. And the next month he sent Ali his air-fare to Athens. Mark had a plan. After a few weeks in Greece, getting used to Western ways, Ali was to fly to London. There, Mark hoped, Blanche would marry him and make him a proper British resident. If she proved unwilling, Ali would disappear into the dark like so many other illegal immigrants. At least he would be earning his living, sending home a few pounds, magnified in Morocco into a decent sum.

Those few weeks with Ali were the most tortured in Mark's life. Ali was straight – yes, he was ready to go to bed with Mark to return an obligation; but that meant, to the Arab boy, a destruction of his self-respect. And Mark loved him just that little bit more than he lusted for him. So they lived as friends, held parties, cooked together, went to tavernas and drank ouzo, rode all over the Peloponnese on a motorcycle. Mark wanted Ali to have the life he had never had, nor, perhaps, would have ever again.

Then Ali left for London. At Heathrow he was asked many frightening questions about his intended stay in Britain. But his intelligence and charm saw him through. Then his baggage was searched and his diary found, and read. Living without his family, the boy had told his journal all his hopes for the future.

The immediate future, for Ali, was detention. Blanche went to see him there and said she had never known anyone look so extinguished.

Mark brought him back to Athens. The boy was half-mad, as if a part of him had been burnt away. Nothing could please him now. He said his life was over, and Mark began to feel the same way about himself. The only way to make Ali all right, Mark knew, was to restore his sense of a future.

When Ali discovered that many of his countrymen had found

work in Italy, which was easier to infiltrate than Britain, Mark let him go, even though he felt that the boy was not ready to be on his own. Perhaps, Mark thought, he should have used the Greek days to train Ali in a skill other than lotus-eating.

But Ali managed very well. He wrote to Mark saying he was happy; every morning he'd buy a supply of trinkets – this was in Naples – that he'd sell for a profit in the day; he was proud to have succeeded. His brave, hoping letters seemed to Mark a dividend on the huge emotional – and monetary – investment he had made in the boy. Until they stopped. Mark had not, now, heard from Ali in more than a year. He had done everything – even written to Morocco in Arabic – and he was terrified that Ali might have been killed in a street-fight in Naples.

In return, I told Mark about something that had happened to me. Three days after I reached London, I was reading Philip Larkin's *Collected Poems* in Honoria Gaskell's garden. A strong breeze blew from a pale high sky and I sat in a well of flowers, magenta and pink. It was like being in an English novel and I thought, this is how I always want to be.

Then, just like in a book, Freddy came out of the house and sat down on the garden-seat, and told me he had some bad news. All I could think was that Honoria Gaskell didn't want me in the house any more, and that would be the end –

My father had killed himself by leaping from a window.

I could hear a bird singing a triplet of notes, and again; how was it possible, I was thinking. In a novel I had written, three years ago now, the father of a boy like me had killed himself by crossing New York's Fifth Avenue, blindfolded. And in that moment I could only think, this means my novel *is* good – how often does Life follow Art?

FIVE

The view from the balcony

My next sightseeing excursion was a visit to Lakeland, where I stayed with Blanche and Freddy in a farmhouse in High Lorton owned by a woman called Mrs Barnlayer (surely, I thought, that could not be: it was like calling Mrs Malaprop just that). The prospect was pleasurable: after all those childhood days spent at Mistletoe Farm, and before that with Little Boy Blue (was he an early version of Freddy?), I was going to whoop it up with the sheep in the meadow and the cows in the corn.

I'd forgotten about the dogs. When I opened the car door and swung my legs out I found myself astride a large black beast that was trying to get in.

'*Sauvez ma vie!*' I shouted in my Owen Meany voice.

Freddy came and shooed the dog away. 'Why did you have to say that in French?' he demanded. 'God! Someone could be murdering you and you'd be looking for the Latin to scream help.'

'The origins of what I said are historic,' I told him. 'Those are the very words uttered by David Rizzio when he was being murdered.' And in Bombay I used them all the time so that strangers would not know what a coward I was.

'Who was Rizzio?' asked Blanche.

I was appalled but not astonished. We had been to Hatfield together and she had asked what Elizabeth I had done to Mary, Queen of Scots. 'Remember I told you about Mary, Queen – '

'Oh yes! And he was one of her husbands.'

'Oh no! He was her favourite secretary and one of her husbands was jealous of him, and the nobles egged him on to plot his murder because Mary was pregnant and they hoped the shock would kill her, and he clung to her skirts, when they attacked him, and cried out, "Sauvez ma vie, madame!" and why can't the English know their history, though this is Scottish, but if you were Indian and had to deal with ten kingdoms every century you'd know how lucky the British are to have these long straight lines running through their past.'

'Bloody wonderful!' said Blanche. 'You could sing that aria from *The Barber of Seville* without the breaths showing in between!'

The Lakes, however, despite having their share of history, got on my nerves – thoroughly spoilt with the admiration and flattery of two centuries. So that Wastwater seemed to sulk mightily and shrug its big black scree-shoulders, but the water was different, unacceptably beautiful, like a young boy who could lead married men astray. Windermere was a woman who had married for money, so utterly changed was its voice from the soft gulps of waves to the tattle of tourists and the blather of motorboats. And at the end of our stay we went to Dove Cottage.

It made me sad to think someone like Wordsworth had to live in that dreary little house. Not that it could have mattered to him, since he was looking at other things. Even that surprised me – his poetry did not seem to be inspired by the Lake District. Instead he seemed to lift the Lakes into loveliness, so that even while his words surpassed the tepid beauty of water and stone, they warmed it into a great roiling vat of imagination whose vapours you inhaled with every breath between his lines.

Going from there to Paul Bailey's party, as we did that night, was like moving from Queen Victoria's Osborne to Oscar Wilde's in Tite Street. We arrived in Hammersmith at about nine-thirty. I saw the name-plates – Bailey, Healey. Paul had dedicated one of his books to David Healey; yet another said, 'David's, always'. Proofs of passion.

Meanwhile, I had a minor passion to deal with. There was

a tall man with us at the door-step, with a mop of pale grey hair in which you could lose your hand. 'I'm awfully late,' he said, 'just couldn't get out of the office – oh, I'm John Walsh.' He had a quick, staccato speech that sounded like a cross between a typewriter and a piano, efficiently pleasant. I gasped furtively when I heard his name. 'He might give you books to review,' Paul had said to me, 'if I sing your praises loud enough.' I needed work like my contact lenses needed their soaking solution. But to work for John Walsh, Literary Editor of the *Sunday Times*, was for me what getting a story into the *New Yorker* was for Truman Capote.

Meanwhile, my chair was being lifted by Freddy and another boy, whom I remembered seeing at the Savoy. 'Thanks very much,' I said, and reintroduced myself. When I first arrived I was desperate because everyone was calling me Fir-daus, making me sound like a conifer. As time went on, I grew to like my new name – I was Fi-rdaus in Bombay – which seemed to say, you belong here; like the Indian husbands who give their wives new names when they get married.

'Are you from Bombay?' asked the young man. 'I've lived there.'

'Really – where?'

'Close to the Gateway of India, one of those sleazy hotels facing the sea.'

'Oh my God, that's where most of my novel happens – and I live close to there. Were you touring?'

'No – I was smuggling precious stones.'

'What!'

'Yes, when I was about sixteen I left home and went all over, doing all kinds of strange things. Bombay – it's a terribly sexy city, isn't it?'

'Oh yes! I'm glad you said it. When I wrote about that everyone refused to believe me; that's because no one talks of sex.'

He nodded. 'You know, I had never had good sex till I came to Bombay. Then I was seduced by this Assamese woman who was three times my age – she ran the hotel – she was fantastic in a Freudian way. She knew exactly what I needed.'

61

I couldn't believe he was telling me this; Britain was the Big Book of Crazy Stories. 'How long did you travel?'

'A few years; then I was in Egypt, and one day I looked at the poor people there, and I thought, I have the freedom to wander through their country but they don't have the liberty to go to Britain, they can't travel. And I came back.'

'Here's the guest of the evening,' said Paul, proceeding to introduce me to a dazzle of people. It was a funny thing, I remembered names in books I had read years ago, but I could never remember the names of people to whom I was introduced in Britain. All my Englishness was a matter of words before eyes, so that in a roomful of people I felt I'd gone deaf; conversations were blurred into a buzz unless they were directed at me. Caroline Michel was there in glorious black – 'I've just read your book,' she said, 'I loved it.' And it was then that she said the fatal words: 'It made me cry.'

'Oh! I'm glad,' I said.

'Listen,' she said, tossing her hair, so confidential, 'one by one' – she mentioned a chain of glittering names and titles – 'may come and sit with you. Make the best of it.' She smiled, I genuflected, she rose.

'This is the man who can give you work,' said Paul leading John Walsh to me.

'Yes, can I review for you?' That wasn't sufficiently oblique, I thought. 'Fiction, modern history, international relations . . .'

'Why not? I've got an Indian novel by Gita Mehta – '

'*Karma Cola* – has she written something new?'

'Yes – would you like to review it?'

'I'd love to.' Even if it were a handbook of infectious diseases and I was a phobic. 'How much will I get for that?' I knew it had to be more than the ten pounds I was paid in Bombay.

'Two hundred and fifty? Will that be all right?'

Surely the only 2,500 per cent pay hike in history. 'Yes,' I said, magnificently English, 'that will do.'

I couldn't wheel myself away from John Walsh, who had this fantastic sexuality, the kind that sweeps you laughing into bed. 'A. N. Wilson – come on! His novels are hardly good,' he said.

'Why does everyone dislike Wilson so much – is it because he admires Thatcher? And he has found God, hasn't he?'

'Yes, all most strange.'

'I think Thatcher is doing a good job.' Everyone laughed at my sense of humour. 'But I do.' More laughs – as if I were insisting that I ate badgers for breakfast.

'Really?' said Paul, 'then you are perfect for the *Sunday Times*.'

'Well, what about Iris Murdoch?' There was a collective groan – the kind you hear in India at the cinema when they are showing *Power Generation in Villages*. 'I think she is superb – no one sees relationships like she does!' A friend and I lived in Murdoch-land. We'd say, 'Ugh! That's Radeechy straight out of *The Nice and the Good*,' when we met a man who spent hours trying to cast spells on his neighbours; and 'God! That's my Beautiful Joe,' I'd moan, watching some young man who was making me suffer. 'Now I know how poor Cato felt.'

A man of about fifty with thick dark eyebrows brushed into his distinguished face was sitting quietly behind me. 'He's a publisher,' said Caroline, giving him a cuddle and a kiss. I was moved by the sight of how far she was ready to go for me.

'Do you think I could read manuscripts for you – edit them – anything?'

'Proof-reading, perhaps.'

Oh dear, I thought, that's the telephone operator's job in disguise. 'I don't proof-read,' I said. 'I don't know how.'

'Tell me,' he said, 'why are you so keen to stay on in Britain?'

I told him. For as long as it takes to boil an egg until it can bounce.

'This is extraordinary,' he said. 'I've never heard anything like this.'

'Do you think you can help me?'

He shook his head. 'I don't think it's any good looking around for bits of work. You should set out – and his arms were wheeling an imaginary chair – 'go all over the country and write a book about it. You've come with a kind of innocence – '

'Would anyone be interested in publishing this?'

'Of course – if Bloomsbury don't, we will, but I'm sure they'll want to. It might be a very bitter book,' he went on. 'You might find a lot of things you don't like, you might get treated badly.'

I wheeled up to Caroline Michel. 'That man, what's his name, thinks I should tour Britain and write about it – '

'Oh – that's Matthew Evans, he's the chairman of Faber and Faber.' And, said my agent later, 'a very good friend of Caroline Michel'. I had been blind to one of the great love-affairs of literary London, and sweet Caroline had not been putting out just for me.

'This is Timothy Mo,' said Paul, grinning at my grin of unearthly delight.

'I was talking about you this morning – how I missed the film of *Sour Sweet*.'

'It wasn't very good anyway; though it had a marvellous script – by Ian McEwan.'

Timothy Mo looked like a letter-bomb: a compact little body, tense and taut, and a face to go with it, so that he looked as if he had taken a sharp breath and was about to spill a secret. 'Definitely gay,' said Freddy, who claimed to have the gift of finding fags in a crowd.

So one day I took Tim Mo for a quiet stroll in the park close to our house in Finchley. He was utterly delightful, talking about money, which we both loved – he had more than he knew what to do with, I had less than I knew how to do without. We went through the tree-thick paths and he told me how he had grown up very rich but had been disinherited because he wanted to be a writer. He had struggled, carried crates, done all sorts of unwriterly jobs, and now he had written three intelligent best-sellers, and there was all that money pouring in. I thought of my father, who was always generous, who thought writing was my kind of craziness which he would indulge only because I had bad luck enough being born with brittle bones. How I had resented that denial of my worth. And now he was dead and would never know what I made of myself.

Feeling particularly tender, I led Tim to the duck-pond; the sight of the ducklings, I thought, might work like the chicks in *Lady Chatterley's Lover*.

And it did. Tim's face turned wistful, and he told me all about his Mexican girlfriend.

The party was going out with the night. Paul was kneeling in front of me. 'Did you get any work?' he said.

'I did, I did – I might have got another book.'

'Oh, I'm glad,' he said; I wanted to kiss him. 'And who's going to look after you when Freddy's gone in July?'

'I'll look after myself,' I said, heroic as I was terrified.

Driving home, Tim Mo told us about David Healey; how he had died some years ago and how Paul could not remove his name from their door.

'Don't wash your hands after you've shaken his,' said Honoria Gaskell when she knew we were going to meet Alan Bennett after seeing *Single Spies*.

It is a comic tribute to the Indian economy that my family belongs to the upper middle class, for we have neither car nor air-conditioning, no washing-machine and no video – only two servants. So that when I went out in London, it was always a pleasant shock to realise that the expensive restaurants were out of reach, or that I'd be sitting in the last row of the balcony of the Queen's Theatre. Nothing is more stimulating than a tumble down the class system – providing you know it's all in fun.

The matchstick figures on the far-away stage were a delight, like looking into someone's house with binoculars.

Mark had carried me up the endless staircase, and that helped to cushion the shock of Prunella Scales's absence from the stage – she had laryngitis. At the end of it all, we went out of the theatre and found Alan Bennett waiting against a wall in the dark. He appeared so defenceless you wanted to carry him home and comfort him with a warm bath. Blanche, Mark and Freddy were ready to fall at his feet; I thought he looked quite terrified of us and the din we were making – we had two other friends with us – saying how wonderful he was. He smiled nervously, shook hands, asked what each of us was doing, muttered, 'Musicians, musicians,' and rode away on a bicycle.

Mstislav Rostropovich, whom I met at the Barbican, was just the opposite. Freddy had accompanied him on a concert tour of India, and while in Bombay we had both been Freddy's guests at a dinner party. Ros-poch, as we called him, was one of my heroes. I had read the autobiography of his wife, the prima donna of the Bolshoi, Galina Vishnevskaya, and I knew how they had been persecuted in the Soviet Union for giving shelter to Solzhenitsyn in their *dacha*. So that Ros-poch, perhaps the world's greatest living cellist, had been banned from performing for any but the most ignorant and uninterested provincial audiences. They had had no alternative but to leave their country, which for Galina also meant the loss of the opera company that had been her whole life. When I met her, splendid and aloof, I asked her how she had been so brave. 'One has to be,' she said. 'What else can one do?'

Ros-poch was full of stories and images – 'These young violinists playing so perfectly – it is frightening, like a twelve-year-old kissing you' – and he smooched the air elaborately, turning his head this way and that – 'passionately.

'The Soviet Minister of Colture has the colture of a – PIG! Yes, I was with him in Washington at a reception, and I say' – he raised his hands – 'thank God I do not have to go back! You know, they would wake us in the mittel of the night and say, "Come here, at once! To play for us, to sing." We would go, and play, and sing, they would not listen, they would be drrunk! But they like the power! Yes.' He nodded like a great bear. 'Powerr! Gilels, our best pianist, requested a holiday in Paris – he was getting a prrize there – the Minister of Colture said, "No! If you go, you must perform! Soon as you get off the plane all will see your violin and demand your violin recital"!'

Ros-poch had sent us two tickets to the London Symphony Orchestra concert he was conducting. We had steps to go down, and needed help. Freddy went and fetched a young man with soft brown hair and red lips. 'This is Ignat Solzhenitsyn,' he said.

'Hello, pleased to meet you,' he said, his voice American.

I didn't know what to do; I would have given anything to tell him to thank his father, but there was no way I could intrude on his careless smile. We had reached the bottom of the stairs. 'Thank you,' I said, going all Indian, shaking my head from side to side. 'Thank you so much.'

After the concert, I was taken back-stage to meet Ros-poch.

'Maybe you should go in and thank him for both of us,' I said to Freddy, suddenly gripped with shyness.

'He'd be terribly hurt' – and Freddy pushed open the door.

'Ah! My friend, my friend!' And I was soaking in his sweat, holding his great bald head to mine. 'How is the book?' he boomed. 'Is it getting published? Yes? Ah! You will send me a copy?

'This, you know who this is? Solzhenitsyn's son, my god-son!' Ignat had been born when his parents were Ros-poch's house-guests and the KGB were trying to flush them out. 'Thank you, my friend, goodbye – send me your book!' And I went out, quite beatified.

My visit to the Shaftesbury Cannon was not as happy. Mark and I had time to spare and food to eat before the show, so we found our way into a quiet churchyard tucked away like a flower behind Theatreland's ear. We had begun tearing the wrappers off the Aero bars when we heard a groan. And a creak; and a sigh.

'Ghosts,' said Mark, his eyes very Greek.

A head appeared over the back of a bench and lolled to one side. Behind us a sleeping body rolled off a stone ledge with the quiet *slomph* of a sack; and when we looked carefully we saw mounds that were men, everywhere, completely grey, a perfect camouflage against the churchyard.

'We've landed in a tramps' graveyard,' said Mark. In the distance we could see a man clutching a bottle to himself, like a comfort to an aching belly.

'Let's go,' I said, apprehending a cosh on the head.

'No,' said Mark. 'They don't do anything. They're fin-ished.'

Finished. I knew what he meant; there were finished women and old men and babies all over Bombay. But Englishmen were not supposed to be finished; this was unnatural, like a slap under the mistletoe. Later, Joy showed me the carcass of a car with a man trapped inside. 'He lives there,' she told me. 'I passed him once and there were hundreds of cockroaches all over him, as if he had tamed them.'

'It's all Her fault,' said Honoria Gaskell. 'Things were never like this.'

I could not agree. I knew, from my own life I knew, what it was to fall apart in a heap of broken bones, and the temptation to stay there on the floor, all struggle ended.

I knew that every day of my life I would have to challenge the victim inside me, the voice that said, so honestly, I haven't got a fair deal, how can I be expected to live as if I had? But I also knew that I had my hand on the knob that could turn that voice to a roar or a whisper, although I could never reduce it to silence. Each twist of the knob was a full day's fight, and it was no metaphor to say that those who would not fight could not expect to live. So while there was no denying that there were some who could not fight – whose minds had rendered them incapable of battle – it was, to me, just as important to remember those who chose to fight lying on their broken backs. Thom Gunn said it in a line, and more memorably than I: 'It is better to be a soldier than a cripple.'

But we were on our way to *Torch Song Trilogy*, my first gay film. Straight people wouldn't find life as much fun if every time they went to the cinema they saw nothing but men swanning around with men or women with women. In Bombay, I used to watch the ludicrous *Dynasty* – 'Such cardboard people,' said Honoria Gaskell – because it had a gay character; that was the only time I could see someone homosexual as real, his romantic relationships as relevant as anyone else's.

We'd bought our tickets and were about to go in when our way was barred.

'I'm so saw-rry,' said the manager to me, 'I know this is absolutely hideous, but we can't let you in. While you have our sympathies, we have our fire regulations. And we can make no exceptions. We shall refund your money. In full.'

I sat there open-mouthed – and it took a lot to get me that way – in the foyer of the cinema. I could not quite grasp that I had actually been turned away from somewhere. I saw his point; the steep and many stairs would be no fun in a fire. 'But my friend can lift me down as quickly as he can run,' I said, and that was the truth.

'I'm saw-rrry,' he said, shook his head and moved away.

'But this is so unjust,' said a young woman, running her fingers agitatedly through her long black hair. 'They should do something about it. I'm so sorry – I wish I could help you.'

'That's all right,' I said, 'we'll go and see some other film.'

She shut her eyes and shook her head. 'How marvellously you take it; and you're smiling.'

I wasn't really taking it marvellously: when it comes to the crunch I always go brave – if only because admiration is medicine, pity a quack cure that gives you a lift, then leaves you feeling worse than ever.

But this was Britain, land of choices, and if I couldn't see a film in one place, within half an hour I was watching it in another. *Torch Song Trilogy* was as schmaltzy as a Parsee wedding, and I liked it for that.

'Too much emotion,' said Mark, shaking his head.

The next day we went to Gay's The Word, the bookshop that was being harassed by the customs authorities for importing gay literature. I had been appalled when I had heard about this. That any published work should be proscribed seemed to me a denial of everything Britain stood for. After all, publishing or selling something is not a coercive act: people can ignore a book more easily than the weather. And it seemed ironic that the same conservatives who were always warning against the dangers of the Loony Left thrusting their version of morality on to families and children were themselves setting a precedent.

I know what the prohibition of pornography does to the human mind – I cannot imagine a people more obsessed with obscenity than Indians. Every time there is a festival of films from France or Germany the scenes outside the cinema houses resemble a food-riot, as indeed it is: a people starved of sexual fantasy seek it in momentary glimpses of bare flesh and moving parts. When some film leaves them unfed, they boo and shrilly whistle their disappointment before moving on to demand their money back.

And pornography becomes a smugglers' monopoly; organised crime produces all the goods that people want and the state will not let them have. The quality is dreadful, with little grey booklets selling on pavements, saying things like: 'Then he was biting my nether regions hotly . . .' Of course, anyone who can afford them buys the glossy magazines from the West, *Penthouse* and *Mayfair*, which the smugglers sell at exorbitant prices. Once again, state controls succeed in excluding only those who do not have the money to circumvent them.

If anything frightened me about London, it was the intolerance. That is an almost insane thing to say about one of the most liberal cultures in the world. Perhaps that is the secret: usually there was no violence involved, no shouting matches or raised arms; in its place there was orthodoxy and a refusal to countenance dissent. Even while the Conservatives were trying to impose codes of ethics on the press, the Left seemed to have hijacked the very concept of good and was claiming a monopoly on morality.

It needed an act of courage to say, in a London drawing-room, that you believed in capitalism; or in selective schooling; or that people who could afford to spend money in pubs and on cigarettes should not protest when they were asked to pay for a part of their medical expenses; or that you didn't think Mrs Thatcher was a she-devil.

I thought Alexander had exaggerated his predicament on that first evening I spent in London; but I was wrong. Again and again I was to see moral intimidation at work. Joanne, a secretary I was talking to, was saying how much she admired Mrs Thatcher, how she thought she was doing a great job, when a friend of mine who worked in television walked in and said, her voice a slosh of derision, 'God, Joanne! Don't tell me you're becoming a Thatcherite.'

'Oh – no, no,' stammered the hapless secretary. 'I was only saying she's a strong woman.'

Every weapon was used to push you off your position except solid facts or logical argument. First, there would be laughter; then incredulity – 'Surely you can't be serious'; once you assured them you were, there were pained faces to sympathise with your stupidity; then polite put-downs – 'Perhaps you don't quite grasp the situation'; when you proved your grasp the ground shifted – 'But everyone I know thinks she's terrible – how can you say this? Do you mean everyone is wrong?' 'Everyone doesn't think so.' 'Yes, but people like us do believe she's a disaster.' And so it returned to the supremacy of one group's beliefs: liberalism was not liberal about those who differed with it. The very people who complained of Mrs Thatcher's 'He is not one of us' attitude had condemned her for not being one of them. Socialism had become the creed of the cultural establishment, and it was as powerful and stubborn as religious belief in the last century, and as irrational. For me, the miracles of socialism were to be seen around the world – starvation in Ethiopia, destitution in India, ruin in Burma, the dead children in Tiananmen Square – while half of Europe was begging to be relieved of the notion that a human being's life belongs to the collective, that it must be sacrificed to the needs of the majority. The illegitimatisation of self-interest has resulted in the abolition of happiness in society after society.

And the bitterest irony was that the opponents of statism, those who rejected the belief that self-interest and personal achievement were evil, were condemned as uncaring, uncompassionate, conscienceless. It was an old trick played by new hands – destroy the argument by impeaching the character.

I, too, was afraid, but I had had a great deal of practice, in Bombay, arguing alone against a roomful of people or hundreds of newspaper columns. That had made me strong. And what made it easier was that so many of the politically intolerant people I knew in Britain were marvellous at a personal level and, like Blanche, were often my friends. 'The only thing I don't like about you is your political stance,' said my editor, who had become one of my closest friends in London; and I could deal with that.

SIX

'You've come a long way, baby . . .'

I had fallen in love. It had taken me time, but it had happened.
London seemed to me now the most wonderful place to make
a home. The stodgy streets made me smile fondly, as I did at
ungainly and much-loved aunts. The Wallace Collection was
wonderful, with a portrait by Van Eyck which looked just
like Blanche. I had seen *M. Butterfly*, the play about a gay
man who is so desperate to be loved tenderly he pretends to
be a woman. (I went with two Parsee friends. One refused
to look when the Chinese actor took off his clothes on stage;
the other couldn't tear her eyes away. 'God knows when I'll
get to see a nude Chinese again,' she said.) I was going to
see *Hamlet* (ah – Shakespeare! In Bombay we talked about
a visiting British performance two months before and three
afterwards) and *Singing in the Rain*, where I was to feel I was
back home: the audience clapped along with the songs, opened
bags of sandwiches and munched them – silently, they were
British after all – and their laughter was louder and more free;
in everything except masticatory politeness they were Parsee
as an audience in Bombay watching a ribald variety revue. As
a boy, I used to squirm when my mother sang along with the
performer on stage; when it happened here I knew she must
have learned the habit from the British audiences that filled
the theatres in the Bombay of her youth.

Always, it was the people who made London lovely – a

taxi-driver told me how much he loved his son and worried when he got home late from parties; a dental nurse who was a waitress at weekends played at guessing where Freddy and I came from (Turkey? Iraq?) and forgot to charge me for a matzo-ball soup I didn't enjoy; with David, a handsome, balding, bearded man who had worked for the British Council in India, I had conversations that left me feeling as if I had listened to Bach's Double Violin Concerto with dark chocolate in my mouth. 'It's such a pleasure to talk to an Indian who can be objective about his country,' he once said to me, and I grinned, thinking of the millions who wouldn't quite agree.

With Mark, I wandered through miles of London. One night we found ourselves locked into Kensington Gardens. We could see no park-keeper, no opening wide enough for my wheelchair. I was feeling cold; because I didn't move when we were strolling, I didn't generate any heat. This was going to be one of those stock situations from the Hindi films: the heroine is dying of hypothermia; the hero raises her body temperature the only way he knows; she – and here our stories must diverge – begins throwing up every morning.

What can I do?' said Mark. 'I can't drop you over the railing, can I?'

'Drops are fatal for me,' I said, outraged by his lack of imagination. Someone in a black leather jacket studded with metal happened to pass. 'Can you help us?' said Mark.

'I'm German,' said the man. 'I'll call the police.'

'I wonder if he thought we were soliciting,' said Mark. 'Oh, here's someone else!'

'Need some help, myte?' said a tall, blond man.

'Yes, could you hold this?' said Mark, handing me over the railing as carefully as a courier.

The next week, at Gay's The Word ('You have to be careful who you meet there,' Honoria Gaskell warned her lodger), my arms were diving into the shelves and coming up with the most marvellous books of gay verse and biography and psychology when Mark called me to him. 'You've got to look at this,' he said, and I hurried to his side. 'Isn't it great?' he said, handing me a cartoon of Ronald Reagan picking his nose.

But later that evening he redeemed himself by reading Wilfrid Owen, in his beautiful English voice ('You mean his middle-class accent,' said Blanche), sitting on a bench on Primrose Hill, and I melted. I could hear that voice for ever, I thought. Mark lifted his eyes from the page and looked into mine. He smiled a small, tender smile and brushed the hair back from my forehead. 'You know,' he said, and I swallowed and nodded. 'You know? You look exactly like that chap from *Star Trek* – the one with the pointy ears.'

But that evening I had the full moon, all London smiling its lights at me, and I was filled with a yearning that had little to do with Mark. Perhaps I was getting nostalgic – for I knew my hopes of staying on were getting paler by the day.

Liz Calder had told me she had tried to get a work-permit for an American girl who read manuscripts in five languages, and that she had been refused; there didn't seem a chance for me. I could get plenty of freelance work, but that would be illegal on my visitor's visa – and I would not break the law.

The prospect was not all dismal, however: before I left, I was to travel all over Britain for Bloomsbury.

'Who should I take with me?'

'Well, I'm off to Banff,' said Freddy, 'Honoria's going to Florence, Joy to Germany, Blanche is flying to Moscow – that only leaves Mark, I suppose.'

But Mark was English – I couldn't possibly travel through the country and expect to be an Indian abroad if I were accompanied by a white man. Besides, I wanted to talk to Asians; the surest way of shutting them up was to have an Englishman behind me. The night before, I had met my first Asian taxi-driver. He was from Pakistan, which was exciting for me. India and Pakistan are like twins separated at birth, and they hardly ever meet. I had cousins in Karachi I had never seen, my mother's best friend lived there, and I was insanely curious about the place. The impression I had grown up with was that Pakistanis hated Indians; that they were fanatical Muslims prepared to kill at the slightest provocation; that they lived in a feudal set-up with mustachioed military-men in charge; that the Parsees

75

there lived lives of unimaginable luxury, but never mind, we had freedom, they did not. A picture drawn with such broad strokes, I knew it could not be accurate.

'This is great,' I said to the taxi-driver, who had a chubby face bisected by a fat moustache. 'I'm from India.'

'You speaking Urdu?'

'No,' I said, switching quickly, 'but I speak Hindi,' which is Urdu without the music.

'Same thing, same thing,' he said. Encouraged, I asked him how long he'd lived in Britain.

'Twenty years,' he said.

'And do you like it better than Pakistan?'

He thrust his palm at me. 'How can you say that?' he said. 'This place is only for money, not for honour.'

'You mean racism is a problem?'

'No, no; but no matter how much money I am making, in Britain there is no honour in living.'

'Why do you say that?'

'See – I'll tell you. Here, even if I make one hundred thousand pounds, I will still have to put out my own dustbin. In Pakistan, I would live like a prince – at least six to eight servants.'

And I thought how tragic that his concept of honour should be tied to a dustbin, to looking after his own life. But then, surely the vision of the good life was always tied to what people around you considered worth having; in California it would be swimming-pools, in Pakistan servants. And if there was anything sad about the man, it was that he still lived by the standards of a society that could not give him the means of achieving them.

Then I thought how much Juice would enjoy this kind of encounter. She was one of my best friends in Bombay – a slim, curly-headed girl with a very un-Indian-woman appetite for experience. She had travelled all over, even to terrorist-infected north India, living in filthy little hostelries, without a man for protection. She couldn't tell Bach from Beethoven or Stanley Baldwin from James, but I didn't need that on this trip. I was a bit like Pygmalion to her; of course, she called it Professor

Higgins. And when I phoned her she said yes, just tell her when.

Part of Juice's gutsiness comes from a kind of innocence about danger. She owes her name to a spot of bother she got into with an Arab. He had stopped her in the street and asked if he could have some juice, orange would do.

'Of course,' she said, 'Come with me.' And swishing her black silk skirt about her hips ('You have a merry-go-round of a derrière,' a lecherous old Parsee had once told her) she walked him through a stink of alleys to a stall where they squeezed fresh fruit before your eyes.

But the Arab blew up. 'What do you take me for?' he shouted. 'A silly savage? A brainless baboon? A hungry hyena?'

Poor Juice – she had another name then – watched his alliterative acrobatics open-mouthed; language was not her long suit. Then she gathered her indignation like her skirts about her and said, 'I brought you where you asked, what are you saying all these clever-clever things for?'

'You most certainly did not!' shouted the Arab. 'I can sue you for false advertising!' and he pointed a hairy finger at her. Juice looked down and saw the bright orange promise on her blouse. 'Del Monte,' she read, and shrieked.

'Now you keep your words,' said the Arab, stretching a well-padded palm towards her, but she kicked off her Bally shoes, bent to pick them up – they had cost her a month's salary – and ran half the way to my house. When she looked back the Arab was splotched on the ground in a puddle of robes and groaning with pain, holding one ankle up to the sky; as far as Juice could see he wasn't wearing anything underneath.

When she got to London, she said, 'Put away that silly map; this is my fourth visit and I know every street. But first, I want to go the Heath – I'm a child of nature.'

The morning was menthol blue, the Heath was ours, we had a picnic of honey-roast ham and bread; then we made our way to Golders Hill Park with its fat sheep and pheasants. Juice fell asleep on a grassy knoll and I attempted to write a blurb for my novel. When I'd finished, Juice was rubbing her eyes. 'Give that to me,' she said. 'Your writing is revolting – I'll copy it out neatly; you can't give it to Liz Calder like that.'

When Liz Calder read it, she looked over her reading specs and smiled slowly, millimetre by millimetre. 'I see you've changed the name of your novel, Fir-daus; it's now called *Trying to Glow.*'

But that afternoon, at the Heath, Juice was at her competent best. 'Now,' she said, abandoning the sandy path, 'we are going off the beaten track straight to the main road.' About ten minutes later I realised the track had beaten us. My wheelchair was lurching like a bullock-cart on a dirt road; the path we were on was narrowing gradually until it could only carry the two left wheels while the other two whirred angrily in the air. And my health insurance had expired the day before.

'I've made it!' said Juice, looking haughtily at the path behind her, missing the jagged stones in front that bit into the tyres and deflated them like gas balloons. We pushed along on the wheel-rims through crunchy leaves and thick-haired trees. 'Oh! We're there! We've come out!' said Juice pointing to the sliver of gleaming road to our left.

' "But westward, look, the land is bright," ' I muttered.

'That's the east, silly,' said Juice. 'God! Your sense of direction.'

The preparations continued.

Nigel Parry came to the house in Finchley, a plump and easy young man. He made me pose sitting on Freddy's piano stool – cheek on my palm, fist under my chin, playing with my collar. And all the while he'd say these marvellously encouraging things: 'You have a wonderful smile!' 'I want to catch your eyes – they're beautiful eyes!' while I rolled over with flattery. When I saw the pictures I couldn't believe my beautiful eyes – there was one that was the best photo I'd ever been in, making me look like a talented teenager. And there was another which made my little nephew scream and run out of the room whenever he interrupted my writing.

But I was unfazed when I saw that. By then I had become a pro at photo sessions. The *Independent* sent Tom Pilston, who had the idea of taking pictures at Waterloo Station, from where I was about to leave for Salisbury on a pre-*Wheels* visit. 'Just pretend I'm not there,' he said, which was difficult, what with the people trying not to look and the way he looked. He had a big smile and a broken nose, a combination most difficult to resist. He sat opposite me on the train. Next to him was a woman whose daughter, looking like a coy Julie Andrews, sat next to me. 'I'm sorry about this,' I said as he began to click.

'Not at all,' said the mother. 'Such good fun! Isn't it darling?' The daughter nodded and looked at her lap. They reminded me of the mother and daughter from *Hotel du Lac*.

'We read such a lot,' she said. 'Six or eight books every week, don't we, darling?' She was the kind of elderly woman, plump and comforting, who would tuck you into bed with a warm drink. I didn't dare to ask what they read. She told me anyway. 'Jean Plaidy – have you ever read her?'

'Oh yes!' I said. 'I learned a lot of history from her when – ' I was a child would have been awfully rude.

'And we love poetry – Patience Strong. And someone gave me a book of Elizabethan love poetry, but you can't read too much of that. Just an occasional dip.'

I talked to Tom Pilston about being a photographer. 'It's awful,' he said, smiling his huge smile, 'you see everything in a square like a photo, and then if you don't have your camera with you it's quite unbearable.' I knew what he meant. I'd never used a camera before I went to Italy, earlier that spring. And it was so addictive – I felt I hadn't seen something until I had photographed it, but of course it was the other way round, I was so busy with the camera I wasn't looking.

'There's been a terrible tragedy in Salisbury,' said the woman opposite.

'The cathedral?' I whispered – and before I'd seen it.

'Oh no – it's the shopping-precinct. A fire, and it was a lovely shopping-precinct, wasn't it, darling?' The daughter's eyes shone and she nodded. 'My daughter loves clothes,' she said. 'Everywhere we go, she buys clothes. She has six wardrobes full – but she looks lovely, and I let her have them. I've never

spoilt her though – she's my only child. I never had enough
to spoil her; I was a widow. And now she doesn't want to get
married – '

'Neither do I,' said Juice, who had exchanged places with
Pilston so he could get my lantern-jaw in profile.

'I don't see anything wrong,' said the mother. 'She and I are
quite happy and she's old enough to make up her mind. How
old would you say she was?'

'Twenty-one,' I said.

'She's thirty!' Her voice was a cry of triumph. 'Oh! Look,
darling, that place we just passed has a lovely shopping-precinct
and we haven't been there.'

I like to think of them always happy, on their way across
the country to new shops, another wardrobe, Jean Plaidy to
bring in the night.

I was on my way to meet Elizabeth, a stunningly beautiful
writer with a face you couldn't take your eyes off – a warm,
pink smile, glossy gold hair, a marvellous walk and a voice
expressive as an actress's. She had brought a friend along to
help me into the van but he kept calling her 'ma'am'.

We were passing through some woods – 'This is where we
live,' said Elizabeth.

'How lovely!' said Juice. 'To have a house surrounded by
woods.'

'No,' she said, and laughed, throwing herself forward. 'The
whole village belongs to my husband, five thousand acres.'

When we got to her house, a sprawling U-shaped building,
I saw a Gainsborough in the hall. 'Is this yours?' I asked
inanely.

'Oh! We had so much that we had to sell; my husband's
parents died when he was only seventeen and the death-duties
came to four or five million pounds. My husband didn't want to
sell the land; he sold paintings and antique services instead.'

There was another portrait, of a rather splendid young man,
eyes flashing as if he were tossing his dark head. 'Who is this
beautiful boy?' I asked.

'My husband.' She had had a romantic life. As a very young
woman she had been one of Britain's most successful models.

She had got married and had two children, after which her husband left, taking all her money with him. She continued working to support her family; then she met a man a couple of years younger than she was and she went out with him for a couple of weeks. He asked her to come with him to Scotland for the shooting. She explained that she had two young children; she had to earn a living and couldn't possibly leave London. 'Then marry me,' he said. And she did.

She was astonished to discover how wealthy her husband was. She enjoyed living with the exquisite crystal and porcelain and the huge dark forest all around. 'Beautiful things make you more civilised,' she said. But she moved like a stranger through the lovely rooms and the garden. When she pointed out a Reynolds it was without pride, as if she were only a guide showing me around.

I asked her about this curious detachment. 'How strange that you should notice,' she said. 'Yes, I never feel that all this is mine, because it isn't. Not that my husband ever makes me feel it is all his. But I know it. I am too much my own person to get absorbed into all this.'

'Were you always writing?'

'No – I was always reading. And somehow I always read good books without anyone telling me to.' I knew what she meant because I had discovered Paul Bailey and Julian Barnes, Martin Amis and Ian McEwan, the poetry of Larkin and Thom Gunn and John Wain without knowing their literary reputation or being led to the library shelves where they waited.

'One day when I was thirty,' said Elizabeth, 'I sat down and started my first novel.'

'Just like that?'

'Yes,' and she smiled, cocking her head. She had shown it to an American publisher. He had accepted it, telling her how she needed to rewrite it. 'He showed me exactly what was wrong,' she said. 'And I sat down and worked it over.' Her book had received some splendid reviews, which encouraged her to write a second novel. But the American wouldn't pay her a decent sum for it. He felt she was his creation, that she owed him all the books she wrote. She was tempted to accept his offer, ridiculous as it seemed, because she knew he had taught her how to write and she knew he would help her to spot the faults in her new novel like nobody could. But her agent went ahead and refused for her; he said it was no good staying with a publisher who was paying her less than she was worth. That could only make for a bitter, resentful relationship. The agent had held an auction and sold her American rights for fifty thousand dollars.

Elizabeth felt very proud; the money was not much by their standards, but she had produced it. Achievement was its own motor. She did not need to earn a penny, but she had known what it was to be a creator, to make something she could exchange for what someone else had made. That was an irreplaceable feeling; neither wealth nor charity could substitute for it. People worked to keep body and soul together, and that meant something more than staying alive. Working was a way of asserting that a person was bigger than his material needs, that, indeed, he had a soul, a consciousness which could only function by proving its own possibilities.

Her second book had also received marvellous reviews, but only in America. It had more or less failed in Britain. She missed her editor and the careful attention he might have given the manuscript, but there was something else. She had shunned all publicity unconnected with her writing. 'They want to feature me in articles about the five thousand acre estate,' she said. 'That's absurd – I don't want to get ahead by telling people how many clothes and cars I have.'

With me, it was wheelchairs. And I was always struggling with this problem. My first novel was about growing up disabled; to that extent my own disability was relevant to the publicity which surrounded it. I also knew that if I had written a book about Martians with carrot-heads my wheelchair ways would still have been of interest – and of publicity value.

So the literary connection was partial; the only way out would have been to declare flatly that I would not talk of my disability, that it had nothing to do with my writing. That would have been falsehood, a brave lie.

Even while I floated across walls of experience in a balloon filled with imagination and observation, the basket where I sat would always be a wheelchair. Iris Murdoch had written *The Black Prince*, a marvellous look at the inner life of a man; James Baldwin had created unforgettable characters who were neither black nor gay; but neither Bradley Pearson nor the white people in *Another Country* would have been what they were if Iris Murdoch were not a woman, or Baldwin what he was.

To have my work judged by lower or easier standards because I was a brave boy in a wheelchair would have been intolerable for me; while I knew Britons were kind, I certainly did not expect them to be foolishly sentimental. At the same time, I realised with pleasure, and despised myself for it, that I was luckier than other new novelists who wrote as well as I did. Quite simply, because my disability caught the eye better than the smartest blurb or brightest jacket. It was an unfair advantage. But I salved my conscience with the knowledge that my head-start could not help me win a race. Once the readers or critics opened my book it would be there, running with all the others, or wheeling behind.

Like a boy mopping up the gravy on his plate, I was trying to cram every last bit of London into the few days I had left.

'Self-created hysteria,' said Freddy.

'Well, I've always been the creative type,' I said sweetly. I was learning to handle his smart-ass ways.

Soon after I arrived Honoria Gaskell had taken me to the May Fair on a show-farm to see the selection of the May Queen. 'Maybe,' said Freddy, 'they'll crown Firdaus the queen.' Honoria Gaskell frowned in puzzlement and wheeled me away. At the farm, they said they were sorry, they knew it was May Day, but they were choosing the May Queen next Sunday, when more people could come and pay and watch. 'How very odd,' said Mrs Gaskell. 'This new commercialisation.'

There was nothing commercial about the costume-show she was giving at a hall in Golders Green; the models were friends or her sons' girlfriends and the costumes were the ones she collected for pleasure. For days before the house was aswirl with silk and taffeta, whalebone and ermine tails, hats and petticoats. Joy was one of the models and I was the photographer. Just before we left, Honoria Gaskell held up a little waistcoat in patterned beige silk with gold buttons – 'Will you model that?' she said, so easily I said yes.

'I don't believe this,' said Freddy. Neither did I. At the end of my post-graduate diploma course in journalism, I'd won more medals than there was space for on my chest. At the prize-giving ceremony I would be given my medals by an eminent jurist who had been India's ambassador to the United States. I would also meet the newspaper editors whose medals I'd won. And I didn't go. I didn't go because I knew the applause and fine words would be for what I didn't have and not for what I had reached.

But when I swept around the hall in Golders Green wearing that waistcoat and with a Victorian shawl over my knees – 'A day at the beach around eighteen-forty,' said Honoria Gaskell to her audience – I knew those days were over when I was a reflection in other people's eyes. And like Helena's brother, celebrating himself, I wanted to fill my lungs and shout that Virginia Slims slogan to the world.

II

ON WHEELS

SEVEN

But westward, look!

'Someone has to invent a new word,' I said to Juice. 'Thank you sounds so feeble and inadequate.' I had just thanked Freddy, who had come to see us off, and it had sounded as idiotic as a tourist standing in front of the Taj Mahal and saying, 'How pretty!'

'I know what you mean,' said Juice. 'You need a real lo-ong word like that thing from *Mary Poppins*.'

I nodded and smiled. A man who looked like Michael Heseltine gone old had slid into the seat opposite us.

'You look like a hunter,' giggled Juice. I frowned.

Paddington Station looked so much like the Victoria Terminus in Bombay it filled me with longing. If only India were more prosperous, the people better clad, more healthy, it could look like this. For me it was like watching one of those computer miracles which showed you your face with red hair and green eyes, or green hair and red eyes – how things could be in another time.

'They call this second class,' said Juice, bouncing in her padded chair, watching the wooden benches and peeling window-frames of Indian Railways in her head.

'Think of the fares,' I said. Back home we could travel the distance from London to Glasgow for little more than a pound, never mind fans that did not work or the passenger who spat betel-juice like a red bullet past your face and out of the window.

We were pulling out of Paddington; I was thinking of Paul Theroux and saying something like that long word from *Mary Poppins* to him for setting out like this to bring back the books I read with such wonder and such envy. 'I think we owe more to those we envy than to anyone else,' I said to Juice. 'No one does as much to help us climb higher.'

She pulled a note-book out of her bag and began to jot that down.

'I didn't know you were planning a book about our travels,' I said.

'Of course I am,' she said, her eyes wide. 'Why do you think I came all the way from Bombay?'

You could have knocked me down with a kitten's paw. 'Juice, are you serious? How do you propose to get this . . . effort published?'

'I won't write it till your book comes out – then if it becomes a best-seller, everyone will want to know my story – I'm sure I'll be able to point out a few fibs – and I'll get a big fat advance, which is more than you have got.'

'And what do you plan to call this thing?'

'*Squeezing It Out*,' she said. 'Don't look so stricken. Since you hardly write like Paul Theroux – '

'Whom you have never read.'

'I've read you and I am not hopeful about the prospects of *Squeezing*.'

The aged Heseltine sucked his cheeks in.

'Are you from Bath?' I asked.

'Oh yes,' he said softly. 'I've been to London for the day.' And he returned to the papers he had spread as neatly as a cloth over the table.

'My maidenhead!' shrieked Juice, and I quickly put both hands on the papers. 'Maidenhead – ooh! Don't you remember the Five Find-Outers were always going to Maidenhead? We just passed it – can you imagine?'

'The next time you embarrass me,' I said, 'you shall get your notice as my research assistant.'

'And that will be the end for your book,' she said, not unkindly, only as a statement of fact.

I wasn't a novelist for nothing. 'Mark,' I said, 'is waiting by the phone to join me whenever I need him.' I wondered if there were phones on the Yorkshire moors where he was walking with his tent on his back.

'Reeding!' said Juice. 'What a funny name!'

'It didn't sound funny to Oscar Wilde – maybe because he didn't say it like you do.' But I was thinking of *Three Men in a Boat*, how I had read it as a boy, glaze-eyed with love for the landscape and the water. The view I could see now was bland, nondescript, with only a sudden shimmer of water like a squirt of beauty in the face.

'No one is talking,' said Juice.

'I'm glad.' By now, in the train from Bombay to Poona, my mother would have exchanged life-stories with the teenager next to her, the deaf old man behind and the young woman with babies like bundles scattered over the floor, while they all wondered about her stuck-up son.

The scene around us in the train to Bath was like a mimed play. Everyone communicated by gestures and smiles. To help someone fit in a large bag between the seats you pointed a palm at the space you didn't need; if you wanted to sit somewhere you pointed at the vacant chair and raised your eyebrows, to which the answer would be a smile or a quick duck into the folds of the *Evening Standard*. A group of children made the only sounds as they clamoured for snacks from the plump young woman with glasses who was escorting them.

'I want jam!'

'This is jam.'

'It isn't; it's some sticky stuff.'

'That's honey – the bees make it.' The little girl grimaced at the thought.

'My sandwich tastes funny.'

'You've got cheese.'

'Oh, look, look! It's rotten; all grey and soft.'

'That's special cheese – people pay extra for the mould.'

'Excuse me,' I said; ersatz Heseltine looked up, his eyes blank, as if he were saying, I've seen nothing.

I showed him a list of hotels with disabled facilities in Bath and asked what he thought. 'Oh, I wouldn't know – the Carfax is good, though. Actually I'm a doctor.'

'Really!' I said, overcome by this shred held out to me. 'Do you practise in Bath?'

'Yes, yes, we have the oldest hospital for rheumatism, dating back to seventeen-forty.'

'The waters were supposed to be a cure.' I said it English-style; in India a kyor is a kyor. 'Are they helpful?'

'Oh yes, definitely.' He was sitting up now. 'They shut the baths; I'm trying to get them reopened. That's what I went to London for today.'

'Why did they shut them?'

'There were amoebas in the water; this was way back in seventy-eight. Then they didn't have any money to do anything about it. Now, we've discovered a new clean source and we want permission to use that water.'

'How marvellous,' I said. He beamed and returned to his papers.

'We are so brave,' said Juice, 'setting out just like that – no travel bookings, no hotel reservations.'

'That's the idea,' I said, and a scare-spasm passed through me. In Bombay I'd stick my brakes to my wheels with glue rather than leave without every ticket and hotel confirmation down to my room number in my pocket. I didn't know how I was going to draw my circle around the country – what if we didn't get the right trains or I didn't get a hotel room that would let me move around, or bathrooms I could manage? All we had were our British Rail Silver Passes. I'd wondered how I was going to wait in a queue for tickets to Bath. In Bombay, if you wanted a seat on a train you reserved it days ahead, going early in the morning to stand in line; the overcrowding was a film-scene, with people travelling on the roofs and footboards, shrugging away the risks of being knocked down by a passing pole or over-bridge.

I had phoned British Rail and they had put me on to a special line for the disabled. 'Just try to get here a bit early, sir – about half an hour before should do. Would you like to stay in your wheelchair on the train?'

'No – *no*,' I said, appalled at the prospect of no conversation. 'I'll move into a seat.'

'Fine – you should have no problem at all.'

And I didn't. They had a bright yellow ramp on wheels that they slotted into a carriage door, and Juice wheeled me, her Bally shoes, made to last, tick-tocking on the metal.

Bath Station smelt of flowers. Which wasn't surprising because flowers were growing, in large earth-baskets, on the railway tracks. 'Just think what *we* have there in Bombay,' said Juice. Railway tracks in India were the longest open-air loo in the world.

'Let me give you a lift,' said old Heseltine. 'I have a car.'

'Oh no!' I said.

'It's no trouble; I'll take you to the Carfax.'

That was too expensive for us, but upper-middle-class Indians find it very difficult to say they can't afford something; their place on the perch is precarious. So I went all English and said, 'I wouldn't dream of bothering you; please carry on.'

'It's no trouble at all,' he said, smiling and shaking his head.

I put out my hand. 'Thank you, so much,' I said, 'but really, we'll be all right.'

'Very well,' he said, 'and good luck.'

None of the cheaper hotels on our list had rooms. 'We'd better look for a travel centre,' I said.

'I'll go,' and Juice was out of sight.

A large lad, his beard wet gold with sweat, was standing next to me. He smiled. I pounced. 'Is this your first visit to Bath?'

'Yes. I'm walking through Somerset – no better way to see a place.'

'I loved his tactlessness. 'So, where are you going next?'

'To Ghana,' he said.

'Walking?'

He nodded. 'And I've come from Australia – where are you from?' I told him. 'Ah! I want to go there. I've heard such terrible things about your country – '

'Really? What kind – '

'I don't want to say till I go there and see for myself – so you'll just have to wait.'

I nodded and he walked away.

'They're shut,' said Juice. 'Someone said we'll just have to wait for them to open.'

'Nonsense,' I said. 'Let's go and see – how can a travel centre shut its doors?'

A porter, white hair under blue cap, approached us. 'Like some help?' he asked.

'Please!' said Juice, handing him our two sling bags while the third slept between the handles of my chair like a hammock.

The woman at the travel centre was cheerful as a cook. 'I'll find you something,' she said, and began dialling. 'You can look at these.'

The leaflets were glossy and tempting. I wanted to go to Glastonbury and there was a coach tour the very next morning. 'Will they take me in a wheelchair?' I asked.

'I don't see why not.'

'Glastonbury!' boomed a voice behind me. 'Can't stay away from that place.'

I turned; a pregnant man in khaki beard and shorts was standing with his hands in his pockets. 'I'm Chris,' he said, 'from the US of A.'

'I'm Firdaus from the R of I.'

But he was not curious. 'The abbey there gets you,' he said, 'and you go back and back and back. I'm he-ere three days, and every day I just go and sta-and there.'

'Oooh!' said Juice. 'It must have got some power like a big magnet.'

'You're right – it pulls you,' and he held his beard and yanked. 'I think it pulled me a-all the way from Nu York. I lost my job there, it was a filthy, menial job, and I went to Aslo – '

'Where's that?' said Juice.

'In Norway,' I said.

'You know, you're right – Norway, that is it. And from there I've come he-ere to answer the abbey's call – see you there tomorrow.'

'Excuse me,' said the woman, 'I think I've got you a room – it's eight steps up but the lady there can help you.'

'Is there a shower?'

'Only a bath-tub, I'm afraid.'

'Will she give me a chair to put in the bath-tub? Or can I put my wheelchair in?'

'Just a moment.' She spoke into the receiver. 'The gentleman wants to know if you can have him in the bath' – Juice gasped – 'his wheelchair, I mean – or could you give him a chair? Oh fine, thank you – they'll be right over.' She told us where we'd find a taxi, and to have a wonderful stay.

The taxi-driver's cheeks were blown out as if they were waiting for a child to deflate them and laugh. I asked him how he liked Bath. 'Terrible place,' he said, and I thought, what a way to start. 'Full of snobs.' That sounded more promising. 'They all have their little cliques, and if you're not in – '

'You're out.'

'Exactly. No good for us ordinary folk. This place is for rich old people in nursing-homes. Everyone who has money buys a house here. You've heard of Barbra Streisand – '

'Yes-yes,' said Juice. 'She was that Funny Girl.'

'Yeah – she bought a house here. Don't know why – never came to live in it. Here's your place.'

'The house looked serenely grey, solid and secure. Juice went in, while I waited in the evening sun, and came back in the company of a beautiful woman with a cap of silky gold hair. 'I'm Liz Gill,' she said.

'That's an Indian surname!' I exclaimed.

'Really! I'm going to India later this year – you are Mr and Mrs Kanga?'

'Nooo,' exclaimed Juice. 'We're just friends.'

'Oh! Then I can't let you share a room – I'm only joking.' Our faces must have worried her.

She helped me up the stairs, lifting the chair – in Britain I never got over this willingness to make things easy for someone.

The first thing I had to check was the bathroom – the chair slipped in. 'Perfect!' said Juice. The room was pleasant, with a television on a revolving shelf and a long view from a large window. 'Oh! Super! Just fantastic! It's too – too good!' exulted Juice. I gave her my jaguar smile; I didn't want Liz Gill to think we'd been living at the Salvation Army Hostel. But Juice had discovered adjectival bliss. 'Marvellous!' she said. 'Wonderful! Fabulous! Cosy! So intimate! Oooh! Such luxury: I just love this!' and she flung out her arms to the television.

After a wash – I was lucky the basin was only as high as my chin – we went out. 'Lovely weather,' said Liz; she had a marvellous accent, clear and expressive with a soft rolling r. I asked her where she was from. 'Scotland,' she said.

'But that's not a Scots accent.'

'It is – we speak like this on the western coast.'

Outside, I unfolded my map; and after that nothing could equal the pleasure of seeing a new place held in my hands, soon to become familiar for ever. So that months later, I would be reading a novel where someone walked down Sauchiehall Street in Glasgow, and I could not only see it as it was, but also how it stretched across the map, where it led and how I had found my way into it and out. I had, all these years, lived without a sense of place and direction. I had never gone out alone, and only when I was twenty-six had I wheeled out without family or friend to show me the way, only a servant to push. That first time I went by taxi to a concert at a hall about ten minutes' ride away, I sat, my palms flat against the plastic seat, my arms a rigid line from shoulder to wrist as I looked at the streets in panic; turns breached the roads in unfamiliar places – did I need to take the first or the next? Alternative routes I remembered were tangled in my terror. When I got there I wondered if it were worthwhile. Now, less than four years later, I was about to tackle a whole country – and remembering the Heath I doubted I should have much help.

A little way down I saw the Sidney Gardens, and, 'Let's go in,' said Juice. There was no one about; so much colour wasted, I thought, watching the spendthrift loveliness of the unknown flowers that would last only the summer. But so much beauty had made Britons blasé; it was all around them, and summer would be back another time.

I put on both brakes when Great Pulteney Street opened out before me; there was something moving about this wide road lined on either side with Georgian buildings, so elegant and proportionate, so intelligently planned and executed, that it was like seeing the music of Bach turned into stone. I found myself reminded of Florence, as if both cities existed for some metaphysical purpose, to show men what they could be. The flower-baskets hanging from the eves, the boys and girls here on holiday from Rome and Salerno talking in their roller-coaster accents, all made the Italian ambience seem almost real. That was only appropriate; surely when Bath was being transformed in the eighteenth century Italy must have been culturally what America is today, and as avidly imitated.

'Grand Parade!' exclaimed Juice. 'Just like our Cuffe Parade.'

'Hardly,' I said, watching the Avon tumble over Pulteney Weir and the park below, luxurious as a private estate for the few who wished to make use of it. Cuffe Parade, a promenade from my childhood, stretching along the Arabian Sea, had been as lovely. The sea broke below it on a rocky strand and on quiet mornings my mother wheeled me there, a very little boy of six, to breathe the sun-salt air and eat peanuts from paper cones. In the evenings we had to dress up to walk on Cuffe Parade. Everyone would be there, the haute bourgeoisie of Bombay in silk sarees and gathered skirts below lace blouses, remembering the soldiers who walked here, not twenty years ago, young men from Birmingham and Liverpool grinning at the girls, tossing compliments into the air as they passed. But Cuffe Parade is gone now, levelled, literally, to widen the road, while the sea below has been reclaimed and taken over by a filth-grey squatters' slum. So things end, in India.

The next morning we woke up later than we had planned. Poor Juice had been walked out. 'You've made me walk the breadth of Bath,' she squealed when she sneaked a peek at the map.

'Wasn't it worth it? The Circus and the Royal Crescent – '

'And the cheese soufflé.'

'Yes; that's the first good English meal I've had.'

'Soufflé is French,' said Juice. 'I think she's bringing our breakfast.'

English breakfasts always made me feel like a Lilliput – the platefuls of eggs and bacon, grilled tomatoes and sausages, the boxes of cereal, the honey and jam and slices of toast, orange juice and tea – it was madness. And Juice went along with it, finishing everything on offer except the orange juice. 'I only have Del Monte, and I won't rest till I find it,' she said. 'The others are just no good.' She was a typical brand-names Parsee – second generation.

When we got to the bus station the driver lifted me in without being asked; he wore specs and a worried grin. He was the jokey type. 'They make the Chiltern cheese here,' he said when we passed the spot. 'Don't buy too much; whenever I take some home my wife asks me why I haven't washed my feet.' The passengers loved it, especially the Americans.

Two of them were sitting behind me; one had a lung-cough, and every time she spluttered I held my breath like a deep-sea driver. I am phobic about germs and falling ill, having spent a good slice of my life laid up with broken bones. But I knew – or believed – that in Britain everything was so much cleaner, and I drank from the tap and shook hands and kissed the Bloomsbury girls without ever worrying about catching something. And the strange thing was, I really didn't fall ill a single day.

'Have you bin to New Hampshire?' the woman asked her neighbour between coughs.

'I haven't.'

'There are no animals in New Hampshire. What about Verma-ant, have you been to Verma-ant?'

'Can't say I hay-ve.'

'Verma-ant has cows.'

'I come from Calif-ornia – you bin there?'

'No.'

'Well, Calif-ornia has fa-aliage.'

'What's fa-aliage?'

'Grass.'

We were entering Cheddar Gorge. 'Lots of folk,' said the driver, 'shut their eyes when we drive in; I always do.'

The Americans shrieked and giggled. 'He a-always does!'

'A lot of people commit suicide here – an ideal spot, considering it's a three hundred and eighty feet fall. If you're lucky you'll get to see their remains. Soon we'll be driving through a canopy of trees – notice the lovely green shadows.'

A little while later the Californian asked her neighbour, 'Is that the canopy?'

'Can't say.'

In desperation, she reached across the aisle to an Englishwoman sitting up straight in a grey pleated dress. 'Is that the canopy, dearr?'

'It must be.'

The plunge into the Gorge was spectacular, almost Indian; the huge cliff clawed by centuries of sea and wind stood unforgiving.

'Is a-all this hay-nd-carved?' said the Californian to the grey Englishwoman.

'No, dear.' A weary sigh. 'It's nature.'

'Oh my Ga-ad! Then we are in one of the wonderrs of the world!'

I thought of Tim Mo telling me to invent dialogue when I wrote about my travels – 'Everyone does it,' he had said, naming one of the best travel-writers I'd read. At this rate, it wasn't going to be necessary.

The Cheddar Caves were open to me – 'Please go in,' said the man selling tickets. 'You don't need to pay because you might not be able to see everything there is.'

There was a ramp to get in; the floor was glistening wet and it was cool. The caves were all right – I liked seeing the stalactites and stalagmites, which I'd always described the wrong way round in my geography exams. What made the place special for me was that I could get in and see it. Across the harbour from where I lived in Bombay is the island of Elephanta, with some of the oldest rock-cut sculpture in the world hidden in caves. And Elephanta is totally inaccessible to wheelchairs.

So were parts of the Cheddar Caves. 'Go up and have a look,' I said to Juice. I like people doing things I couldn't; that makes me feel I've gone there too.

A young woman, with her hands held behind her back, came up to me. 'Are you enjoying yourself?'

'Oh yes! Do you work here?'

'Yes – nice and cool, isn't it? And in winter it's warm and cosy – the temperature is always the same, about sixteen degrees.'

'Then you're lucky to be working here.'

'Oh, it's just for my holidays. I'm studying.'

'Where?'

'In Weston-super-Mare; it's lovely. We have water fights on the beach between lectures. Your friend's back.'

'Oh! It's just wonderful up there,' said Juice. 'Let me carry you.'

'Are you crazy?' What with my brittle bones, everyone had refused to renew my medical insurance when it expired in London. I had taken an insane risk setting out on this tour.

'Help!' shouted Juice. 'I'm sliding away!' She was slipping on her Bally shoes, clutching the railing with one hand; with the other she held one handle of my chair, which kept twirling around, threatening to shoot away down the wet slope, leaving me spilt and smashed.

An unlikely rescuer, the grey Englishwoman, came and steadied me. 'Let's do this together,' she said, in a voice she might have used in an air-raid shelter.

The main street of Cheddar was given over to tourists, but only a little way; after that it was quiet, and you could imagine someone planning a bridge evening or writing a love-letter inside the self-possessed houses. We found a church smothered in flowers, but its doors were locked; the vicarage was tempting and I longed to be invited in; instead we had tomato soup and apple tart at a pub.

Glastonbury was not far away. 'A mystical centre,' said the driver. 'Look at that tor which the pilgrims climbed with peas in their shoes for penance.' In India people walk around a sacred hill barefoot. 'And on the summer solstice the mystics gathered there and danced.' The Americans were awe-struck into silence.

The abbey at Glastonbury was too much of a ruin to move

me, and it made me angry, all this talk of spiritual force attached to the place, and the mythical King Arthur's tomb in which were buried two bodies some monks had discovered in the thirteenth century, in the reign of Edward I.

Which was an inappropriate response, surely, but I knew it was a reaction to the world I came from, where superstition had been elevated into spiritual truth. When my friend had chickenpox his mother ate chicken every day to get it down; smallpox was a visitation from a goddess (now dead!); yellow jaundice was 'cured' by a bowl of water placed below the patient's bed with prayers to turn the water yellow instead of the man.

The evil eye was an almost universal belief: children went around with black spots disfiguring their temples to keep it away; some women were accused of having a black tongue which only needed to speak to curse; most women fasted once a week so their husbands would not die on them, for widows were inauspicious, their presence an invitation to misfortune; pride in achievement was hubris, to be punished with a fall; and once a year all the evil in the house was encapsulated inside an egg that was broken on the door-step.

All ferociously funny if you did not have to see your family, your loved ones, your neighbours debase themselves, leaving you alone, clutching reason like a flag you were embarrassed to fly because you knew there was nothing extraordinary about the way you thought. Not in the real world, the Western world, at least.

While I could understand that the poor quality of life made superstition a psychological means of survival, of keeping disease and early death and failure away, I could not accept this kind of thinking from people as educated and comfortably off as I. A brilliant young woman I knew stoutly opposed eye-donations and cornea-transplants for the blind on the grounds that they would constitute interference in God's plan; an advocate commented when he heard this, 'And who knows what use that blind person will make of my eye – he can do the most evil things with it and it would all go to my divine record; after all, those eyes were given to *me*, not him.'

I knew that there were people in Britain who believed this kind of thing, and I knew Glastonbury was my best chance of finding them. I had spotted a weird book-shop on our way into town, and we walked down to it from the abbey.

'Ga-ad! I can't stay away from this place,' said a voice, and it was Chris the American from the travel centre in his khaki beard. 'What did you think of it?'

'It was all right,' I said, and he held his hand to his heart to say I'd hurt him there.

The book-shop was large and dark with titles like *Why Women Hate Men* and *I was Married to a Witch* peering at you from the shelves. Besides Juice and me the place was empty. I saw three people walk in and move to the shelves with the assurance of book-buyers. I wheeled closer – there was a man with eyes widened as if he were watching a horror movie in his head, a thin, middle-aged, black-haired woman in black, and a younger woman, her long dark hair stiff as if it had been combed with glue.

'Excuse me,' I said; they turned, fixing me with three identical pairs of eyes. 'I'm from India,' I said, and they nodded and shut their eyes for a moment. 'And I want to know about this old religion, this spiritual world – can you tell me anything about it?'

'It's Glastonbury,' said the man. 'Our centre, all the force-lines gather here – '

'Do you know about force-lines?' said the younger woman – his daughter?

'Of course; and what do you do?'

'We used to be terribly popular before Christianity,' she said, while I watched a figure large as a child's hand that hung from her neck. 'And the Christians took over all our festivals – there's a huge force at Christmas, which they mis-use – '

'Christ was a good man,' said the older woman, whose eyes tilted dangerously at the corners, 'a healer. But for his followers religion is only about power – do you know the Christians bless aeroplanes and wars?'

'How awful! And how do you keep your religion alive?'

'We heal – there's a goddess, Sulis, here,' she said. 'These are her headquarters and she helps us heal – '

'The skin – ' said the daughter.

'Yes, Sulis sent us a message saying she would heal a woman of a skin disease. And on the summer solstice she was cured!'

'How did she send you the message?'

'We are mediums,' said the man and woman together, 'and she is able to sense the spirits.' The daughter nodded shyly.

'Do you get a lot of messages?'

'Oh yes! Poor thing, she gets quite exhausted conveying them to us – '

'I have my own aborigine,' said the daughter.

'Yes, she does, and I have a Red Indian chief who went to the Canadian High Commission to find out more about him – '

'Yes, and would you believe it? There was an exhibition with a portrait of our chief!'

'Do you look into crystal balls?'

'No,' said the man. 'We are beyond that – '

'On another plane,' I said.

'Exactly!' they all said together. 'Dowsing, crystal-gazing are for lower spirits.'

'I have a cat – ' said the girl.

'Yes, we all have to find religious perfection through animals, and you have to find an animal that is compatible with your spirit.'

'What are you wearing around your neck?'

'That's Isis, my goddess from Egypt,' said the girl.

'And what is that you have in your ear?' I asked the man, watching a dangling silver Celtic cross.

'It's the key of life,' he said.

'Isn't it a Celtic cross?'

'Oh no!'

'Never!'

'The Christians stole the symbol from us,' said the man.

'But we have our friends,' said the daughter, 'from our previous lives.'

'And they slip into us whenever they feel like it,' said the mother with a complacent smile.

'Thank you so much,' I said. 'This was so valuable.' I wheeled towards Juice.

'Those were two witches and a wizard, weren't they?' she whispered.

'Sort of – and he's called a warlock.'

'Why are you shaking? Oh! You're laughing – I thought they had done something to you!'

The cathedral at Wells was silent. 'Can we stay for evensong?' I asked.

'Of course,' said the verger, 'it's a spoken evening.'

'Then we are not interested,' said Juice, and I hurried her away. 'Look at that lace,' she said, pointing at a large square, frail with figures of the saints. There was an inscription which said there was a businessman and public servant of Madras, Sir Stuart Town, who when he left India took up bobbin-lacemaking. His wife, who did not want to compete with him, took up needlepoint, and this was her handiwork. I liked this feel of weaving into each other's lives, India and Britain, like a parted couple who can't resist looking back.

On a walk in Wells, I saw a Conservative Party club. There was a stout man at the door. 'Can I talk to somebody inside?' I asked. Might as well, I thought; I'm not going to find too many Conservatives up north.

'This is just a social club,' he said. 'The agent's office is further down the road.'

'Is Mrs Thatcher popular among the members?' I asked.

He shrugged. 'She's going to win the next election,' he said, 'because there is no one else.'

The agent was almost too blue to be true: his blond hair was smart and short, his eyes clear, cheeks pink, shaved smooth as his shirt was ironed. He was very gracious, fascinated by the idea of my book.

'This is a Conservative stronghold,' I said. 'Does that make your job easy?'

'Most people are apolitical here – especially young people. Our members – we have about three thousand – are mostly in the fifty-five to sixty age-group. Of course, this constituency had the biggest increased majority in the Euro-elections last month, when we were losing all over the country.'

'What about Mrs Thatcher – how popular is she?'

'I think a lot of the members are alarmed by the new policies on health, education, privatisation – '

'Is that because they are new or because they don't believe in them?'

'I think they don't. I mean, there is a latent belief, but no, not for these new directions.'

'Don't you think the Conservatives are losing the game because they are not putting across a moral message – that it is honourable to be self-responsible? They always seem to be saying, vote for us because our policies work. But that's not what people want; they need something to fight for, like socialism used to be.'

'I know all this,' he said patiently. 'But I can't be a spokesman for the Party; my job is to be a good listener, to tell people I'm with them, sharing their worries about the Party.'

I asked him if there was the kind of moral intimidation against the Conservatives that I'd seen in London.

'Not at all,' he said. 'Not here in Wells.'

Back at the cathedral, waiting for the coach, we met the Californian dressed in red and yellow sweatshirt and white trousers; with her was a little, wizened Southern belle. 'Sounds lahk you've been to a real good school,' said the belle. 'You speak English lahk the English.'

'We went to school in India,' I said.

'Well, I never! Mah God – did you hear that? They learned to speak lahk that in India.'

The Californian nodded impatiently. 'Tell me,' she said, 'what you think of the English.'

'They are rather dowdy,' I said, and waited.

'You've said it! Ga-ad! I'd never have dared to, but you're dead right – a-all those greys and browns. Enough to get you down. Now look at me, I love colour.' She lifted her blouse at the shoulders. 'They call this gaudy – I think it's cheerful. All of us old girls in California dress this way.'

When we left the coach in Bath I thanked the driver who

had been lifting me – and my chair – in and out all day; and gave him ten pounds. 'No,' he said, 'this was my pleasure.'

'Don't insist,' said the Californian. 'It's his pa-alicy never to accept – we tried too.'

'Can you think of a nahs place to have dinner?' asked the old belle.

'Number Five at Argyll Street,' said Juice. That was where we had eaten our cheese soufflé the night before. 'It's super, it's fantastic – '

'It's rather nice,' I finished firmly.

'We'll trah that,' she said, and we parted ways.

I saw a book-shop; in London I had kept myself away from Foyle's and Dillons because I knew by the time I got out I'd only have enough money left to take a taxi to the airport and fly home. But this was a cut-price book-shop called Good Buy Books, and Madame Butterfly was singing inside.

The young man at the desk was holding his forehead and shaking with laughter. When he saw us he said, 'Sorry.'

'What are you reading?' I asked.

'Something by a chap called Paul Bailey.'

'Oh! What?'

'Have a look,' and he handed me a pink book entitled *An English Madam*. It was the biography of one Cynthia Payne, who advocated sex on the NHS. I asked Paul about it when I got back to London. He chuckled and said, 'I keep quiet about it!'

'Is this your shop?' I asked the young man, who had gone back to giggling. He had the flat chin and tilted nose of the English schoolboy.

'Oh no!' he said. 'I just work here from six to nine – it's good. I can read and listen to opera.' I wanted his job.

The books were affordable, even for me. I asked him if I could choose a dozen and they'd post them to London for me.

'I'll have to ask the owners,' he said. 'Could you come back tomorrow?'

'Yes,' I said, pleased.

'You only want to go back for that boy,' said Juice. 'Don't deny it – I know your type.'

We gave Number Five at Argyll Street an encore; the Americans had taken our advice. They spaded through a four-course meal while Juice and I agonised over whether we should share a dessert or not have one at all. Juice said, 'How dare our rupees be so little-little!'

When we got back John Gill was waiting to help us up the stairs. He had a raddled, handsome look about him; he was about forty with a big nose, wide lips, plenty of laugh-lines down his cheeks. He had been a steward on BOAC in the old days; now he manufactured trays and cups that airlines used. 'I've been to Bombay,' he said, sitting on the steps while I tried to call Liz Calder. 'We used to stay in the hotel called Sun-'n'-Sand, do you know it?'

'Oh, yes, though I've never been there.' It is at the other end of the city from where I live. When I was a boy it was the place to hold a wedding reception; and my friends and I used to throw fantasy-parties by the pool there.

I asked John about politics. 'This is a blue-door household,' he said. 'What we need is strength, and Thatcher is strength.' I wondered how that would play in London. 'Look at us,' he said. 'We run a bed-and-breakfast, though it's very hard work with two little children, because we want to send them to private school and that needs a lot of money.'

I nodded vigorously and we glided up the stairs. Juice was right about our room. At night the lights of Camden Crescent floated in the sky outside our window, like ships on the horizon.

The next day we went to Street. I had met a pianist in London whose husband taught at Millfield, 'the most expensive school in Britain'. 'You must see it,' she said.

The taxi-driver was disgruntled. 'I'm a Labour man,' he said, 'and all that these Conservatives do is support business and the tourist trade. What do I care about the tourists and the shopkeepers? I need someone who does things for me.'

'But surely tourists are good for your taxi too,' I said.

'I suppose so – you know the last time I went to Millfield I took a Spanish woman and her daughter. They'd flown in from Madrid just so the girl could have a look and make up her mind if she wanted to study there. I waited two hours at the school, then I took them all the way to Heathrow.'

We were passing a little village full of square, heavy houses. 'Used to be a mining village,' said the driver. 'They shut down the mines, they shut down the trains coming here. Everyone has to use a taxi now, whether they can afford it or not. And they've sold the miners' cottages as fancy houses – they've good, solid walls, three feet thick. I've got one too, beautiful view from the back – fields and hills. Too bad the miners can't enjoy them any more.'

Millfield seemed like one of those country hotels which dot the Indian hill-stations; small bungalows breaking through the trees. The headmaster, Brian Gaskell, was square-faced, square-jawed. He spoke slowly, with assurance, his chunky appearance lending weight to his words. He was appalled that I had come without reading up Millfield. 'I thought you would have done your homework,' he said.

Five Indian princes were the first pupils at the school, which now had twelve hundred boys and girls. The headmaster didn't like calling it a private school – too dangerous, I thought – Millfield was an independent school, he said. And, 'No, we are not the most expensive in the country – there are one or two others which charge more. We are paid less than eight thousand a year.'

'What's special about Millfield?'

'It's not like the other public schools – much less snobbery and mindless discipline. And we don't demand only academic excellence – sports and music are as important. And I feel every pupil can climb a notch or two higher if he's given the right environment. That is why we offer bursaries – about forty per cent of our pupils are on bursaries.'

'Do they study free?'

'No, but some of them pay as little as twenty per cent, others perhaps forty or sixty per cent. You'd be surprised how many parents come to us and say, "We can manage five thousand pounds a year – there's no way we can pay the rest." If we feel the child deserves the education here, we take it.'

'Does the school make a profit?'

'It's run by a charitable trust – so whatever surplus we have is ploughed back into the school.'

'What about discipline? That can't be easy with so many adolescents.'

'It isn't,' he said. 'We have a few rules and we are strict about those. No sex, no alcohol. Drinking is difficult to supervise because boys can go into town.'

'What do you do if you catch them?'

'Well, there's gating. They're not allowed to go out of the school premises for a certain period. If the offence is repeated, we suspend the pupil.'

'Do you ever expel anybody?'

'Oh, yes – sex or drugs result in immediate expulsion.'

'How often does this happen?'

'Not often,' he said. 'Perhaps once or twice a year. Suspensions are a bit more common – six or seven, I think.'

'What do you think of the state system?' I asked. 'Do you think it should be expanded, or do you think there should be more and more – independent schools?'

'That's a political question,' he said, and sat back, silent.

'Oh no! What do you think might be better as far as education is concerned?'

'I feel independent schools have a duty to show the way, to set standards of excellence so that state schools can rise to their example.'

This reluctance to defend individual choice and the right to run private and better schools for those who wished to pay for them disappointed me. The argument that independent schools served state schools as shining lights was so flimsy a justification, it could be blown away by any determined egalitarian. But that is how it was – individualists were playing the game on the collectivists' ground, dragging their feet but sliding inevitably towards the flat, impoverished, unvarying landscape of egalitarianism. For the levellers had the courage to fly their principles from the rooftops, while individualists only dared to mutter theirs behind their hands, in furtive whispers.

'I'll call the senior English master,' said the headmaster, 'and he can show you around. It's a pity there are no pupils – school broke up only last week.'

'Do you have a uniform?' I asked.

'No, but we have a dress code. The girls are asked to dress like smart secretaries – ' Juice nodded approvingly – 'while the boys wear jackets and ties. You, for instance,' he said, his eye on my tieless pin-striped shirt, 'would not be admitted.' We smiled.

'What about pupils in wheelchairs? Have you ever had any?'

'Yes! A girl – and she managed very well. Teachers moved classes to the ground floor for her and she had no trouble at all.'

The English master, David Rosser, was a body-builder, the headmaster told me. He had the look of a man you would accompany down the Amazon without a worry. He had come from the north of England where, he said, there was very little cultural difference between the working class and the middle class except that the latter had bigger cars and better televisions. Only the university teachers were interested in books or serious theatre.

I asked him what he thought of the young Briton's ignorance of history; for Blanche and Joy and Mark, and so many others I had met, the past was an empty corridor receding into the darkness.

'Yes,' he said, 'and then you have no sense of who you are.' He told me about a friend of his who was on the Scientific Advisory Council to the Indian Prime Minister. He had two gentle, intelligent sons whom he wanted to send to Millfield. But the boys were so steeped in Hindu culture – they could relate myths in marvellously involved detail – that Rosser had felt their removal to a British school would be a terrible shock for them; and he had dissuaded the father.

'What a pity!' I said. 'If you're brought up in that kind of Indian culture you never find your way out.'

'But they are growing up with a knowledge of their past,' he said. 'Isn't that invaluable? Isn't that what British children don't have?'

'Yes,' I said, 'but India's is a closed culture; it doesn't help you to connect with the outside world. British children have the universe around them, their society is wide open – a sense of the past can only enrich them.'

'If you don't know your own culture,' he said, 'you can't appreciate anyone else's. Like a language – if you're not fluent in your own, you'll never be good at a foreign one.'

'Yes, but if you grow up too comfortable in your own culture you never gain the ability to be at home in someone else's.'

He said it was a pity no one knew the Bible any more. He was a sceptic, but he felt the Bible lent a cohesiveness to British society that served a very valuable purpose – everyone shared the same myths and parables.

'I suppose societies move on,' I said. 'They can't remain in cultural cages.'

'Yes,' he said, 'it would be wonderful if people knew the Bible without being religious.'

We went to see a lecture-room. They had a teacher, for their hundred and twenty second-language students, who was a genius. He could talk a dozen languages, and was now picking up Swahili. The foreign students did well, but they were often clannish; Millfield had had a lot of trouble with American students and drugs.

We had seen the gigantic chemistry laboratory; now we went to the art room. The abstract paintings were so professional, I wondered how much the artists would achieve when they went out into the world, with all the imaginative nourishment it had on offer.

The library rivalled the best in Bombay – there were computers and video-tapes to choose from.

Outside there were deep green woods. 'Do you ever have trouble with homosexuality?' I asked.

No, he laughed, heterosexuals were enough. The school was very strict, there was no question of first warnings, 'Because they'd use the first warning!'

Rosser thought Thatcher was wonderful. His only worry was that if she went out things would backslide. She had made money respectable, he said, and that was right. Because money was our last absolute, the only thing you couldn't bend – you had to make it to spend it. Through my whole stay in Britain, he was the only person I talked to who said this kind of thing.

'What about the Church?' I asked. 'How do you see it?'

'As the natural ally of the Left,' he said. 'It's so foolish of the Tories to keep insisting theirs is the party of the Church.'

He showed me a golf-course, two swimming pools – one indoors for the winter – and a television studio where the pupils could shoot their own films. I was overtaken by sadness. 'It's all so ordinary for the children here; and I think of the children back home making their lives out of so little because wealth which can make something like this is considered filthy. Are the children here blasé about all this?'

'They're bound to be; they've grown up with it.'

'Yes, like we have with the poverty,' I said. But poverty is not something you can make use of; opportunity is. And to ignore it seems, paradoxically, to be a greater fault.

Bristol was not part of my journey, but when the Labourite taxi-driver told me it was less than an hour's drive away I had to go.

My mother was no longer an heiress. Her cousin had died while I was in London and she had inherited her wealth. You couldn't have afforded a studio flat in Chelsea with it, but it was a lot of money in India. And Amy, who had left it to her, had studied here; I had grown up with her thirties accent and the cheese-rolls and mince-pies she had learned to bake in Bristol.

Our new driver was an old man, with a thin, smiling face. He had bought a taxi after retiring, and when he was younger he had served in the British Army on the Rhine. Before that, during the war, he had gone on a holiday, only to find his house had disappeared when he returned. 'Bombed out of sight, by the Germans,' he said. 'And now look at them, lording it over us with all their money.' But Thatcher was going to set things right – she had done a marvellous job for the area, he said. 'No one is unemployed who doesn't want to be.'

We were surrounded by the Mendip Hills, large and soft so you wanted to stroke them gently.

Bristol seemed charmless, without the gumption of the big city or the intimacy of a town. We had to get a map and we went into a newsagent's. 'Look,' said a man with a lopsided smile, 'don't buy this from me; it'll cost you a pound. You can get a free one from across the road at the tourist centre.'

At the door, a black man stopped us. 'I heard that – the tourist centre is on strike. Just thought I'd save you the trouble of crossing the road.'

'Thanks very much,' I said, and wheeled back into the shop. 'I heard that,' said the man with the crooked smile. 'Please take this map – no, don't pay me for it. I won't accept any money.'

'Too-too kind,' said Juice, and he grinned all over his right cheek.

We found our way to the waterfront; I'd never seen a waterfront outside of Paul Theroux. It was the ugliest little bit of landscape possible – video-game arcades blinking their dead lights like zombies and an electronic organ playing all the tunes ('Come September', 'Never on a Sunday') that give Parsee weddings their Philistine flavour.

We had lunch in a big, bare café, dreary as a co-operative canteen. When I went to the disabled loo I got trapped inside. The door, on springs, was so heavy that every time I pulled it my wheelchair rolled away; if I braked there was no space for it to open. Juice had helped me in; now I had to wait till somebody needed a wee. Five minutes later, a suspicious, mustachioed young man let me out.

We walked to St Mary Redcliffe, which Elizabeth I called 'the fairest, the goodliest, and the most famous parish church in England'. I was wheeling down the aisle watching the high ceiling criss-crossed with gold; when I looked down I saw a little inscription that said this was Thomas Chatterton's church. I liked the idea of coming upon it so by chance. Chatterton fascinated me – to think this was the very church from which the fatherless, poverty-stricken boy had stolen parchment to write the poems he passed off as the work of a medieval monk called Rowley. His work was much admired and yet, when he wrote as himself, his poverty starved him into suicide.

I had read Peter Ackroyd's evocative novel *Chatterton*, a confluence of fact and fiction, and being here somehow made me feel like a character in his book, coming upon Chatterton as his protagonist had. Later, we went to see the house where the poet was born, an elegant one-storey rectangular building with perfectly placed windows punched into it. A man emerged from the door. 'There's nothing to see inside,' he said. 'And anyway, it's been shut for years. Chatterton didn't live here very long. His father was the schoolmaster and this was a schoolhouse, but his father died before he was born.' I looked longingly, but it didn't work.

Earlier, in the church, I met the verger, a slim, bespectacled man, and his wife, plump, a little bland. They had worked in Ghana. I asked them how immigrants, of which Bristol had a large population, got on with white people.

'We respect all religions,' said the wife.

'Our children were told strictly never to disturb the Muslim servants when they prayed,' said the verger. 'And we had such good Pakistani friends. When they moved into our neighbourhood no one would talk to them; but we did. They were splendid people but the others wouldn't admit that – '

'Yes,' said the wife. 'We had to suffer our neighbours' wrath for our friendship.'

'But there is a kind of reverse racism,' said the verger. 'West Indians are lazy, they are quite unemployable, everyone knows it but you can't say it.'

'Surely,' I said, thinking of my London taxi-driver, 'it isn't West Indians who are like that but some individuals – it's very unfair to tar everyone with the same brush. How outrageous it would feel to be honest and hardworking and still be considered good for nothing because you were West Indian.'

'Yes,' he said, 'that is very unfortunate – that people who are doing wrong are doing it to innocents in their own community.'

'It's a cultural pattern, I think,' said the wife. 'Even in Africa they'd be thieving, no matter how much you gave them.'

'But that's Africa, these people are from the Caribbean.'

'Yes, but it's the same culture.'

'And they're so quick to accuse you of discrimination,' said the man. 'I was working with the local council and this West Indian accused me of racism because I didn't give him a job. Luckily, I was able to prove my innocence – the council had a policy of never hiring without advertising. And we hadn't advertised for two years. So I had sent him away because there was no job to give.'

'It's the same with the lesbians – ' said the wife.

'Yes,' he said. 'They want special treatment so the council has set up a committee for lesbians. That's outrageous, I think. Mind you, we have nothing against gay people – everyone's private life is his own.'

We wanted to go back to Bath by train, since we had rail passes; but it was the day in the week for the rail strike. All that summer, in London, people would ask each other, 'Is there a tube strike tomorrow?' as if it were the end of the world. And reports of tailbacks many miles long made it seem so.

We took a taxi back home and the driver insisted I was an actor he had seen on television. No, he didn't know his name and, well, if I said I was not, he'd have to believe it.

Back in Bath, we took a cruise up the Avon in a large motorboat. 'How do I get in?' I asked.

'Not to worry,' said the captain, lifting me into his arms.

He was a handsome man, with silver hair, pink cheeks and Wastwater-blue eyes, and Juice sat next to him, mouth avidly open, listening to his commentary.

The reeds and rushes and water reminded me of the film *Hope and Glory*, the little boy escaping the London Blitz for the serenity of his grandfather's house by a river in the country.

'There was a woman called Sally who was burned there as a witch,' said the captain pointing to a hill. Everyone laughed; I shuddered. Women are being burned as witches even now in India so that their brothers or other male relatives can grab the lands they have inherited from their fathers.

'Those hills are honeycombed,' said the captain. 'They were meant to be the government's refuge in the Second World War –

113

the Admiralty uses them now.' I looked at the hill, green and ordinary, nothing to indicate it was just a shell of earth.

When we got out of the boat we were stopped by an American woman. 'Did he give you a ca-ammentary?' she asked.

'Yes,' said Juice. 'He was fantastic.'

'Just look at that! And our man sat like a dummy through it a–all.'

'Where are you from?' I asked.

'From Liverpool; but I've lived in the States for fifteen years – my husband's American.'

'We're going to Liverpool,' I said. 'Have you been recently?'

'Yes, it's gone down – Britain's gone down. In Liverpool they've built this Maritime Museum and it's a–aful. If only the Americans had done it.'

That night, 4 July 1989, I read a newspaper article about James Goldsmith, who had made the biggest takeover bid in British history – thirteen billion pounds for the BAT group. He was, David Rosser had told me, a Millfield boy.

The shower-curtain rod fell on my nose when I was in the bath-tub next morning.

'Aaaeei!' screamed Juice. 'You have a hole in your nose.' And she held up a ring-sized circle of finger and thumb.

'Do you think it's broken?' I whispered.

'Feel it, feel it.'

I touched my Jewish nose gently; a smear of blood appeared on my finger-tip. 'The hole is smaller than I thought,' said Juice, disappointed. She brightened. 'I know what! I'll write a chapter called "A Bath-tub in Bath".'

We joined a walking tour later that morning. About five dozen tourists were waiting for the guides. When they arrived we broke up into groups; I chose a plump, greying woman because she had the best-looking boys in her bunch. She also had the worst voice, a hissing whisper that blew away with the breeze. And my ears were at her waist, which didn't make it easier.

Some students had inscribed the Magna Carta on a long wall

in a narrow street. One of the clauses said a widow would not be forced to remarry. In India it is the other way round; a widow is a slut if she expresses her desire for a second man. And if the Magna Carta came from the thirteenth century, in India, today, women in villages have to shave their heads, sleep on the ground, wear no colours or jewellery; they can never participate in any celebration lest they pollute the happiness with their misfortune, for a husband's death is blamed on a woman's evil destiny.

The Royal Crescent, a sweeping curve of lucid thought turned into buildings, had a lawn large as a park, marked private, on which a couple was strolling. I thought that was beautiful – a world without privileges would be life without incentive.

Adjoining the Crescent was the Royal Victoria Park; Victoria had visited Bath as a princess, heard somebody refer to her short, fat legs and never returned. By then, Bath had lost its royal popularity, which had begun with the visit of Charles II's queen, Catherine of Braganza, looking for an infertility cure from the waters. The same queen had brought Bombay to the British as part of her dowry; I liked the connectedness of things.

And yet I could feel no literary connections in this city of Jane Austen. Sitting in the Pump Room, thinking of Catherine from *Northanger Abbey* passing coy glances and smiles, I could not bring the two together. And more recently there had been Iris Murdoch's novel *The Philosopher's Pupil* placed in a thinly disguised Bath, and even that did not touch the real place. The fault – if it could be called that – lay, I knew, in the fact that I had read English literature more imaginatively than the English ever could. Not only were plot and character fictional for me, but so was place. Bath or Hyde Park or Kensington were as much part of an imagined reality as the conversations and conflicts in a book. And when I looked at the originals they did not merge into the fiction, but lay quite compatibly side by side. So that every time I heard the strokes of Big Ben, I'd think of Mrs Dalloway and how 'the leaden circles dissolved in the air', but I could never see her walking the streets I was passing through; Clarissa Dalloway still strolls through other streets that stretch before her in my head.

When I returned to Bombay and began reading them again, I discovered that English novels had become less real to me even as I could see the Chelsea or Oxford through which the characters moved. The experience of places had reduced their imaginative impact, so that novels read like skilful journalism rather than fiction.

The water from the springs at Bath tasted like liquid metal. It was from a new bore, sunk recently; and now a new concession had been granted to a private firm to tap sources and open a new bath. But it would be expensive and do the locals little good. The bath I saw, the unusable one, was as green as the celery soup I had once had in London. 'It's the algae and the sun,' said the guide.

For the first time in my life I had a lady taxi-driver; she was only thirty-eight but her eldest son was twenty. She and her husband drove their taxi a half-day each. They had made enough money to buy a large house on the other side of Avon. It had become increasingly impossible to buy property on the fashionable side of the river; a three-bedroom semi-detached house cost ninety thousand pounds. Dead cheap by London standards.

We went to the American Museum because I was horrified by the idea of such a thing in Bath. But the lady there explained that two Americans had set it up precisely because they knew people thought nothing beautiful was ever made in America.

There was a doll's-house which fascinated me; I longed for a larger version for myself. It is hard for people to imagine what it can be like to live in a world where tables are always too high, bookcases too tall, armchairs too deep.

There was an old couple with an even older woman whom they both called mother. They had stopped in front of a huge black fireplace and were shaking their heads, horror in their faces. 'I remember,' quavered the mother, 'how my mother used to make me kneel in front of one of those and black it every Saturday – '

116

'And you know how I wept,' said the daughter, her head thrown back to remember.

'Yes.' The mother smiled and turned to me. 'Her aunt left her house to my daughter, and the first time she lit a fire bats fell down the chimney and she had soot all over the room. She ran all the way to my house and burst out crying and shouting – oh, what a day that was!'

Cathy, the taxi-driver, came to take us back before I had quite seen the museum; that, I supposed, was better than being stranded there and wheeling down the steep hillsides.

She took us to see Prior Park, a palace masquerading as a mansion; beyond it the ground sloped away to a little bridge with cows grazing in the distance. Below that lay Bath, its honey-coloured stone sensuous in the sun.

Later, I sat in the piazza in front of the abbey, the Pump Room on one side, while Juice went shopping. 'I'll only buy if I get something from Marks – I don't wear other makes,' she said.

I wheeled into the centre of the piazza. A lone piper stood directly opposite me; above him and the music the abbey soared, the stone like a gigantic pair of arms folded in an Indian *namaste* enclosing the long stained-glass window. Angels climbed ladders on either side, as if they were making for the mosaic sky, triangles of enamel blue and immaculate white. I put on my brakes and waited till it all became ordinary for me again.

A man with long golden curls, wearing a long black coat, stopped two Italian boys in front of me. 'Will you give me a cigarette?' he said.

'Don't have any,' and they laughed and pointed at the coat that touched his knees.

'You are tight – aren't you?' he shouted. 'I hope someone refuses you – remember they refused Jesus. And see what happened to him!'

The Italians laughed in his face and turned away with a smart shrug.

I wheeled myself next to an empty bench and waited. I wanted to see if anyone would come and sit next to a wheelchair. In about

117

two minutes a bird of a man alighted on the seat; he had a small bald head and a long thin nose. 'Nice evening,' he said.

'Wonderful.'

'Pity I can't enjoy it much longer – have to start working at seven.'

'What do you do?'

'Nothing important – some menial job.'

'How does that matter? Surely the important thing is to work and earn.'

'You're absolutely right, you know. That's why I don't mind being an attendant at a petrol pump. Better than being out of work. And I'm earning as much as I did when I was doing a proper job – you know, using my mind. I must go,' and he flew away.

'This is a comfortable corner of England,' the man at the Conservative Party Association had told me. Surely the availability of work created an appetite for it; people usually move towards the possible. But they also create their own world, and perhaps the attitudes to life here had helped to make this area prosperous as it was.

Juice had joined me, and as we left the piazza I threw back a grateful look at the Pump Room. It had the only disabled loo I had met with sliding doors through which I could glide.

EIGHT

Who cuts the grass above Tintern?

The pale golden moustache of the young man sitting next to me was blowing under his breath; he turned and smiled and turned away. We were on the train to Cardiff and Juice and I were sitting away from each other so that we could meet other people.

'Are you from Cardiff?' I asked the young man.

'Yes', he said. 'I'm going back after a long time.'

'Where do you live then?'

'In Cardiff,' he said. 'But I've been away.'

'In London?'

'All over – I've been all over.' He nodded at the end of every sentence as if he were glad it was over.

I told him I was from India and this was my first visit to Wales.

'It's my first visit,' he said, 'in two years.'

'You must be very excited about meeting your family.'

'I am,' he said, and his moustache fluttered. 'I've got my future wife there.'

'Really! How marvellous!'

'And our daughter.'

'That's lovely.' I tried to keep the surprise from my voice.

'I've seen her only three times.'

Across the aisle from me two adolescent boys sat down with a dozen cans of lager. One was white and fat with a plump smile.

He kept giving me the thumbs-up sign – I grinned. Every time I looked at him he pointed at the window and said, 'Wales!' He pointed at his friend, who was dark like a shadow. 'He doesn't know Welsh,' he said.

'Are you fluent?' I asked.

'Oh yes! It isn't difficult – anyone can learn but they don't want to.' The shadow shrugged. 'You should know your own language,' he said. They went on drinking and laughing, but when an old lady needed help with her wrist-breaking bags they jumped up to assist.

'What do you do?' whispered the young man next to me.

'I write – my first novel is out in February.' I had started my sales pitch early. 'What do you do?'

'Nothing. I've been drifting!'

'Oh – wouldn't you like to learn something?'

'I have been, I have been – I've done a course in bricklaying, City and Guilds, and I've got City and Guilds in Maths and English.'

'Then you should be able to do something – '

'I want to,' he said, and his hand was a fist on his lap. His face tightened. He shut his eyes as if he were trying not to groan. Then he said, 'I was in a rehabilitation centre.'

'And you are out of it now.'

He rested his head against the back of the seat. 'There are two ways in life,' he said. 'The right way and the wrong way and I took the wrong way. But now I want to go right.'

'And that's all that counts.'

'Yes – sixty pounds, I used to spend sixty pounds a day before I went in. And now they pay you thirty-five pounds a week on the Youth Training Scheme – that's nothing. What can you do with that much?'

'Yes, but you are learning something which will make your future better.'

He shook his head. 'You learn nothing – unless you watch carefully. You've got to make a big effort or you come out as unskilled as you went in.'

'I suppose that's with any job.'

A young woman looked over the top of the seat in front. 'I've been teaching retarded children at Yeovil,' she said.

'That must be very satisfying.' I was beginning to feel like a counsellor.

'It is – but you don't know the hard work. It's no good being patient with them. You have to develop a different understanding of life altogether.'

'What did you teach them?'

'A lot. Some of them even join the YTS!' She disappeared behind the seat.

'You know,' said the young man, looking at me directly for the first time. 'You are the first civilian I've talked to in two years.'

Cardiff Station was confused – everyone we asked for the way to the travel centre pointed to someone else. Up and down we went by lift, following pointed fingers, trying to look beyond the shrugs.

'This seems familiar,' said Juice grimly.

Finally we went to Mr Evans, the station-master. He got us our onward reservation in less than a minute. Then he got up to hold the door open – 'Have a wonderful stay, and if you have any problems with travel come to me.'

Things worked like that in Cardiff. It was no good approaching someone with a formal request. But if you went up to a man and said, 'Could you help me, please?' he'd drop whatever he was doing, run to call the lift, slide the door open, lift the luggage and say, 'You know where to find me if you need any help.'

On the way out, I felt a tap on my shoulder. It was the young man from the train. He shook my hand. 'Thank you very much,' he said. I saw him walk away, one arm around his girl whose hair he was kissing again and again, the other pushing their daughter in her pram.

'Hey! You need to wipe your specs,' said Juice.

We walked to the tourist centre – Cardiff seemed new and ugly – where they found us a hotel. There was a short man with a thick dark moustache at the enquiries desk. I bothered him with questions for twenty minutes, about Caerphilly, about Cardiff – where could I hear a choir? – about Swansea.

He phoned Swansea and asked if they had a Dylan Thomas museum. 'Yes,' he said, holding the receiver, 'it's at the Marina.' I stood up on my arms, so I could jump at the prospect. He smiled. 'You're going to have a good time, I can see,' he said, and called us a taxi.

'It's not far,' shouted the Turkish taxi-driver into Juice's ear.

'We've got luggage,' she said.

'It's not far, I said,' he yelled.

'Just take me,' shouted Juice, and I ran my wheel into her foot.

The Riverside Hotel was red and hot. The ruby walls and carpets seemed to make the temperature rise, and it was warmer than Bombay in the summer. Our room had a ceiling a tall man could reach by lifting his arm and small windows that looked on to a sun-baked wall. All I could do was take off my shirt and lie flat on the bed until we went out.

The streets of Cardiff seemed like a foreign land. The people looked so different – short and scrawny, hollow-cheeked, with soft hair and moustaches like snuffling animals. There was an unmistakable colonial air about the city, and it could have been my imagination, but the people seemed to have been robbed of their pride so that they moved slowly, gently, like victims. Again and again, I was reminded of India. An imperial occupation had done something to the people, ruined their sense of efficacy, of being able to run things, so that they had withdrawn to an area of self where they were still effective. In all Britain I did not meet a people as caring and as affectionate as the Welsh; there was a sweetness about them, smiling and intensely personal.

I had come to Wales without the slightest sympathy for the nationalists, whom I thought of as a lunatic fringe. And I had felt it absurd that after seven centuries people could still talk of a foreign occupation. Now, seeing the stolid colonial architecture squatting stubbornly in the civic centre, or the castle, huge and unapproachable, I was overtaken by a sense of oppression and impotence.

122

The peacocks on the castle lawns did nothing to make me feel better. The Tower of Silence, where the Parsee dead are laid for the birds to eat, flocks with peacocks as it does with vultures.

We escaped into Bute Park, where I saw a circle of stones with a flat one in the centre like a miniature Stonehenge, but no one I asked seemed to know what it was. Cool breezes and lengths of water made the park lovely. We had walked, exchanging smiles with strangers, for about fifteen minutes when we saw a fat woman with pale curls and matching specs stretched out on a bench, waving at us.

'Can we sit down?' said Juice, and the woman drew her feet in.

'This is a lovely place,' I began.

'Yes. I come here' – her voice was high, like so many women's in Wales – 'to forget the bad strokes people done me.'

'Like what?'

'Come at me with a carving-knife.'

'Is Cardiff dangerous?'

'No. That was my husband who attacked me. And I put my parents in trouble to marry him. I stole from them, you know.' She spoke with the dip and swell of a rhythm. 'So they had to sell their house, poor things. After adopting me and sending me to private school – Roman Catholic.'

'I hope you left your husband,' said Juice. 'No use staying on with these – '

'Course I left him – but the court gave him one son; said the child would make him a better man. And you know what he did with him – he molested the boy. Can you believe such evil?'

'Imposs!' said Juice.

'But there are people like that in this world. A mongoloid girl came to see my husband – in a wheelchair she was, and she fell down the stairs; separated from the wheelchair, poor thing. And what would you think he did? Pounced on her and raped her.'

Someone had uncorked a bottle of giggles inside me, and the bubbles were bursting in my chest.

'All the while I was making a life. I kept lodgers to pay off the mortgage, I did. But the lodgers did such bad strokes to me – one who came from Iraq kept five people in his room. Is that a decent thing to do? The next one forged my name on a rent-receipt, said he was paying me double what he was. So I kept a girl instead and she blew up my cooker and sued me for the damage to her face.'

Laughter poured out of me in a gush.

'Some may laugh,' she said, laughing, 'but I have suffered. My father died because they didn't have enough money and I locked myself into my house, so depressed I was. I ate and ate and became like this – I had a Tory boyfriend before, when I was like you, slim. And I watched the television. Then my ceiling fell in, my bed broke, someone kicked in my back door. So I decided that's enough. I better get out and about.

'The first time I left my house a car ran into me and I was in hospital for a month. But I gave all the nurses and doctors cake to eat when I left.'

'That's so thoughtful,' I said.

'Isn't it? All my life I've been good and all I've got is – '

'Bad strokes,' said Juice.

'Yes. My poor dog tried to eat his way through the door when I was in hospital so they put him down. And then I took this job on the Employment Scheme – looking after old people, doing their shopping. Ten more pounds each week; I thought, I'll buy bicycle parts – I go round on this bike all day. Now they tell me I have to use a bus and buy a bus pass for four pounds. The people who train me have a secret agreement with the bus company.'

'So what are you going to do now?' I asked.

'Maybe I'll leave the job. I've still got my house – did you know my house was selected by the BBC as the worst house in the street?'

'Such a pleasure meeting you,' I said. 'We must be going.'

'Come back tomorrow,' she said, 'if you have the time. I'll be waiting here till nine in the evening.'

We walked by the river, glad of the silence. There was a bearded Asian sitting on the grass while his little boy played.

'Are you his sister?' he asked Juice. She shook her head. 'Very good of you to take him out.'

We walked on. Then I thought, well, why not. So we turned and I asked him, 'Are you from India?'

'Pakistan,' he said; his beard was trim, his eyes large and sad.

'We're from India.'

'No! But you speaking like English.'

'No-no, we are from Bombay,' said Juice.

'Hindu – Muslim – what it matters?' he said. 'When I was boy, in Pakistan, even next village was foreign – don't talk with them, don't do this with them, that with them. When I come here so many people help me – they never ask, you Hindu? You Muslim?'

'What about the British – are they racist?'

'Never!' he said. 'Most polite and helpful people. I went to Pakistan last year – there, people are so rude. I went to telegraph office, the man shouted at me. I thought, have I hurt him in some way? Here I go they fill the forms for me. You also must like it better here, in wheelchair.'

'Oh, it's heaven,' I said.

'Yes, I know. In Pakistan also no one does things for handicrafts – they just lie on the ground, no wheelchair, no crutches. It is very hard to be a handicraft in Pakistan.'

I told him about our tour round the country. He shook his head and his eyes filled. 'You are a fine gentleman,' he said; and to Juice, 'You are kind but you must be learning so much from him!'

'Too-too much,' said Juice eagerly.

'He put out his hand. 'I wish you all the luck in the world,' he said.

Back at the hotel we had dinner in the pink and white dining-room. We were late; the other tables had been set for breakfast. The waiter was a boy with smooth red cheeks and short hair rising at the crown. He was talkative, and Juice and I made it easier. 'You're from India?' he said. 'Wowoo! The furthest I've been is Greece. You should've seen me when I came back – what a tan I had, a real wicked tan and rippling muscles. All the girls flipped over me.' He laughed, bending over and slapping his knee. 'I'm saving money to go back – that's why I'm working here in my holidays. I also work at the Holiday Inn.'

When we'd finished eating he said, 'Care to come to the cocktail lounge?' I was amazed and delighted. In India a waiter was as likely to propose an after-dinner drink as he was to suggest sex.

'I don't drink,' I said, 'but we can chat.' I was very impressed by the holiday he'd earned himself; in Bombay boys didn't have money to go to Kashmir but they wouldn't, or weren't allowed to, do anything to earn it. 'And,' said Juice, 'you wouldn't be feeling this way if he did not look like he does – those dark eyes and rosy skin.'

We sat in the hotel lounge. 'I don't know what I'm going to do,' he said. 'I want to go for a year on the *QEII*.'

'That sounds great,' I said, 'but you must be sure you'll go back to studying when you return – a lot of people can't.'

'You're lucky,' he said, 'you know what you are. I've got a friend like that; he thinks he's a writer. He writes all the time – can I show you his stories? Maybe you can tell him if he's good or not.'

'Of course I will,' I said; whenever I was asked something like that I became the young writer I had been, and I felt the old fear and exhilaration and mad hope which so often came true.

'You're like my grandpa,' he said. 'He reads all the time – big books from the library. I live with him to help him sometimes. And he tells me all these things I never knew. Like the Germans invaded England in the war at Portsmouth – they did,' he said, watching the look on my face. 'They were defeated – you know how? By setting the sea on fire – no one talks about it, but someone who was there told my grandpa. He hates Maggie Thatcher – he screams when he sees her on the telly. "Lies! Lies!" he shouts, and stamps his foot.'

The next morning I woke up saying, 'The dawn came back, the cock on his shoulder': I was going to Swansea, to Dylan Thomas.

But first we had to go to the launderette a street away from the hotel. When we stepped into it someone started screaming with the most remarkable breath control. 'It's my fire-alarm,' said the woman there cheerfully. 'Nothing we can do about it – it goes off just when it likes, it does.' Two Chinese children, a black baby and I sat there with our fingers jamming our ears, a new kind of multiracial protest.

When we got out we realised we had just ten minutes to catch the train. Juice teetered across the bridge over the dried up Taff in record time. When we got to the station we couldn't find the platform. When we found the platform we needed the lift. When we got into the lift it was the wrong lift. A chunky young man from British Rail offered to take us – 'Run!' he said. We got to the train and heaved a sigh of relief. Juice tilted my chair to get it in and the train slipped away, wheels laughing with the tracks. 'I'm so sorry,' said the man. 'Can you wait another hour?'

'We'll go to Tintern instead,' I said.

'The train to Chepstow!' said the man, snapping his fingers, and we began another rush down by lift. When we got to the train I was shoved into the first-class carriage.

'But I'm a second-class passenger,' I said, visions of fines and punishment looming before me.

'Don't worry, sir. Have a good journey,' said the man waving us off.

Travelling first class was a bloody bore – there were two other people in the carriage beside ourselves and they were sitting at the other end. 'Take a picture,' I said to Juice, striking a Truman Capote pose. She held the camera with one hand and her eye shut with the other and clicked.

Chepstow came close to nothingness; so much of Britain was like that. Twenty or thirty minutes away from a busy town, the countryside swept over the landscape like a vengeful sea, so that you were left with the impression that the towns were precarious reclamations, hardly holding their ground. And that was strange, because the towns were old, rooted in history, or at least the Industrial Revolution. Perhaps it was the contrast with India, where small is always big, that made British towns tentative for me, as if they hadn't quite said yes to urbanisation.

127

'The most beautiful scenery in Britain,' said the driver of our taxi, rushing through the wooded hills, the sun on the throat of the valleys. I liked this part of Britain, because it made no claims to overawe you with splendour, as the Lake District did. There, I was always waiting for the cannons of grandeur to go off; when they did the sound was no louder than a pistol-shot.

Here, above Tintern Abbey, nature made no promises it could not keep. The trees, the silence, the sky melting as if it were made of blue butter, all humming to themselves; you stopped without invitation.

Tintern itself seemed an angry ruin trying to outlast old age, its skeleton stubbornly clinging on while the flesh had withered away. The ground around it dipped and swelled, blocks of stone and masonry making it impossible for a wheelchair. We tried going down a path – there was a bridge ahead, an old lady told us, and a wonderful walk – but we found ourselves stopped by private houses. Finally there was the river, wriggling in the sun; I could see it only through a single gap in the greenery. And I sat there clutching a copy of Wordsworth's poem, reading it to the water. I could not resist the temptation, though I knew I was taking the risk of casting the lovely lines into reality, where they could get tangled, lost.

On our way back the driver pointed out the Severn, large, slow, heavy, like robes spread out on the surface of the water. Suddenly I was about ten, lying in bed with one of my fractures which came every year like Christmas, and a bit more often, when I was a boy. It was afternoon and hot; I was watching the whirring fan with intense concentration, knowing that somehow it would make me forget what was happening in my hip-joint. Then I picked up a book about a boy who sailed out on the Severn. I went with him and the pain grew more distant. By the time I finished the book the pain was gone. After that, the Severn was a charm for me; if I saw it flowing through a story, my day was brighter.

Juice was munching a cheese sandwich in the back seat when the driver pounced. 'Do you mind waiting?' he said in a schoolmaster's voice. 'We don't allow food in the taxi.'

'I'm so sorry,' Juice said. But she was thrown. When we got on the train to Cardiff, she was restless, worried about missing our station. 'Let's go!' she said, helping me back into my wheelchair. We got off. But Cardiff Station had shrunk while we were away; most of the porters had left, the lifts had vanished.

'We are in Newport,' I said.

By the time we got to Swansea I was seeing Dylan Thomas in every face – but there really were boys with the large eyes and mouth of the young dog.

We had a lady taxi-driver. 'Never read Dylan Thomas,' she said. She took us to the Marina. We found a theatre with a poster of Dylan Thomas outside. The doors were locked; I could see only darkness through the glass panes.

We walked around it; a bearded man stopped us. 'Are you looking for something?' he asked. I told him about the Dylan Thomas Museum. 'Never heard of it,' he said. 'Dylan Thomas – he was a poet, wasn't he?'

'Yes,' I said faintly.

He thought he'd cheer me up. 'Why don't you come and see the Maritime Museum?' he said.

'I don't think so,' though I knew I was being cussed, like a child who wouldn't have vanilla ice cream because he couldn't get his favourite chocolate-chip.

I couldn't stick the Marina – it was meaningless, with a basin of water clogged with boats and the waterfront sweltering warm with crowds. There was a loud sound behind me, as of something heavy falling. I looked back and couldn't see Juice. Panic under the sun; I could imagine calling my publishers from a phone-booth, asking them to drive down from Soho Square to bring me back.

'It's finished,' said Juice, and I swung my chair around, hitting her in the head. She was crouching over my bag, which lay on the ground, a dead octopus with its torn straps stretched out like tentacles. Her eyes were wide with horror, like mine. It was a very special bag that I had bought in Florence because it could hang from the handles of my chair without touching the wheels. In it was money, my taped notes, all the medicine my phobias said I might need, addresses and phone numbers, Aero bars, sweaters to protect me from the unfaithful weather, Palgrave's *Golden Treasury*. 'What are we going to do?' I said.

'You sit with it, of course,' said Juice, plonking the octopus-corpse behind me. That gave me about four inches of space to sit on. Even with my mini-car version of a body that was tough; every time the chair took a bump, I felt the edge of the seat against my tail-bone.

'Any shop, any price,' I said to the taxi-driver, who wore a tantalising sweatshirt made of white net through which I could see whorls of dark hair and smooth knots of muscle.

We found a bag and I bought it, though it said 'SPORT' in large white letters and I hated the idea of getting a brave-boy smile. But the price was amazing – just £1.99. British prices were strange – a hand-mirror in Oxford Street cost £10, and I could get that in India for 75 pence.

'What about Dylan Thomas?' I asked the taxi-driver. 'Doesn't Swansea have anything to do with him?'

'Never heard of the chap,' he said.

Actually I liked disappointments; they made me feel I was a traveller – as did the doors at our hotel in Cardiff. They were the exact width of my wheelchair. Every time I needed to go through one, Juice had to rush it and withdraw as I lurched forward with the impact. We'd have a second go, and a third, until suddenly I would shoot through. But the Battle of the Doors was to me what sore feet were to Paul Theroux, and I was glad to fight it.

Roath Park back in Cardiff made me sick with envy. The gigantic lake, sloping shores held back by trees, the breathing space. India has its loveliness, but not this kind – safe, easy, welcoming to my wheelchair. The lake was too large for Juice's legs to circumambulate, so we stopped at the memorial to Robert Scott, a lonely island in the vastness of water. Scott of the Antarctic was a childhood history lesson I never forgot, because it had moved my teacher to tears and I, eight years old, had been fascinated by the idea that history could make anyone cry. Later, that took me to the books from which I learned my British history, which, of course, was no longer taught in India.

That night we ate at Wimpy's. One of the most pathetic things about being excluded from the life of the West was the pleasure Indians took in its rubbish. So that back home girls would gurgle with delight at the sight of a garish American hair-clip, and men show off their clownlike T-shirts from 'over there'. Exclusion made for enchantment, and people were reduced to the state of children who, bleary-eyed, pretend to enjoy a late-night party which they have fought to attend.

Fast-food chains from the West are forbidden to operate in India, and McDonald's is like Maxim's for us. Eating our local burgers we dream of Big Mac; sipping our milk-shakes we talk of the ones 'you get *there*, like melted ice cream in your mouth'. So that in Rome, the sight of a McDonald's café drove me wild – this was a light-hearted version of everything I had been denied because I was born in Bombay: the books, the ballet, the theatre, conversation about these, BBC television, the London Philharmonic, Van Eyck and Rubens . . .

That evening in Rome, I pretended not to notice that the Chicken McNuggets tasted a bit like chewing-gum after the flavour was gone. But after three and a half (I couldn't finish my order) visits to fast-food joints in London, I knew the truth.

So Wimpy's in Cardiff was a kind of giggle at myself, at the glamour-struck guy I had been only twelve weeks ago. The café was a pedestrian precinct on Queen Street. It was a Saturday night, heartbreaking in its hope. Wimpy's was full of young people, and they were dressed as if they were going for a night out in the West End. But all they were doing, before or after their burgers, was parading up and down the piazza, the boys slick-haired in pin-striped shirts and midnight blue jackets, the girls in chic little black dresses well above their black-stockinged knees. The boys walked with boys, flicking smiles at the girls walking with girls; sometimes a smile would be held and flicked back, they'd stop, exchange eager looks, exaggerated compliments, excited laughter and move away with candlelit eyes.

When we finished, a plump, black waitress came up. 'I

charged you less, only take-away prices,' she said. 'Saved you ten p.'

I was appalled and moved.

'Do you think we look poor?' said Juice, surreptitiously glancing at her Bally shoes.

'No, it's the wheelchair,' I said, uncertainly. In London, Freddy had ordered fish-and-chips at a café and had been given a double portion. 'You need it,' said the woman at the counter, watching his shirt with its frayed cuffs and washed-out collar.

'She thought I was a tramp!' he shouted. 'I was so embarrassed.' And the next day he marched into Marks looking for clothes to become a person again, all the Bombay horror of poverty breathing down his neck.

'Take these with you,' said Anthony the waiter, dumping a rustle of papers in my lap. 'They're my friend Claudio's writings. Then tell him what you think. Is that all right?'

I smiled. 'I can't take these,' I said, 'but I'll read what I can.'

What I read was enormous fun, full of energy; the story wasn't farm-fresh – the burly bully at school gets his come-uppance when one of his victims reveals that his name is the shamefully frail Rupert – but I liked it. I thought Claudio could write. Though literally speaking he couldn't – his spellings were worse than an American's (I have a friend in New York who writes Cawsway for Causeway and except for accept, as in 'Your friends will have to except you, so what if you're gay!').

The story I read was only one of more than a dozen he had done about the same gang at a school. And there was a novel he had started on. He was fifteen, and I wrote to him saying if he worked hard he might get somewhere, but he must not stop studying. I couldn't believe the number of people I met in Britain who had dropped out of school, when it was free, and reasonably good. A teacher friend told me how she had to cope as Walkmans competed with Wordsworth in her class, and pupils snored softly through it all. Did it, I wondered, have something to do with the fact that if you don't have to pay for something you devalue it? Quite unconsciously, you feel that if you were being offered something worthwhile surely you'd be required to give something in return. I had seen something of this in India. Our servants would never be satisfied with a free pair of spectacles, which they broke within a week, or the vitamin tablets they were given without charge by municipal doctors. Then you took them to a private doctor, they saw you pay, and they came out saying they were already feeling better. This time the spectacles were real, they would last.

That morning, my first Sunday on tour, I wanted to hear a Welsh choir. Llanduff Cathedral, said everyone, and we got there when the service had started. 'I'll help you,' said a smiling woman in pink, looking at the stairs.

'Please go ahead – you'll be late,' said Juice.

'Then we'll be late together,' she said. And that was better than any sermon, I thought. Though I understood what Sunday service could do for someone. Not many people stood outside themselves to look in, if only because they didn't have the time. But this hour, one morning a week, gave them an opportunity made easier by the exhortations to self-examination from the pulpit.

The choir sang so well you had to shut your eyes. Across the aisle a beautiful woman in a long white shirt and with short gold hair was singing perfectly in tune; I wanted to wish away all the spoken slices of the service.

A tall black woman, regal in robes, walked up the aisle; on her way out she stopped and said, her voice deep, 'Do you remember me?'

'No – I'm sorry.'

'At Wimpy's yesterday,' and she swept on, having shown me what the Church could do.

We took the train to Caerphilly. The air there was light, transparent, so that movement felt strangely effortless and the views of distant hills were sharp as the sight from a telephoto lens.

We were desperately hungry and we went to a pub; nothing but desperation could take me to one. 'You'll never be an

Englishman,' Freddy had said to me. Part of the dislike was that I didn't drink. 'You have moral objections,' said many a Briton to me, nodding understandingly.

'No – I just don't like the taste.' And yes, I did find it strange that perfectly lovely people should drink so eagerly, as if they wanted to alter the way they were. Perhaps it had to do with being perfectly lovely – in my four months in Britain I didn't once meet a loss of temper.

Pubs always had a peculiar smell for me, something like a cleaning liquid, or perhaps polish. Or the food, which was quite unbearable, overweight, and modest of intent.

But the pub in Caerphilly could afford to be disdainful of food. Perched on the edge of a moat, it possessed a perfect view of a castle, vulnerable, with a leaning wall, handsome grey against the delicate blue sky.

I was wary of castles that didn't let me in, so we went to the tourist office to find out its intentions. The only person there was a woman who looked like a genial Mrs Thatcher. She was delighted that Caerphilly was going to feature in a book. 'There's a ghost in the castle,' she said. Her accent didn't have the Welsh lift and fall. 'A few years ago some workmen refused to stay inside because they had heard music and smelled perfume.'

'Oooh!' said Juice, rubbing the goose-pimples off her arms.

'Yes, it's the poor Princess Alice who fell in love with a Welsh prince, though she was married to Gilbert de Clare. And she confessed it to a monk who broke his vow and told her husband. So he exiled her to France, away from the man she loved.'

'Too-too sad,' said Juice.

'Not really, because her lover got his revenge. One day he ambushed the wicked monk and *hanged* him. We have a place called the District of the Monk.'

'We must go inside!' said Juice, her voice wobbly.

'Oh, you can – there's a way for the wheelchair.'

'Do you enjoy this job?' I asked.

'I love it. I'm not here all the time. I take tourists all over Wales.'

'Do you take Americans?'

'Oh yes! They're so sweet. Would you believe, the last group I took tipped me three hundred pounds. And how they love Britain! They have read all about it and it's like coming home for some of them – they go crazy over things like the farmer getting a shouting from his wife for entering the house with his muddy shoes on.'

I told her about Cheddar Gorge. 'Well, yes,' she said. 'These people I took last week kept asking who cut the grass on the hills around Tintern.'

'Why does the castle wall lean towards the moat?'

'The castle has been slighted – Cromwell's men did that so that if it were recaptured by the royalists they wouldn't find it very useful.'

'We must go,' said Juice.

'Look out for the witch!' she said. 'She lives in the moat and shrieks horribly.' Then, seeing Juice's face, she added, 'It's just the suction of the stream that feeds the moat when the tide runs a certain way.'

Caerphilly Castle was a pet, quite literally so. It was tame, domesticated, like a huge kind dog kept to play with the children. The ghost and the witch must have fled long ago; old places like the abbey at Glastonbury had atmosphere, a completeness about them that disdained visitors as irrelevant. But Caerphilly Castle belonged to the tourists, its colourful pennants wagging in the breeze. An American boy in scarlet shorts had climbed to the top of one of the battlements, and I was shot with envy. It always hit me like a bullet, the longing to do something with my body that was laughably impossible. I took a photo instead.

That afternoon we drove down to the beach at Barry Island with a taxi-driver from Pakistan. He had a thick moustache that seemed to be reflected in his dark, troubled eyes. 'I've been here fourteen years,' he said when I told him I was an Indian. I always had to tell people since Parsees look like oriental Jews. 'Fourteen years and now I'm going back.'

'Don't you like it here?'

He shook his head mournfully. 'Can't practise my religion here.'

'Why is that? I mean, you don't have to do anything you don't want to – drink or things like that.'

'But I see people doing them – that is also a sin,' and he pointed at a skimpily clad girl crossing the road in front of us. Perhaps the exposed sexuality of Britain was confronting him with a temptation that he found both difficult and necessary to resist.

'I'm going back in January,' he said. 'Funny thing – I married a Pakistani girl living here because I was too poor. My family was labourers, six brothers, sisters. I came here without English. Now I have two shops, two flats that I rent out, this taxi. Know how much I make? Two thousand pounds a month. And that's nothing.'

'That's a lot,' I said.

He liked the approval in my voice. 'I've spent one hundred and fifty thousand pounds on my family. Every time there was a wedding I went home – six times, three months for each wedding. What to do? Had to help them. My brothers and sisters are still poor.'

'Do you have children?'

'Yes – boy of thirteen, girl of nine – '

'Don't they want to stay on?'

'Doesn't matter what they want – I have to take them away before I lose control over them. Once they are sixteen or so there is nothing you can do.'

'But there's so much more opportunity for them here.'

'They'll have a good life in Pakistan – a big house, at least two servants. I'll send them to a proper school. I can't keep them here – the West destroys our children.'

'Will you be selling your shops when you return?'

'No; I'll keep one to make money. Will you come to Newport, to my house?' His voice was warm, sincere, and I knew enough about the culture he and I came from not to be taken aback by his invitation. 'You will make me so happy,' he said. 'You can meet my family, eat something under my roof.'

How I longed to see his house, meet those children, but something in me was resisting, saying, 'No, no, thank you –

we don't have time. But do give us your address – if we are ever in Cardiff again, we'll surely – '

'How could you be so stupid?' said Juice. 'That was a chance in a million.'

I knew that; but listening to that man I had felt a terrible fear. The world he spoke of was the world I was returning to in a month's time. My life, my ideas, were not his, but in India people like me survive precariously on the knife-thin westernised edge of an irrational universe. In India, the body is snatched away from the mind so that people turn to reason – as the taxi-driver had to the West – only in order to make money, to survive. The rest belongs to religion, to tradition, to unthinking. So that the man I had just met had to abduct his children from the West before they learned to think too clearly. Thought, like thirst, is fatal in the deserts of sand and soul.

My first glimpse of the sea in Britain was also my hundredth. All my life I had seen it, first in my childhood picture-books and juvenile readings of Masefield, later in novels like *The Sea, the Sea*. And it was so different from the Arabian Sea, paler, with a cold, glistening surface. There were cliffs and a headland reaching for the horizon. It made me nostalgic for the days when my imagination bobbed on waves like these.

At the beach, my wheelchair sank into the sand, immobile as a dinosaur. All around me the Welsh were roasting themselves, turning a *tandoori* red under the spit of the sun. Juice managed to heave the chair out of the sand and climb back to the promenade.

Barry Island was a happy place – boys played games on the promenade, a ball floated into the air again and again from the invisible – to me – beach below, a thick red man sat fishing on the rocks at the end of the promenade while behind him a couple exchanged luxurious kisses. Every little while a public-address system would request parents to bring their children close to shore while official white boats patrolled the water.

There was an amusement park where I wanted to go. 'Yes, we'll enjoy the rides,' said Juice. 'I love them – in Bombay I buy three tickets to the Giant Wheel so I don't have to get off.'

We bought two tickets and I approached what we, in Bombay, called an aeroplane: boat-shaped seats connected by long rods to a central pole around which they would swing gradually higher and higher. I had sat in one as a boy on my seventh birthday, but everyone thought it was too risky with my bones. When I went to Disneyland five years later, my big sister wept as I whirled. 'You're so light,' she sobbed, 'the wind will carry you off!' That was my last ride. After that, no one would lift me into a fairground ride. 'Sorry, but suppose something goes wrong?' they'd say.

I went up to the aeroplane. There was a laughing young man in charge, wearing a cheerful yellow T-shirt. 'Could you help me in?' I asked.

'Of course. Let's go!' And he lifted me into the air and the aeroplane.

'What about my wheelchair?' I said, thinking of all my notes inside the new bag.

'I'll take care of that – you enjoy yourself.'

As the plane took off, sweeping over the abandoned ground, I thought, this is the life! But Juice's hind legs had collapsed, as they say in Gujarati. 'Oh! Mummy! Save meeee!' she screamed. 'Please stop the machine! Help me down! Get me a parachute! No! No higher!' But the plane, with the insouciance of the deaf, climbed beyond the perpendicular above the roofs. This was a drug – now I knew how Britons felt when they drank, though I was still sober enough to look for my new bag at every round, the one that said, not inappropriately now, "SPORT".

'That's the end,' said Juice, marching me out of the park. 'I'm going to be sick any moment.'

'What about those three tickets to the Giant Wheel?'

'I'm not sure I really did that.'

'I can take the other rides alone – see how easily that man helped me?'

'And he asked if you had a good time – why didn't he ask me?'

'I'm sorry about that – anyway, I'll try that water ride next.'

But I was out of the gate.

'Remember, you are uninsured,' said Juice.

We walked to the other end of a waterfront lined with rocking-horses and shaking-cars. Behind them were bingo parlours and gambling dens with games like Cakewalk, where a machine shook as if it had Parkinson's disease, dropping money into a tray at random while bug-eyed men felt for it with groping fingers. Gambling is all right; it's fun if you gamble with somebody, and you lose and he wins or whatever. But to do it with a machine, and endlessly? When there are public libraries and museums and art galleries waiting? What good did it do to climb into the monetary middle class to gain leisure and squander it like this?

But I also knew that money was a pre-condition of a better life, not a guarantee. As it reinforces the future, it also prises it open, so that the children of the parents playing bingo on the waterfront might grow up to play bridge. How many of the literary women I knew might have had grandmothers who first bought a book by Marie Corelli?

NINE

For the love of Liverpool

I woke up grinning, the next day. The night before I'd been saved from a dunking. Juice, pushed beyond endurance by my mockery of her courage-credentials, had brandished a glassful of water clonking with ice across the table at the swanky Italian place we were eating in. The dark-haired waitress rushed over and held her hand. 'No violence, please,' she said, and turned away as if she had seen nothing.

We had a new waiter at breakfast, tall, fair-haired, fine-boned. His name-tag said Anthony. 'Anthony the Second,' said Juice.

His predecessor had told us about him. 'You sing well, don't you? The other Anthony's been telling us.'

'Oh yes! I do!' He had a witty, crooked smile; his voice was low and very clear.

'And are you hoping to make a career of your singing?'

'Yes,' said Anthony I coming in and sitting at our table. My Indian heart was taken by surprise. 'He's fantastic – he sings and dances in the street.'

'They think I'm mad, they give me dirty looks. Cardiff is like that, small and small-minded.'

'That's why he wants to go to America.'

'Lionel Ritchie – I've met him and given him a tape. Now I'm going to the States – my uncle's a big boss of the Greyhound company. I can make it in America, I know I can.'

'There must be a lot of competition,' I said, feeling like a sprinkler at a fire.

'There is, but you can get ahead if you're good. In Britain you have to be super-good to get anywhere at all.'

'Went to town, yesterday,' said AI. 'God! The girls there!'

'We go to Catholic schools,' said AII by way of explanation.

'Yes, his is stricter than mine.'

'I was only dancing the other day with the statue of May-ry – she's Madonna too – and I'd put some lipstick on her. And this nun came in – "Aaah," she screamed. "You're in league with the Devil!" And my religious education teacher went mad, she had to be put in hospital – '

'Religious obsession, like,' said AI.

'Yes, she thought we were all possessed and out to get her. "You're destroying me!" she'd shout. "All of you born with your parents rolling in the gutter."'

'They don't let us read the *Sun*,' said AI, 'because of Page Three – you know Page Three?'

'I've heard of it.'

'I told the nun you can take Page Three, let me read the rest, but she banned the *Sun* from the school.'

The train to Liverpool was waiting. 'We have to go,' I said.

'Oh! That's sad,' said AI, sagging in his crisp white shirt.

'Come back to Cardiff,' said AII. 'I won't be there, but if I make it big in the States, I won't forget you.'

For someone who hates partings this kind of travel is not a good idea. I left a tip for AI with a note asking him to have a meal in Athens and remember me.

We were late at the station, but someone from British Rail was waiting for us. 'We'll get you in with a minute to spare, sir,' he said.

Opposite me in the train was a kissing couple; the boy about eighteen with a wispy blond beard, the girl looking like Petra Kelly, short hair, bright eyes. In between the smooching sessions the boy worked on equations in a large book, the girl read a horror novel.

Thirty-four kisses later I asked them if they were from Liverpool.

'From Germany,' said the boy, whose name was Hans. 'We are touring Britain.'

'So am I!'

'Have you been to Stonehenge? It's a rip-off – they make you stand ten metres away behind a fence.'

'Like Lendzend,' said the girl.

'Yes, we had to pay to go there.' He spoke slowly, translating before talking.

'And where are you off to now?'

'Lake District – '

'And Scotland.'

'Then the money will be over and back home.'

I asked about East Germany – did they go there?

'Oh yes!' said Hans and giggled. 'I go to the East and sell my Western marks in the black market – I get seven for one. Then I go back and the official rate is one for one so I make a profit, have an expensive dinner.'

'Aren't you afraid of getting caught?'

'No – nothing will happen.'

'My mother,' said the girl, 'she escapes without getting caught – only a suitcase she comes with.'

'Ja,' said Hans. 'Her mother escaped in fifty-two – not so hard then.'

'All her relatives she loses,' said the girl.

I thought of those lost relatives that night in November when the Wall was punctured.

'What about the Wall?'

'Ja,' said Hans. 'But it is not so bad behind it. We feel it because we are used to colour, attractive packaging. You get things there, as good, only so badly wrapped in paper you don't want to buy.'

'But the freedom – '

He shrugged. 'Life is old-fashioned in the East – but they have beautiful buildings.' The thought of those monuments made him feel better, less guilty about the countrymen he could do nothing about.

'Is it difficult for you to think about the war – do you feel guilty?'

'Not at all. You make up for it by fighting war, joining the peace movement. But lots of people don't feel guilty because they like the past. Even young people, like my age.'

'I wish we can talk like you English,' said the girl.

'We manage okay,' said Hans. 'Only in Wales people talk slang – you ask beg your pardon four times, then you get fed up.'

'We have to change trains here – good luck!'

They went out and stopped by the window. Hans was wearing his knapsack on his back. He gave me a thumbs-up sign and Petra Kelly smiled and made a fist.

I turned to the fat old woman across the aisle. She was from Liverpool. 'Go to Blackpool,' she said, 'and the Albert Docks; they've made them all new, you'll loov them.'

'Are there a lot of bed-and-breakfast places?'

'Oooh, hundreds! They'll ask for eighteen pounds but you be firm; they'll come down to four pounds a night.'

'She's a time-traveller,' said Juice from behind me.

Lime Street Station was very friendly but not too efficient. There was a bell we had to ring for disabled assistance but no one was there to hear it. About ten minutes later a grinning face appeared behind the glass. 'I've been dealing with five people and you are the sixth. Welcome!'

I told him we needed a reservation for the train to Glasgow.

'I might not be able to get you seats together.'

'That's perfect,' I said. 'I love talking to strangers.' An American behind me guffawed. 'That's purr-fact, he says!'

At the tourist information centre they said they could get us a room. But there was a problem.

'A common loo and shower!' I spluttered, horrified.

'That's all we can get for now – I'm sorry, sir. And the room's all right for wheelchairs.'

'We'll take it,' said Juice.

Back at the station I was surrounded by taxi-drivers while Juice went to collect our bags.

'How can we help you?' said a robust sixty-year-old.

143

'Yes, just tell us and we'll do it,' said a weedier version with a cigarette in the corner of his mouth.

The robust one tried getting me into his black cab. 'It won't go,' he said. 'Never mind – we'll get you into one of the new ones.' He hurried towards a Metro cab. 'Gentleman for you,' he shouted. And the cab cruised over. 'Let's get you in,' he said, tipping the chair. The weedy one shut the door and grinned, clutching the cigarette between his teeth. When Juice emerged from the station she was open-mouthed to see me caged in the cab.

'Thanks very much,' I said to the drivers.

'Our pleasure,' they chorused.

'Liverpool is like those men,' said our plump, bespectacled driver. 'Friendly.' Every time he braked, my chair tipped back against the grille and fell forward. 'Take care,' he said, 'you'll end up going through that – come out the other side like potato cubes.'

'What do you think of the local council?' I said, knowing it was Loony Left.

'Doing a great job,' he said. 'Only they don't have enough money.'

The Bradford Hotel couldn't decide how to welcome me – through the garage or through a revolving door or through their restaurant. They decided on the last. It was our first big hotel, in size, at least.

The doors were all right and the lights were bright. There was a wash-basin that sang in the middle of the night whenever anyone else used theirs. The panelling on the walls was cheap, but there was a wide view with a big sky and I liked that.

We went walking through the city watching the people; a remarkable number seemed to be overweight. I wondered if that was a symptom of poverty, the diet too rich in fats, low in protein. Buildings were dirty, black with pollution, signs on shops played Fill in the Blanks, and the streets were littered, puddled. Liverpool did not seem to live in 1989 at all but in some other, darker, era. People smiled all the time but they were slovenly in dress, quite different from the modesty of London or the swish of Bath. Dogs barked down alleys, wild boys chased each other and shrieks filled the evening air.

The town centre with the mammoth St George's Hall and museum and library was heavy, gloomy. A sharp wind stirred the clouds into a grey porridge. A woman with tiny eyes, thin blouse shivering, was hurrying home. We asked her the way to the waterfront.

'Where are you from?' she asked. We told her. 'I was born there,' and she put her shopping bag on the ground.

'Where?'

'In Jabalpur.'

'I have a friend who was born there.'

'I wouldn't know; I left before I was one – Independence came.'

'And you've never been back?'

'No; I'd love to – only thing Indian about me is my birth certificate, and it mentions caste; everyone says what's this?'

'Have you always been in Liverpool?'

'Oh no! I grew up in Birmingham. I went to live in Norfolk – it was awful, very unfriendly. If you talked to somebody at the bus-stop they'd think you were mad. I love Liverpool. There's always something going on and the people are marvellous.'

She worked at the library. 'Everything is going to be shut tomorrow, the museum and all that. There's a local government employees' strike.'

I asked her about Toxteth, which had seen some terrible riots a few years ago. Could I go there?

'You have to be a bit careful. It's a rough neighbourhood – not dangerous. I must go – my daughter's waiting. So good to meet you.'

We walked down to the waterfront. The Mersey was filthy, but there was something brave and moving about the way it opened itself to the sea; you could imagine the courage of those who set out from here into the cold.

We sat on a bench facing the water with two old ladies. The one next to Juice was short, dark, with a moustache; my neighbour had river-green eyes and a smile that could light a candle. They were sisters, Hattie and the lovely Lucy, who told

145

me she had retired a few years ago. 'Worked for sixty years from fourteen to seventy-four. Never been on the dole, I haven't.'

'That's wonderful – is Mrs Thatcher very unpopular here?'

'Oh no! She isn't – plenty of Conservatives around. I loov her – look at the renewal she's brought – the spirit we lost after the war.'

'Was Liverpool badly bombed?'

'Oooh! Yes! It was. And I would sit in the shelter with my three-year-old son, and pray that we'd be taken together if we were. How brave we were, singing in those shelters. What happened to us after that?'

'You mean young people?'

'Oh a lot of them are loovly, but then so many cheat the dole – that's wicked, isn't it? That means there's that much less for those who need it.'

'What about the health service? Do you feel that's falling apart?'

'There's a shortage of nurses – but I've never been sick; hard work never harmed anybody.'

'Do you go out much?'

'Who wouldn't in this weather? And my sister and me, we have our boos-pass; we can travel anywhere, free! Can you imagine that? But we'd be glad to pay a pound each week – every little bit helps, doesn't it?'

'And do you ever travel out of Liverpool?'

'Every Tuesday to Southport; there's a band there and a woman with a loovly voice who sings old songs. You pay just seventy-five pence and listen for two hours. We take our little picnic and sit on the deckchairs. And we go to Blackpool when they have the lights. All the nursery rhymes – "The Cow Jumped over the Moon" in lights. It's beautiful, isn't it, Hattie?'

Hattie nodded. 'Quite a one for talking, your friend is,' she said to Juice.

'But we won't go out in winter,' said Lucy. 'It's so dark – '

'And dangerous,' said Hattie, clutching her throat.

'My sister's scared since our house was robbed – but it was all insured!'

'You don't know which is more dangerous, staying in or going out and getting mugged,' said Hattie.

Lucy dropped her voice. 'I used to spend one night each week with my son and my five grandchildren – now I can't; she doesn't feel safe without me.'

'So you have a lot of family, that must be a pleasure.'

'Sheer delight, and my granddaughter is courting now, would you believe it? And my daughter-in-law is so good; of course, you must know how to deal with them! I've always lived in a large family – my parents had six children. We meet all the time at the bingo parlour. I haven't won yet. My sister-in-law won five hundred pounds, she did. Gave it all away to the family – we got our share too.'

'Is that Birkenhead across the river?'

'Yes; and New Brighton. Our parents took us to New Brighton, every month. We can't go there now – '

'Why not?'

'They took away the ferry, I don't know why, but they took away the ferry.' I wanted to fly her across right then. 'But doesn't do to grumble. There's so much good in the world, isn't there?'

'I think so.'

'We enjoy television and I have my son, my only son, but God knows! I loov him. And if I have him and me boos-pass what more can I ask for?'

Toxteth was a ghost town in the hot sun. The streets had no one I could talk to and the taxi-driver insisted I stay in the taxi. 'It's rough,' he said, as we drove past the burnt-out buildings and the police station where the riots started. 'Lot of West Indians here,' he said. 'But they're quiet now, and peaceful isn't it? You wouldn't tell it all happened – '

He took us to the Protestant Cathedral, which had a marvellous reproduction of Epstein's Holy Family; the young couple watching the child in their arms. I knew the look on their faces. When I lay in bed with a fracture, my parents watched me with that despair redeemed by an unbending love.

We went looking for the Roman Catholic Cathedral. From

afar we could see its strange steeple like a crown of thorns –
'The Wigwam' everyone called it. On the way I spotted a
sign saying 'Trade Union Community and Unemployment
Resources Centre'. Juice went in and emerged with a tall
young man. 'I'm Bob,' he said, 'would you like to take a
look?'

The centre was clean and white and busy with sounds.
'Those are the children,' said Bob. 'We look after them while
we're teaching their mothers all sorts of skills like working on
computers.'

I asked him about unemployment. 'It's very high on
Merseyside, about twenty per cent. Out of half a million
people ninety-seven thousand are not working.'

'Is it worse for immigrants?'

'Oh yes, there is fifty per cent unemployment among them.
The only thing that can help them is job quotas – but that
makes white workers angry.'

'Is that because of racism, or are they unemployable?'

'Both, I think. We hope to change things with this centre.'

'Are you funded by the Labour Party?'

'No. Mostly by the local council – of course, that is run
by Labour. And then we rent space to various organisations –
War on Want, the Campaign for Nuclear Disarmament, the
Communist Party.' That was ironic, considering the way com-
munists had treated trade unions all over Eastern Europe.

They had a huge drama-room. 'The unemployed put up
their own productions here. They even write them. And then
we sell tickets.'

'What sort of plays?'

'Well, recently they did one called *Snooper*. That was about
the inspectors the government sends to harass unemployed
people to find out if they are working on the side.' If they were,
I thought, then they weren't unemployed. On the other hand,
state benefits were not lavish; the temptation to supplement
them must be irresistible.

'We have a sports centre,' he said, 'where unemployed people
can keep themselves fit – that's so important.' I liked him; he
was serious about what he was doing and well-intentioned.

There was a painted ceiling by an unemployed artist who was the son of Jack Jones, the trades-union leader. It was a circle of loud colour and crude caricature, like a propaganda poster, depicting the Slave Trade and the March for Jobs.

'Do you feel satisfied with what you are doing for unemployed people?'

'Our whole thrust is to make them employed again. But while they are not we try to keep spirits up, to give them a feeling of doing something worthwhile.'

After this and Toxteth, I wanted to meet black people. Bob gave me the address of a Community Relations Centre, a dirty yellow building in a decrepit street. A beautiful girl, black and glossy, came out. 'I'll help you in,' she said; her hair was huge as a monsoon cloud. She manoeuvred my chair through a stable of big old cars.

Inside, a man called David ushered me into a large, quiet room. He had a tired face, the creases ironed into his forehead. 'I'm sorry, I don't have much time – we can talk for about twenty minutes.'

I stayed for an hour and a half. 'Are you West Indian?' I asked.

'No, I'm British black. My mother was English, my father from West Africa – he came here in the First World War.'

'And do you find a lot of racism in Liverpool?'

'Oh, it's rampant.' He had what Blanche called a middle-class accent.

'Is the prejudice against colour or culture?'

'Colour mostly.'

'Then why do you think Asians are doing much better?'

'They are more passive; black people stand up and fight. But even Asians when they assert themselves – like in Bradford – get into trouble.'

'Do you think West Indians are often aggressive? I've seen that. The only times I've met rudeness is from black sales people – a lot of them are, again, very helpful.'

'Wouldn't you be aggressive,' he said, 'if you were treated badly for no reason at all?'

I am, I thought. 'I understand, but for their own sake, don't

149

you think they should be encouraged to tune their responses? Assertion in the face of ill-treatment, not aggression as a habit!'

'But it's very difficult,' he said, running a hand through the ripples of his short hair. 'Their parents were different – if they were denied entrance to a club they walked away; these youngsters shout, sometimes turn violent.'

'Doesn't a permanently aggressive stance contribute to racism by strengthening stereotypes? I mean, here are liberal white people saying black people are no different from anyone else; but this sort of behaviour is different – rudeness in the street, in shops and, of course, physically they are often bigger and stronger – '

'How liberal are white people?' he said. 'Most of them have been pushed away from racism only because black people have made such a noise. How many of them will rally to the support of a family whose house is attacked in the next street?'

'Do you think this anger is an element in keeping black people unemployed?'

'Their parents weren't aggressive – they tried to get ahead in their menial jobs but they didn't get too far – '

'Some of them did – you, for instance, belong to the middle class.'

He looked indignant. 'I don't think so,' he said quietly. 'But as I was saying, the children saw their parents working well and obediently and getting nowhere. So they decided they weren't going to do menial jobs, they would rather remain unemployed; some of them opted out altogether, they wouldn't even stay on the dole.'

'If their parents were as passive as the Asians and yet received more racial ill-treatment, doesn't that mean there were aspects of their culture which Britons found unacceptable? I mean, there is this widespread view – I've met so many white people who feel West Indians are lazy and dishonest. This can only be a stereotype, but do you think there is any reason why people should think like that? Are West Indians more laid-back?'

'There is a cultural trend not to lay store by success or work or earning. But it's been fed by the absence of jobs, of employers who turn you away just because you are black.'

'And what about criminalisation?'

'Well, it's all a circle: people don't get jobs, they feel hopeless, the feeling spreads so that young people begin to say, "We don't want jobs from those who don't want to give them to us," and turn to easy ways of making money – theft, drugs. I'm not justifying crime – no amount of racism can justify that – but this is an explanation. And it goes back to childhood – '

'Values picked up?'

'No, just that black youngsters are treated worse by the authorities, who feel if he's black he's a troublemaker. If a black boy breaks a window the police are called in, he might even be taken away to a juvenile correction centre. If the same thing happens to a white boy he'll be kept in after school or given a spanking at home. And the black boy grows up already seeing himself as a petty criminal – that can be devastating.'

'I know,' I said. 'What about street-life? That is very much a West Indian thing. Do you feel it contributes to young people going out of control?'

'What you call street-life is also a sense of community – if both parents are out, everyone's watching the children. But yes, this is something brought over from the Caribbean.'

'What about serial monogamy – the fact that so many women live with a sequence of men, have children by them, the children grow up without a proper sense of family?'

'It happens,' he said. 'I'd call it an extended family – and the mothers do their best to give them a moral framework. Then they go out and they are told they are rubbish and some of them start acting that way.'

'Is there a way out?'

'It's very hard – Asian youngsters move towards business or the professions. For black children there are drugs or music, which is again drug-related, or religion, which not many care for in this modern world, and sports. Not many can excel at sports.'

'Do you feel if racism disappeared from Britain black people's problems would be solved? Or would their culture still hold them back?'

He smiled. 'I think we'd be fine once racism vanished. A very small part of our problems come from our own culture.'

Perhaps that was true in a sense. On an island where their culture was predominant it might not have caused problems. But the reality was that black people were a minority in an island with a sharply defined, and contrasting, culture. A culture in whose material success they wanted to participate, as so many Asians did. But the Asians had grasped something important: that success has no nationality in a relatively free economy. What works is education, industry, savings, the postponement of satisfaction, stability in the childhood environment. To flout these values was to commit economic suicide in the new Britain.

Racism is an unmitigated evil, a negation of mind and morality, perpetrated by those who have nothing to be proud of but the pigment of their skin. From my own life I knew what it was to be a lesser being in the outside world; how much harder it might have been if my parents had been disabled as well, and my relatives and my friends. The bigger world would have receded almost out of sight, as it had for so many young black people.

But if happiness is the goal, there is only one way to break out of despair – and that is achievement. Success requires the same values from the disabled or blacks or whites. For some of us the struggle is greater, but there is no substitute for it.

The only answer to racism is a sense of individual self; not a drowning in a collective identity, the hiding of heads in Afro hair-dos. The best refutation of a racial stereotype is the intelligent, responsive face on which no mask can be imposed.

One of the reasons why racial prejudice continues to survive is that its enemies have driven it underground, so that it can no longer be fought out of existence. Someone like me can talk with a certain amount of immunity about the shortcomings of immigrant cultures because the Holy Trinity of Liberalism resides in me – I am gay, Asian and disabled; I am on the right side. But for white people to discuss cultural patterns in other communities is fatal. I remember an afternoon I spent at Kew with an Indian woman and her liberal English friend. She and I discussed English people, their social habits, their attitudes, their quirks. Later that evening, her friend John said, more in sorrow than to blame, that statistics proved again and again the gradual criminalisation of young West Indians.

'I'm appalled to hear you say that,' said my Indian friend, red in the face. 'You are repeating white people's lies about black people – I can't imagine how you, of all people, can do this!'

'All I'm doing is what you've been doing all afternoon,' he said. 'Generalising about people, finding patterns – I'm sure neither you nor I are saying that individuals can't differ from cultural trends.' But she would not give him a hearing.

And that is disastrous; because when strange cultures share a living space the scope for misunderstanding is huge. Asians see whites as promiscuous and blacks as lazy; blacks see whites as selfish and Asians as pushy; whites see blacks as dangerous and Asians as miserly. How much better it would be if everyone talked freely about what they thought without feeling every time that they were guilty of racism. That way, differing attitudes could be understood in their contexts; and comprehension is halfway to acceptance. Condemning racism cannot mean outlawing prejudice. As long as people live with each other they will take irrational dislikes, they will generalise and treat strangers with suspicion; it happens between people from the north and south of England. The important thing is not to let prejudice become insidious, something to be scrawled only on the lavatory walls of the mind, to be conveyed subtly by a look or a shrug or a tone of voice. As my taxi-driver had said, no one treated him badly, but racism was there, he could feel it. It was, to exaggerate, a crime without fingerprints; and the way to deal with it is to bring it out into the open, to make it amenable to argument and proof and change.

The Big Top seemed to be a more appropriate name than the Wigwam for the Roman Catholic Cathedral in Liverpool. The altar was a stage in the centre of a gigantic hall with candles awaiting a birthday cake. The walls were decorated with cute collages, mosaics sprinkled with silver dust, banners and light sculptures. I sat there aghast, thinking of the churches in Rome, wondering if the Baroque seemed as outrageous when it was introduced to an age of classical loveliness. But, I had to admit, vulgarity was part of the British scene, on the waterfront, in the shopping-precincts. The Americans have made a style out of vulgarity that is glamorous and energetic. It was the weak-tea version, timid and self-conscious, that made British vulgarity so annoying, like a half-hearted liar.

There was more of that at the Albert Docks, which had been renewed into ugliness; a combination of red-brick and Ristorante-type fake-ethnic cafés.

After that the ferry to Birkenhead was a relief. I sat by the railings, feeling the boat under my chair like a huge vibrator. The skyline of Liverpool, with the Town Hall and the clock tower, was out of *A Letter To Brezhnev*, a film that had given Liverpool the lustre that had drawn me here. Standing next to me was an old woman clutching the collar of her black coat in one hand and a faded blue handbag in the other. Her face was pale, her eyes small but steady. 'Do you live in Birkenhead?' I asked.

She shook her head. 'I'm here just for the ride. I love the ferry and it gives me something to do.'

'Doesn't Liverpool look lovely from here?'

'Yes. To think what it was like in the war. We had a seven-day blitz, night and day. They wouldn't report it on the radio, felt it might please the Germans. I was thirty then, with a little son. And I'd wrap a scarf around his ears but he wanted it off! "Let me hear the guns!" he'd say; anti-aircraft guns, you know.'

'Was it a terrible time for you?'

'It was – two of my friends hid under a table all night till the bombing stopped. They only came to their door at dawn and a bomb scored a direct hit. Killed both my friends on the spot.' She looked down at me and slowly smiled. 'Doesn't do to think of these things, does it?' she said. 'And yet you can't forget, can you?'

'No,' I said, thinking what war had meant to my family. The British soldiers swarming over Bombay brought a touch of romance to my mother's teenage years; her cousin, back from Bristol, drove an ambulance in Poona, bringing wounded soldiers from the trains to the hospitals. She worked in a canteen, organised the Women's Voluntary Services, arranged social evenings for the soldiers. 'I was so light,' she'd say, 'when I danced with an Englishman, my feet never touched the ground. Those were difficult years – but what a good time we had!' My uncle, in the Merchant Navy, might have differed from her – his ship was torpedoed in the Bay of Bengal.

'Have you ever taken the ferry to Belfast?' I asked.

'Oh no!' she said. 'Would you believe Ireland was neutral in the war – the South, I mean? And they left all their lights on, which guided the German planes to Liverpool!'

'What do you think of Mrs Thatcher?' I asked.

'Are you a council man?' Her tone was wary, and the ferry had reached Birkenhead. She was hurrying away. 'No,' I shouted after her, 'I am not!'

'Behave yourself,' said Juice. The evening before she had asked the waiter at the hotel to make her bread 'nice and hot-hot'. I was outraged because everyone at the hotel thought she was my wife, and I was by association a hot-hot type as well.

Birkenhead seemed to be unpeopled. We walked down a long road without meeting anybody. We discovered a garden bright with begonias and roses in a square of handsome early Victorian buildings. 'This won't do,' I said. 'We have to explore.'

We entered narrow lanes with burnt-out houses and boarded shop windows. There was a Lady Margaret Hairdresser nailed firmly shut, a Jacket Potatoes place locked and barred. I couldn't understand it.

'This place is a spooky,' said Juice. 'I'm afraid – I'm my parents' only child. If something happens to me here, they won't forgive you.'

'They won't mind,' I said. 'Parsees honour an English grave.'

'But they've never heard of Birkenhead.'

We floated back in the ferry.

155

Later, we stepped into the glasshouse called St David's Centre. It was a kind of supermall. We went through the shops selling strange vegetables. In London, Blanche had served me artichokes, which we never ate in India. I thought they were good for sadists who would enjoy plucking out the flesh and, finally, the little heart.

I needed a battery-shaver and we went into an electronic goods shop where a woman in a saree with a glossy black bun on the nape of her neck was talking on the phone in Punjabi; unfortunately I didn't know the language or I could have eavesdropped to pass the fifteen minutes she kept us waiting with her red-lipsticked smile.

'So swarry,' she said. 'But a call from a-broad, from my native land. What can I do, good sir?' I asked her if I could have a look at different models of shaving-machines. 'By all means, sir.' And she unlocked the glass case in front of her.

'Are you from India?' said Juice. 'We are.'

'From Pakistan.' Every time someone said that I held my breath; somewhere I still believed they all hated us.

'How long have you been here?' I asked.

She smiled and danced her eyes. 'You guess!'

'Twenty years.'

'Ri-ight!'

'That's a long time – do you miss home?'

'Not at all. If you lowe a place it is with you all the time – how can you miss it?'

'Have you been back?'

'Wery often. I lowe travelling; I've been to America so many times.'

'To India?'

'Yes, I hawe.'

'How did you like it?'

'Wery nice, but . . . how shall I say it? Pakistan has made a lot of progress in the last fifteen years.'

'I understand.'

'And there are too many people in India. What caste are you?'

'We're Parsees – do you know Parsees?' Nobody ever did,

156

and I couldn't blame them. We were about eighty thousand in a population of eight hundred million.

'Of course I know Parsees! Our Qaid-E-Azam, Pakistan's founder, Jinnah was married to a Parsee, Rati Petit. You know that?'

My mother could never tire of telling me how the middle-aged sophisticate had eloped with the lovely young daughter of Parsee aristocrats, her father a British baronet!

'Yes,' I said. 'I'll buy this. Have you always lived in Liverpool?'

'Southport, much more pleasant. Hawe you been to Pakistan?'

'No. I wouldn't like anything better.'

'Go, go! You hawe a beam in your eye that tells me you will enjoy wherewer you go. I will remember you in my prayers; remember me in yours.'

TEN

Salaam Glasgow

In the morning I decided to leave for Glasgow. Unlikeable, unforgettable Liverpool had given me enough of itself; I felt I didn't need to stay longer. But our British Rail reservations were two days away. I phoned, and the man behind the disabled window recognised my voice. 'I can't give you a reservation,' he said, 'but I'll wire Preston where you change and I'll wire Glasgow. You should have no problem at all.' How easy everything was in Britain. What a tangle this would have been in Bombay, a confusion of queues and servants and recalcitrant clerks made amenable by bribes.

Next to me on the train was a Scotsman snatched out of a pictorial encyclopedia, with a flat chin, a strong nose and hooded eyes. He was groaning and shutting his eyes and shifting in his seat.

Across the aisle was a young man with a craggy face and a little girl out of a Miss Pears advert. He smiled. 'Going to Glasgow, are you?' he said.

'Yes, are you from there?'

'No, I live in Carlisle – a quiet life. I'm a market gardener.'

'Do you grow vegetables?'

'Not any more – not much money in that. I'm growing decorative plants and herbs now.'

'What's herbs?' said the little girl.

'Something you add to your food to make it taste better –

that's my little girl. She lives in London; I'm taking her to Carlisle for the summer. You aren't – are you English?'

'Indian. I live in Bombay.'

'My grandmother was born in India – her father was a chaplain in the army. He had a wooden sword because he didn't believe in bloodshed.'

'What's bloodshed?' said the daughter.

'Hurting people so their blood comes out.'

'Is Mrs Thatcher very unpopular where you live?'

'Terribly, terribly!' he said. 'There's so much poverty – not your kind though, I mean, not like in India.'

'I think not.'

'I saw a film about where you live, *Salaam Bombay*, about all the street children, how they survive. It was very depressing and I keep reading it has a message of hope. Have you seen it?'

'Yes, it's very depressing. But we hardly ever see that part of life.'

'There are a lot of poor crofters in the Highlands.'

'Where you live do you have neighbours?'

'Don't need any. I love being on my own – I was snowed in for two months once. That was heaven! I could walk out but no cars could reach me. Before that I lived in Lockerbie, right where the plane crashed. My friend was living in my cottage – he saw everything!'

The sighing Scotsman next to me had opened his eyes. I got ready. He turned his head and looked at me.

'Are you from Glasgow?' I asked.

'Used to be – I'm from Muswell Hill now, London.'

I thought of my first evening in Usha's flat; I wanted to rewind time, live it all again. 'Are you going to Scotland for a holiday?'

'No, I have to drive a lorry to London.'

I froze, my Bombay snobbery caught unawares. In India there was as much chance of my talking to a lorry-driver as there was of the Queen appearing on *Wogan*. 'Have you,' I said, 'worked in this . . . line for long?'

'I've worked since I was twenty. I was in a shipyard then and there was a strike; I worked three months in two years.

159

That's when I decided I didn't want anyone ruling my life, no more unions for me. I'm on my own, I work in the building trade. And I make two thousand a month.'

'Oh my God, that's fantastic!' I was sounding like Juice.

'Oh, yes! And I've got a pension plan – not like these whiners who finish all their money and complain when they can't work. If I can't work my pension will give me as much as I'm earning for six months; then it'll taper off. If I die each of my two boys – they're six and nine – will get a hundred thousand apiece. Even my ex-wife will get something.' He smiled a reluctant smile and scratched his calves below his knee-length shorts. His accent wasn't easy to follow and he had three teeth missing, perhaps because he didn't want to waste money on getting new ones.

'I've used my car for twelve years,' he said. 'Not like these whiners who keep buying what they can't afford. And it works fine, my car; every month I drive the children to Scotland. I have a house there and it's good for them to see the country – education.'

'Why don't you bring them by train? It can't be easy driving two young children.'

'I *hate* trains,' he said. 'This journey is a torture for me – sitting like this, can't move your legs, can't move your bum. And I hate the idea of my life in someone else's hands. I take the children by car – we reach Scotland in three days. I say it doesn't matter if they lose a few days of school.'

We were pulling into Glasgow and I asked him, perhaps because I knew what he would say, 'What do you think of the Prime Minister?'

'She's all right,' he said. 'Not a whiner, that woman. But I don't like her poll tax; it's going to make me pay more than I do now, sharing a house with three men.'

The tourist office in Glasgow had a huge flight of steps, but even as I looked at them angrily someone was helping me up. Before I could say thank you he was gone; Glaswegians were like that – helpful, not friendly.

I went to sleep at the tourist office because we were tenth in the queue and they were taking about ten minutes to find each person somewhere to stay. There was a golf tournament going on, and rooms were in short supply. I had a marvellous nap, which was funny because I am one of those persons for whom falling asleep is a long, hard climb into nothingness. In Bombay, I lie in bed and wait stoically. But then, I always have an afternoon nap, and I do so little, physically. In Britain, I slept at once, quick as switching off the lights, woke at eight, spent the whole day out watching, listening, thinking, napping in lonely railway carriages or outside a loo while Juice made up her face.

An hour later, we got our turn. There was no hotel, no bed-and-breakfast for what we wanted to pay, and certainly nothing suitable for a wheelchair. 'I know what!' said the girl at the desk brightly. 'The university hostel – you won't mind that, will you? And it's less than what you want to pay.'

'I don't want something for less,' I said indignantly.

'Oh – I thought you'd be glad.'

I couldn't possibly say that I did not stay at cheap hotels back home. 'Is it clean? Is it all right?'

'Of course! If you don't like it you can come back to us and we'll try and find you something else.'

The prospect of that was worse than the common loo and bath the university's Baird Hall of Residence offered.

There was also a bare, bleak lobby painted jaundice-yellow and sick-green, hung with gloomy portraits, brown and dusty. A Heep-humble man apologised for asking us to pay our four-day charge in advance. The room was meant for the colour-blind – blue doors, green walls and orange curtains. The loo was not disabled, so doors swung in my face while my wheels got stuck in a little dip at the threshold. The bathroom was out of a moronic movie: if I went in the door wouldn't shut; if we shut it by force the chair wouldn't move. The plastic chair in the bath-tub swayed so that I had a shower on a see-saw or, as the Americans more accurately call it, a teeter-totter.

Glasgow wore a confident face. People walked on the streets with their heads high, their backs straight. Scotland, unlike Wales, seemed to be undefeated, and quite distinct from England. The people were different: quiet, proud, self-possessed. The English are really a talkative people, silence like shoes they want to kick off. And they are self-critical, always doubting their attitudes. 'What do you not like about us?' they would ask me, soon after they began talking. Getting someone in Glasgow to talk was not easy; they would nod, say a word and walk determinedly away.

The women were more stylish than in London, less girlish than in Cardiff. The men were shockingly handsome, their faces cut in pale, polished stone, unlike Englishmen, who are carved from a softer substance, like snow mixed with earth.

There was a haunted-house quality about the gabled buildings of Glasgow – black, curling, saying beware! The red brick gloomed over the streets, which sloped viciously.

St George's Square was different, the buildings clean, flowers staring down the imposing architecture of the City Hall. And the great men standing everywhere. Each name was like a socket into which some plug from my childhood fitted. I did what I wanted, and stuffed the silliness of it; I said 'Lochinvar' to Scott and 'My love is like a red, red rose' to Burns, thinking not of boys, for once, but of Britain.

The next day we were late for breakfast because the shower-head came off in my hand and I had to screw it back. I once asked Freddy why British plumbing was so awful – hot water turned a sudden cold shoulder or ran out altogether – and he said it was because Britons rarely showered, perhaps twice a week or so. In Bombay the reputed frequency of British baths is once a fortnight.

Quite often I would interrupt conversations with questions about ablutions. 'Daily, even twice a day,' said my editor, Mary, indignantly when I told her what people in Bombay thought. But then, to my horror, I discovered The Wash.

'You fill the basin,' said a young man I found devastatingly attractive, 'take a flannel, rub soap on it, then rub it on your body, rinse it in the basin, rub off the soap, rinse it again, rub on the soap, wash your feet, rinse it in the basin – no, you don't waste water emptying the basin every time, that's absurd. You go on like this for twenty minutes and then you're clean.'

'No, you're not,' I said, unshakably Indian, for once.

But it didn't matter. You could be in a crush at Oxford Street or packed tight with people in a train and you'd never need to hold your nose. In Bombay, you'd be wishing you had a bad case of catarrh.

The breakfast at the Baird Hall of Residence was served in a large bare room, proletarian as a Soviet canteen. The waitresses were like something from a gothic film, one limping around stoically, the other so cross-eyed I didn't know if she was taking Juice's order or mine.

The evening before I had phoned the writer Alasdair Gray. 'He's so funny, you'll love him,' Liz Calder had said, giving me an uncorrected proof copy of *1982 Janine*. 'It's very precious,' she said, scribbling 'This is Liz's book' on the flyleaf. 'If he autographs it, you can keep it.'

Alasdair Gray was most gracious. 'I shall come wherreverr you arr,' he said over the phone.

'I don't think that's a very good idea,' I said. 'This place is quite unpleasant.' The receptionist gave me an Arctic glance. 'Perhaps we could visit you.'

'I don't think so,' he said. 'I live upstairs in a tenement.' A tenement? I was horrified – that was where poor widows and servants stayed. 'Perhaps we can take a walk,' he said.

'Oh yes! I would like that.'

'I'll come at eleven,' he said.

'I think you should stay at home,' I said to Juice. A writer in London had told me some very exciting things about Alasdair Gray.

'I won't miss this man for anything,' said Juice. 'I'm going to wear the peach frock I bought from Marks in Bath.'

'At your own risk.'

We waited in the entrance hall. An old woman with a stick hobbled in; two shabby bearded tourists wandered through the door; then a tall smiling man smoothing his silver hair walked in. I moved towards him; the tourists, who looked like trolls, bore down on me. They had huge noses and stomachs; one of them wore a shirt that had half-found its way out of his waistband. The other one bowed and I could see streaky hair plastered to his skull. 'I am Alasdair Gray,' he said.

Juice gave a tiny shriek; I knew she was wishing she hadn't worn the peach frock.

With him was his friend, Tom, who was a poet published by The Galloping Press. We went into the warm day. 'Is Britain like you imagined it would be?' asked Alasdair Gray.

'I suppose everyone knows by now – at one level the Britain we imagine exists only in India, tennis and tea on the lawns served by liveried butlers.'

'Yes,' he said. 'Saki wrote a book, *When William Came* – it was about Britain being occupied by the Germans and the Empire shifting its capital to Delhi.

'We feel Britain has gone down,' he went on. 'There was a tradition that the state maintained public amenities like parks, and all that is disappearing so that one wonders if Britain is a civilised society any longer. Once upon a time, public services were paid from unearned incomes.'

'There is nothing like an unearned income,' I said, sounding like the Big T. 'Someone made the money and passed it on. Surely one of the reasons why we want to make money is to give our loved ones a better life?'

'Obviously you come from a background of some wealth,' said Tom.

I hesitated. Our recent inheritance was in the foreground, surely. 'I don't,' I said. 'My grandfather went bankrupt. My father earned his way through college and I've always earned as well.'

'Yes,' said Alasdair Gray, sounding alarmed. 'This is the West End.' Around me stood buildings beautiful as rejects from Bath. 'We'll go to Kelvingrove Park. You can see all of Glasgow from there.'

I asked them about Scottish politics. 'The Tories are irrelevant,' said Tom. He had an accent that sounded like a snarled cassette tape. I could understand regional pride but what, I wondered, was the point of talking in a way that no one outside your own world could understand properly?

Tom was very bitter about the Labour Party. 'They are the

conservatives of Scotland,' he said. 'They've been successful for so long now. And they co-operate with the government on everything.'

'Surely not.'

'Oh, yes – look at what they're saying – they're not going to renationalise industry, they don't believe in unilateral disarmament. They're not socialists any more.'

'That's because they want to get elected.'

'By whom? They're deserting their supporters to catch the voters in the south-east of England. They have betrayed the welfare state that brought them up – what would they have been without the free education, the health service?'

'But that's all right,' I said. 'Because Labour's traditional supporters will go on voting for it; they have nowhere to turn to, and anyway I don't think they'd want to vote for anyone else. Labour is a habit.'

'A habit they can break,' he said. 'Scottish Nationalists have defeated Labour recently.'

'I think the Nationalists are the only hope for Scotland,' said Alasdair Gray. 'We don't want to be ruled by England. Certainly not by Mrs Thatcher – she condemns Scottish nationalism but she's an English nationalist.' I could sympathise with that – Scotland, with about as many voters as Greater London, had been rendered irrelevant by the logic of political arithmetic. And the fact that it gave the Conservatives fewer seats with every election meant that it counted for less and less in their political calculations.

'We must have our freedom,' he said. 'I don't mean for foreign affairs and defence – we don't want to build ships and planes – but everything else.'

'The English keep frightening people,' said Tom. 'When we had the referendum on devolution they said there would be a flight of capital if Scotland went its own way. And then capital began flowing out anyway.'

'That was because it was being inefficiently used here.'

He disregarded that. 'The English love a leader,' said Alasdair Gray. 'Give them a leader and two dozen of them can squeeze into a jeep – they just have to follow him.'

'We are different,' said Tom. 'We must go our own way – it's no use relying on Labour; we need a real party of the Left. Not people who are ashamed of socialist policies, who are trying to convince voters they are not really socialist.'

'That's because socialism has failed,' I said, so loudly birds began to twitter.

'Oh, no – I don't agree,' they said together.

Kelvingrove Park was misty and mysterious, with a small dark river creeping through a tunnel and plane trees and elms everywhere. The park climbed higher and higher and the two men kept lifting me up the stone steps, wheezing and gasping. 'A touch of asthma,' said Alasdair Gray.

They loved the blackened buildings of Glasgow. Tom felt they should be kept as they were as a reminder of how things used to be.

We walked back into town. 'Would you like a cup of tea?' said Alasdair Gray. 'Or would you like to rest now?'

'I think I must,' I said. 'I'm rather tired.' And I was, but not in my back or my bum as I usually become after hours of sitting. This was another kind of exhaustion, something I was familiar with from India. A sense of hopelessness that comes from looking at faces turned towards the past, towards dogma and defeat, so that the real, changing world is the enemy. Scotland was relatively poor, and it was so easy to make England the cause. There were examples enough to follow. Like a criminal blaming his toilet-training for his actions Africa and India use the ready-made excuse of colonialism for the corruption and poverty that are savaging their societies. As the imperial childhood recedes their cries become more shrill, more unbelievable. Yet there is no attempt to look honestly at themselves, to admit that before the imperial masters there were the native tyrants who looted and ravaged as effectively as their socialist heirs were doing, statism the justification, always. The remedies I had just heard put forward here in distant Scotland were familiar by failure – renationalisation and more of what has not worked anywhere in the world.

In the lobby of our hostel Alasdair Gray autographed the copy of his book – 'For a very pleasant conversational outing' –

and I was seized with guilt-cramp. When you are disabled and people are so good it seems somehow ungrateful to think of them as anything but kind and correct about everything. To be critical of them or their ideas makes you slightly ashamed of yourself.

We left the hostel about five minutes later and headed for an Indian restaurant. In Britain, Indian food was what silky-headed blond boys were for me in India. I drooled. I wouldn't, couldn't, eat the same food in Bombay; I found it too dangerous. I had had two attacks of amoebic dysentery and was unwilling to prove myself a third time unlucky; Indian food with its extravagant spices and uncertain hygiene made me nervous. But here in Britain the spices were subdued, the cleanliness apparent, English food boring as an evening of Snakes and Ladders. And I went back to my culinary culture, tongue hanging out.

While we ate, that afternoon, the manager, a bald, harassed man of about fifty, was being begged for a job. A hollow-cheeked Asian boy of about seventeen was saying in Hindi, 'I'll do anything, inside-outside work, dishes, shopping, serving, cleaning, and for less than anyone else.'

'Yes–yes,' said the manager. 'You think I don't want to keep you? It's to my advantage also, no?'

'Then why don't you? I can start today.'

'And tomorrow the police will come – you're employing man without work-permit, they'll ask. What will I say? What face will I show them?'

'When the police come I'll stop work – I'm not telling anyone about this job – '

'No – no, you go back just now, see if you can get a proper work-permit, then come here – '

'I can't go back,' said the boy, his voice breaking. 'There is nothing for me back there, no future, no life.' He brushed the back of his hand angrily against his eyes and ran out of the restaurant.

In the street outside I saw an elderly man wheeling himself up the pavement, ahead of us. He stopped at the kerb and looked back. 'Do you think you could help me down?' he asked Juice, smiling against the sun.

167

'Of course,' she said, tipping him down.

He kissed her hand. 'Thank you,' he said. 'Now you give me a kiss.' Juice walked fast and backwards away.

We went to Glasgow's oldest book-shop, John Smith, huge as a public library. A lovely young woman with plump curls and sparkling eyes met us. 'I'm Fiona Stewart,' she said, her accent the kind you hear on BBC programmes like *In Scotland This Week*. Liz Calder had told me I could meet her.

'This shop is incredible,' I said; it was my first big British bookstore.

'Oh, this is just the ground floor, there's much more upstairs,' she said, and laughed to see my face.

'Do Glaswegians read a lot?'

'Oh, yes. Of course, it's best-seller time now, the summer always is, but people here read a lot of serious literature. And especially Scottish history and culture – that's very popular; we have a whole section for that.'

'Do you know anything about the gay life here?' Somehow Glasgow seemed Victorian, as distant from homosexuality as the Marquess of Queensberry.

'I wouldn't know much about that,' she said. 'But there is a book-shop close by that is run by a gay man – he's wonderful, I'm sure he can tell you a lot. Do you know that a gay novel is selling very well just now? *The Swimming Pool Library?*'

'I reviewed it.' God! What it had meant to me. I had read a review by Edmund White, then Freddy had got it for me from Sydney. And using the little bit of influence I had I'd reviewed it for a Bombay newspaper. I liked doing that; letting homosexuality out of the closet, the subject being brave as I am not.

'Where are you going after Glasgow?' she asked.

'To Edinburgh.'

'Awwh! Glasgow is so much more friendly – you know, they say when you visit someone in Glasgow they put the kettle on; when you go to meet somebody in Edinburgh they ask you if you've had your tea!'

We went back to the tourist information office. The Hall of Residence was impossible; I could not endure the thought of

another bath on the see-saw, or of witnessing another beheading
of the shower. I was getting tired of my wheelchair version of
sore feet and wanted to be sure of a proper place to live in
Edinburgh.

It didn't take long for the tourist office to find us a place.
'It's a bit away from the town centre,' said the girl there. 'But
then, you're paying about half as much as your limit.'

'We don't mind paying more,' I said.

'There's no need,' said the girl. 'They're willing to let you
have the room for this much.'

Outside, the offices had shut and the streets were fluid with
people. I stopped somebody to ask the way but he walked
on, not noticing me at his waist; then it happened a second
time. The third time I asked I was gasping with laughter and
my voice was high and sharp as broken ice, and three people
stopped at once.

Hans, who ran the book-shop Fiona Stewart had told me
about, had green eyes and a mouth etched in pink. His pale
gold hair fell over his eyes and down his neck, and he was
wearing a long loose grey jacket over a T-shirt. He looked
like an overgrown, knowing page-boy. He was in a bit of
a hurry, but the sight of my wheelchair slowed him down.
He was Dutch but he couldn't stand Holland; it was small
and suffocating and everyone knew or tried to know what
everyone else was up to. He had come to Scotland for a holiday.
Glasgow was the worst place to go to, said his friends; all the
faggot-bashers lived there. 'Let me go and see for myself,'
he said. And he had stayed for ever. The weather was all
right for someone who came from Holland. He liked the
big-city feeling and Glasgow was alive. 'Not like Birmingham,'
he said, covering his face with his hands. 'It's awful, it's
dead.'

I asked him about the gay scene in Glasgow. He sat with
his legs crossed. 'I don't know – I'm not part of it any more,
going to bars and all that. One gets old.'

'And there's AIDS – '

'Yes, we all know someone who has died of it, but I don't
know how that has affected life. Anyway, there are very few

169

new cases among gay men – they were the first to adopt safe sex.'

'Is it easy to be gay in Glasgow?'

'Not as easy as in London – but it depends on your class. If you're from the working class it's still difficult; if you're in the arts world nothing could be easier.'

He suggested I look around the shop. It was white and bright and spacious, the jacketed books multi-coloured, easy to find under carefully labelled sections. The whole place was like Boots with a k in place of the t. There were ramps going to the upper level, so steep that as soon as we approached them, a young man jogged over to lift the chair up the steps. 'No one dares to use the ramps,' he said grinning.

We went down the streets, tilted like sliding-boards, to the Clyde, and crossed it. I saw a sign saying Gorbals Street and caught my breath. In the forties, when British audiences still made ballet part of Bombay's culture, my mother had danced in an excerpt from *The Miracle in the Gorbals*. Indian men thought ballet was sissy, so she cut off her hair and danced the male lead. As a boy who couldn't walk the story was irresistible to me, and I began reading everything I could find about the ballet. People visiting us thought it was terribly poignant that I should be mastering ballet technique, like a famine-child reading Julia Child; I thought it was enormous fun. Dance was one of those things, like tennis, that I could be madly enthusiastic about without feeling I had a duty to myself to be more than a spectator.

We went to the Gorbals; the slums had been raised into towering blocks under the blue-grey sky. We met an Irishman, short, about sixty. 'We have to pay rent to live here,' he said, 'but it's marvellous. Lovely flats. Used to be dreadful at one time. All public housing, everything done by the council.' His wife was a social worker with a disabled club. He was retired and he spent his evenings at the pub. 'I meet an Indian chap there,' he said. 'Very nice man – they live in one of these too.'

Juice was getting scared. There were no other people to be seen; everyone was snug in their council flats. And she was hungry. 'I'm going to have a baked potato, tonight,' she said. There was a Spud-U-Like not far from where we were staying. She didn't mind climbing the streets back; the thought of the hot-hot potatoes kept her strong. We reached the place at about ten. 'Sorry,' said the woman at counter, 'we've run out of potatoes.'

ELEVEN

Swishing it in Edinburgh

'Didn't you know from the start?' said the no-longer-humble man at the reception desk when we told him we were leaving a day early. 'The check-out time is ten-thirty and it's already past that.'

'That's all right,' I said. 'We'll pay for another day, but we'll leave in ten minutes.'

'Certainly not,' said Juice. 'I'm sure you can allow us ten minutes' grace – that's all we need.'

'I suppose I can,' he said dourly.

'Good!' said Juice. 'Now, may we have our day's advance back?'

The taxi-driver who took us to the station hoped we had enjoyed our stay, and I didn't have the heart to say no. 'You'll see,' he said, 'how much better our city is than Edinburgh.'

But, 'The best thing about Glasgow is the road to Edinburgh,' I heard later, and I had to agree. The train sailed through seas of mist like a submarine and when we got to Waverley the welcome was unmatched anywhere in Britain. As soon as he saw us a boy with clipped golden hair ran across the platform holding his blue BritRail cap. 'I'll be back in a minute to help you,' he said, and listening to his accent I sank back in relief – gone were the words twisted out of shape. Someone else in uniform walked over. 'I'm busy,' he said, 'but I'll send somebody immediately.'

'Don't worry,' we chorused, for once. 'Someone is looking after us.'

The boy with the cap was back. 'Where would you like to go?' he said.

'To the travel centre to book our onward reservations.'

He sauntered along with our bags. 'It's a long queue,' he said. 'Why don't you go to the station supervisor? He'll do it much quicker and you've got the wheelchair too – I'm sorry, I would have come along but I have to do something else.'

'Where shall we leave our luggage?' said Juice.

'With me?' offered an American girl with crinkly yellow hair. Juice and I looked at each other, suspicious as Indians; in a poor country anything is worth snatching and selling. 'If you like,' said the girl.

We nodded, and rushed across. Outside the station supervisor's office a BritRail man stood stiff as a guardsman under fire while a short, fat American spat, 'I don't give a fuck for you, for the rotten rat-race you run, I won't stand in any fucking queue, do you get me, what're you watching me for, as if you're freeze-dried?'

And so he was; in Britain, exhibiting bad temper is like belching aloud (though I did know a very well-educated Englishman who enjoyed ferocious fist-fights with his wife – 'It's a pity I always have to wait for her to start: gentlemen don't hit first' – and was planning to buy a cheap china cup to fling at her when she returned from a holiday in France).

When we got back from the station supervisor – 'We'll have somebody to help you waiting outside, and he'll roll you into the train' – the girl with the bags was still there. And running over to us was the boy with the cap. 'I got away,' he said breathlessly. 'Where would you like to go now? I can carry your bags anywhere.' And he escorted us to the taxi.

If Glasgow was a man sitting in a deep armchair telling a ghost story, Edinburgh was a great lady in grey silk swishing her pleasure through life. Everything was cool and cloudy and I needed to wear a pullover for the first time in many days.

Mayfield Gardens had houses that were elegantly solid, like handsome men in evening clothes. Mrs Telford, in whose house we were staying, kept shaking her short brown hair and apologising – the beds were still unmade. She had just had a shower cubicle installed and she brought a chair for me to put inside. But it wouldn't go through the sliding glass door. 'Done in a minute,' she said, climbing on to the loo-seat with the chair in one hand. She raised it over her head and lowered it through the roof of the cubicle, pausing to give us a bright smile from her pedestal.

This room was to the room in Glasgow what the *QEII* was to a tramp-steamer. There were old-gold damask curtains over french windows that opened on to a moist green garden and the wide avenue beyond. Inside, the walls were the colour of ripe peaches, and there was a huge fireplace. The television, for once, was at my level, and there was a large low table of gleaming glass and varnished wood. 'Let's stay in all day,' said Juice, bouncing on the unmade bed.

'Someone like your Arab might have slept here last night,' I said, and she bounced right off.

Edinburgh seemed wealthier than any other place in Britain – you could feel the money in the cut of women's hair, the collars of men's jackets. We went to the Waverley Shopping Centre, gliding up and down in the glass lift, smiling through the spray from the waterfalls. I knew it was all plastic but I soaked it in like a village boy; glamour, I thought, is as much a part of the human hunger as laughter, and in India we had so little.

They had run out of haggis at the restaurant in the precinct and I sighed and ordered a cutlet, which turned out to be a little cut of meat on the bone; in Bombay a cutlet is a patty, and everyone calls it a cut-lace, while patties are crusty and are called pattice.

We went out and into George Street. Juice meanwhile had found a bargain – a map of Edinburgh that sold for £2.50 she had got for 20 pence from the tourist office. 'You must write this,' she said, 'to help future generations of tourists.'

'They,' I said, 'won't be travelling on a Bloomsbury budget.'

George Street was wide enough for a million pairs of lungs, with statues of Pitt and George IV supervising the length of it. We found our way to Waterstone's to meet the manager there but she was away. Instead there was a young man, Duncan Furness. 'I'm the assistant manager,' he said. I told him who I was, or rather who I was going to be. 'Would you like some coffee?' he said. Juice hesitated and I refused for her.

I asked him about the contrast between the two cities. 'Well, in Glasgow,' he said, 'the public housing is at the centre – it can be seen everywhere; in Edinburgh it's kept hidden outside the city.'

'What about churches? I want to go to Sunday service.'

'Then you must go to St Giles' – it's severe and dour but the atmosphere is wonderful.'

'Do you know anything about the gay life here?'

'Well, there is this marvellous book-shop, West and Wilde – you know, Mae and Oscar – there's someone there who can tell you.'

There was. He was talking on the phone to somebody with problems. 'Yes, I think you'll just have to get over this . . .' His voice evaporated. The book-shop was narrow and dark and I found a book I hadn't been able to get since I was sixteen and knew I was gay, Gore Vidal's *The City and the Pillar*.

The phone-call had ended. I asked him what it was like being gay in Edinburgh. 'It's no problem,' he said. 'People are very tolerant – they have a history of tolerance.'

'Really – you mean even in the Victorian days?'

'No, I mean going back about ten years.'

'And getting jobs wouldn't be difficult if you were gay?'

'Not at all; in fact the civil service has a lot of gay employees, the trade union insists on that.'

'What about this shop – do you face harassment?'

'No, never.'

'Gay's The Word in London does.'

'I know, isn't that strange?'

'What about coming out? Do you know anyone in public life who has come out?'

'No, I don't think so – it depends on your social background; it's harder if you're working class.'

'I believe so. Are there any gay bars here?'

'There's the Laughing Duck – you must go and see it. They

send people here, we send them there.' He marked it on the map for me.

'What will happen to me?' said Juice, outside the Laughing Duck.

'Nothing you can't handle, I'm sure.'

A tall dark-eyed man helped us into the dark. There was a bar at the far end with coloured lights above; everything else was glow and shadow.

I followed the man who had helped me into the bar. I thought he'd appreciate the direct approach. 'I'm writing a book,' I said, 'and I wonder if you could tell me something about the gay scene here.'

'What?'

'Is it easy to be gay? Can you get jobs?'

'I'm unemployed,' he said, 'and I have a boy waiting for me.'

I retreated to a table. Juice was sitting on a sofa against the wall. Next to her two women were trying to erase each other's lips with their mouths. A pale boy with dark hair sat opposite me – he was handsome in a film-star way, huge eyes, flaring nostrils, glossy lips, square white teeth. 'Are you gay?' he asked. I nodded. He turned to a woman with corrugated lips who was sitting on a high stool between us. 'Are you gay?'

'Certainly not,' she said, and lit a cigarette.

'Do you live here?' I asked.

'No,' he said, 'about twenty miles away. It's a village, it's awful, they don't know what being gay means.'

'That must be very hard for you.'

'Oh, it is,' he said leaning forward. 'And I've lived in London so I know the difference. Used to be a courier,' and he winked. I wondered for what. 'I want to get back to London, to the bars there – would you like some poppers?'

'No, thank you, I'm quite full,' said Juice, and I spluttered into my orange juice.

'What about you?'

'No, thank you.'

'What a bore.'

Juice was making funny faces over my shoulder. I looked

back – three men were sitting on each other's shoulders and giggling. Someone came and sat next to me; with him was a man with flat hair and he sat next to Juice.

'I'm from the UN,' he said in a peculiar accent that I couldn't place. I remembered how Liz Calder had introduced me to a woman who had written a book about Peru, at a party in the Groucho Club. She spoke slowly with a funny accent. 'How,' I asked in my camp way, 'did you ever manage to get a work-permit?'

'I'm British,' she said. 'I was born in the East End.'

The man from the UN said he was a doctor, he had lived all over the world. He kept looking at me through a square made with his index fingers and thumbs. He asked Juice to join him on the dance-floor, which didn't exist. 'I'd rather not,' she said, and wiggled, which made her say yes.

'Just five minutes,' he said. 'Just one dance.'

'I'd rather not,' said Juice, and he got up and left. Must have been English, I thought.

The man next to me was also English, in his late twenties, with a thin, sharp face, a pointed nose and fastidious lips. He lived in Edinburgh and thought it was charming but loved Glasgow. 'In London,' he said, 'they have two attitudes – either they make you a celebrity because you are gay or they bash you up. The Scots treat you as queer, but I prefer that to the English extremes.'

'Do you come here often?' I asked.

'Every evening.'

'Oh my God! What about the straight world – aren't you missing out on a lot of interesting people? I mean, straight people are often wary about making friends with homosexuals; surely this is the same thing in another direction.'

'I know what you mean, but I feel it's better in terms of personal integrity to stay in the gay world; outside you don't remain yourself.'

'But all my friends are straight. They know I'm gay, and I never have to pretend with them.'

'Maybe I should start,' he said smiling. 'It's not as if I don't meet straight people. I work with the DHSS, dealing with personnel; everyone knows I'm gay, though I've never said so. There are some people I don't get on with but I suppose I wouldn't have even if I were straight.'

His name was Stephen; his father had been an urban vicar. 'We were middle class, but we were poor,' he said, encapsulating the irony of the British class system. His accent was clear and precise, and he had read a great deal. 'I met Alan Hollinghurst at a signing session,' he said, showing me an autographed copy of *The Swimming Pool Library*.

(When I met Alan Hollinghurst it was at a trendy restaurant in the City and he asked the waitress for a salad.

'We have a flower salad today, sir,' she said.

'What flowers?'

'Pansies, sir,' and she was as innocent as someone who has never read a book.)

'We talked of Anthony Burgess. Then Hollinghurst said he'd be back in a moment and never returned. I suppose that's the only way you can manage to meet everyone.'

A man with a peeling red nose stopped by us. 'Do you go to church?' he asked Stephen.

'I used to – not any more.'

'Well I do, and I'm so worried they'll find out I'm gay – I've told only two people.' He had a sandpaper voice. 'What will I do if they know?' And he shuffled away.

'The Church of England is pulled,' said Stephen, 'in various directions, some condemning homosexuality, others condoning it, everyone quoting chapter and verse to prove their point. And the Roman Catholic Church is even worse – they want you to confess not only what you've done but also what you haven't, as long as you've thought of doing it.'

'Christianity is very narrow,' said a girl in black sitting down next to Juice. 'I'm Tom.' She saw my face and patted her short dark hair. 'I wanted to change sex, I went on hormones; but I decided I liked my man's body too much so I'm Tom again. As I was saying, Christianity is so narrow, which is why I left the Catholic Church and took up Hinduism.' He produced a book with images of Indian gods; I made a face. 'Your friend,' he said to Juice, 'is very snobbish, I think. And anyway, he's found somebody for the evening.'

'I despise people,' whispered Stephen, 'who go to India to look for salvation and ignore the poverty around them.'

'I despise people from the West,' I said, 'who come to India and tell me, so what if Indians are poor, they are rich inside. I want to tell them the poor would rather be rich outside, just like their admirers.'

'I wouldn't want to go to India,' he said. 'I like my creature comforts too much.'

'What do you think of Mahatma Gandhi?' I asked.

'He was such a sham.' And he crossed his legs and folded his hands on his knees. 'He knew he could get his way with the British, because they wouldn't kill like the Nazis or the Soviets.'

'Actually,' I said, 'he advised British people to let the Nazis invade and then defeat them by passive resistance. What do you think of Mrs Thatcher?' He shook his head. 'Don't you think she has done something for Britain that needed to be done?'

'Yes, but I wish the Left had done it, they would have been gentler. I think the social cost of Thatcherism has been too high.'

'I don't think Britain could have been set on its feet gently; what do you think of people who cheat the dole?'

'Well, the ones who get caught are usually the poor, who are trying to supplement what they are getting – the rich cheat their way through. And isn't it wrong that Mrs Thatcher is trying to reverse progressive taxation, where you pay more if you earn more?'

'Which means the better you do the more you're punished. No wonder there was a brain-drain.'

'There is a brain-drain because people at our universities are being starved of cash.'

'The brains you find in universities are not the only ones – those who create businesses and jobs and wealth are also very good brains.'

'I suppose so,' he said, distracted by what was going on.

The woman with the corrugated lips had become increasingly irritable. 'What sort of place is this?' she said loudly. 'Don't any men come here? My sister told me this was a good place to find a friend, so I came. And it's a long distance for me to travel.'

Juice was open-mouthed, and so was I, in my head. And then, as if she'd been heard, a middle-aged man sat on the sofa, between Juice and her, and looked deep into her eyes. They began talking. About thirty words later, he pulled her from her stool to the sofa and they began kissing like something from *Fatal Attraction*.

'I'm a Zoroastrian, though I'm not a believer,' I said to Stephen, so I wouldn't be impolite and keep watching. 'Do you know about us?'

'Oh yes,' he said, 'the ancient religion of Iran, isn't it? Still practised in India?'

'Yes, just a few thousand of us left. I'm surprised you've heard about us; almost no one in Britain has.'

'Hindus don't like Parsees,' said Tom. 'They are too indulgent.' I supposed he meant that Parsees never fasted or did without sex.

'Do you find us very reserved?' asked Stephen.

'Not a bit – I mean, not really. There is a pleasant kind of restraint, but British people are so in touch with their feelings, they can't ever be cut off from people.' He smiled. I said, 'Do you think the British are vulgar in a mild way?'

'Oh, yes!' he said. 'China dogs and lace-poodles over the toilet-seat, even dolls with crinolines to cover them up.'

Tom was telling Juice, 'A friend who saw you here this evening saw you earlier, in the city. And he told me you were so attractive – let me put my arm around you.'

'It's nine-thirty,' said Juice. 'We'd better be going.'

'So good to have met you,' I said to Stephen.

'A pleasure,' he said, drawing in – everyone in Britain did that. As if, having kicked off their shoes, they found themselves barefoot when it was time to leave.

There were china dogs at breakfast the next day, snarling and sniffing from the mantelpiece in the dining-room. I had seen them at Barry Island behind shop windows, carrying little messages in their paws – 'I love you Mother' and 'Give me a cuddle', just the kind of thing Bombay Parsees display in their 'halls' (in India there are no sitting-rooms or drawing-rooms).

A little boy crept in, trying to be discreet as he rummaged through a drawer. 'Are you looking for something?' I asked.

'Yes, my special paper – I'm making money,' and he held aloft a blue-green scrap. 'That's ten pounds. Now I'm going to make a hundred.'

We called a taxi to take us to Edinburgh Castle. I had seen it the night before, floating like a golden chandelier over the city, and I wanted to know how accessible it was for someone like me.

The lady taxi-driver was very friendly; she talked rapidly, tucking the words away into her plump cheeks. 'Such good weather . . . bit late . . . April . . . daughter's wedding . . . my son couldn't fly out . . . stuck in France . . . serious boy . . . no games . . . only Trivial Pursuit.'

'I enjoy that too,' I said, thinking of long, laughter-filled evenings with Honoria Gaskell's family. 'How old is your son?'

'Six,' she said, and Juice giggled into her palm.

The wardens let the taxi drive up to the castle because of the chair. It was like a royal motorcade, crowds on either side watching curiously, trying to guess why someone was being given this privilege. And I didn't have to buy a ticket – but that night I ate at the Caledonian and I thought how absurd it was to consider everyone who was disabled needy.

The castle was not meant for wheelchairs but the wardens and the American tourists everywhere helped me see almost everything. There was a family from Boston, looking around, and whenever they saw me stuck before steps, the father would tell his teenage sons, 'Go ahead! Work up an appetite!' and they'd lift me as easily as a bag of cotton-wool.

There was a memorial to the Scottish men who died in the Great War with long lists of names and inscriptions like 'Their grave shall be the sea', and I thought of Wilfrid Owen saying, 'Weep, you may weep, for you may touch them not.' It was awful not being able to pray there, to have no one to pray to; instead I said Owen's 'Futility' and moved into the sun.

All of India's defeats were celebrated at the United Services Museum – Seringapatam, Mysore, Lucknow. And there was the sword of Tippoo Sultan who had died fighting the British . . . but I had also been shown his sword at Hatfield House. One of the two had to be fake, unless they'd captured a gleamful of weapons. And there was a portrait of the Sultan, the Tiger of Mysore, painted in happier days by a Scottish officer's wife, his face upturned, eyes fierce as the moustache that almost reached them. The Tiger had, in his heyday, turned English captives into dancing-boys, so he could relish the humiliation of the would-be conquerors of his realm.

There was a wedding photograph, in the museum, of a Scottish family with Indian servants in turbans and sarees in a corner. I was amazed, thinking of Parsee wedding photos, which are just like that, the servants called out of affection and gratitude to make the group. Even as we think how gracious, how liberal we are not to leave them out.

'Would you like to see where Mary, Queen of Scots, lived?' a warden asked me.

'Yes, please.'

He called a fellow warden and they lifted me up the right-angled steps into the royal apartments. I had read Antonia Fraser's gripping biography of the Queen during a visit to New York as a boy of twelve, getting jerked out of the sixteenth century every time I heard the film-familiar police-siren in the streets of Manhattan. And now, seventeen years later, I was sitting in the room where she had given birth to James.

I was not meant to glimpse the Crown Jewels. At the Tower in London they hadn't let me into the rooms where the jewels were kept because it was down steep stairs and much too confined for a wheelchair. Here, in Edinburgh, they were up a spiral staircase – 'Sorry, sir,' said a warden, 'I doubt we can get you there.'

But at Holyrood House, the guide swooshed me up in the Queen's own lift. 'For Her Majesty's private use,' he said, smiling, while I thought of my father, and how when I was a boy he had brought back from a visit to London one of those mock newspapers, which said, 'FIRDAUS KANGA DINES WITH THE QUEEN'; for weeks afterwards I had the time of my childhood, inventing the story of my evening with Her Majesty for dizzy-eyed aunts.

But Holyrood was special for me because of David Rizzio and our shared cry for help. Here, it had all happened, and as we made our progress through the dining-room with its portraits of Bonny Prince Charlie – a lesson from my Radiant Reader – and the apartments Charles II had had prepared for himself and his Bombay-bestowing bride, I could feel my anticipation in goose-pimples that could not wait. I smiled at George IV, florid in tartan, and at Lord Darnley's bed, air-conditioned to preserve the sixteenth-century stuff with which it had been restored. 'And that,' said the guide, 'is the way to the room where David Rizzio was murdered. And here, young man, is where we part company – you won't be able to get up the stairs. Be careful, everyone, you can bump your head – '

'Go!' I whispered fiercely to Juice, so that I could blow my nose. Hard.

Jenner's, the department store in Princes Street, where we had lunch, made me feel better very quickly. There, from the vantage point of seventy-five kinds of shortbread (I am exaggerating, by about five) and a child's dreamful of chocolates, I was amused to find that Harrods seemed a poor and distant cousin. I loved Edinburgh for its wealth; for someone like me it was a refutation of all the misery I had grown up among, as if the world were throwing a fist into the air and shouting – yes!

There was a drizzle by the time we got to Princes Gardens. But there were rows of people sitting on benches like an audience at a play they didn't like very much. Occasionally, someone would look up at the sky, purse his lips, straighten his back and look down.

By the time we reached the National Gallery the sun was out again, shining on the face of Indiana Jones, to which a blond young man with yellow teeth was putting the last touches. Remembering the gods and goddesses that sleep in technicolor

chalk on Bombay's streets, I stopped. 'This is very good,' I
said, looking into the seductive gaze of Harrison Ford's eyes.

'Thanks – I hope it doesn't rain though.'

'Couldn't you cover it?'

He shook his head. 'There's a law against that – I don't
know why. They'd penalise me.'

'Have you been doing this long?'

'All through the summer – I'll be making a lot of money once
the Festival starts. Are you going to be here for the Festival?
Ah! You should. The Fringe is wonderful – all over this piazza
you have jugglers, acrobats, dancers.'

'Do you think you're lucky to live in Edinburgh?'

'Oh yes! I haven't always lived here – I'm an art student.'

'What are you going to do when you finish art school?'

'Paint, I just want to paint.'

I wanted to give him five pounds. Then I thought it would
look frightfully vulgar next to all the 10-pence pieces glinting
in the tray at his feet. So I made it a pound, and thought I was
becoming more English in a way I didn't want to be.

The National Gallery was a jewel-box. I was surprised. I had
expected the English to have carried everything worthwhile to
London. But looking down at me was Gainsborough's *The
Hon. Mrs Graham*, pale and proud as a Parsee. (It was only
much later, on a visit to Luton Hoo, that I realised I was seeing
pictures differently from everyone else. In the chapel there an
early Renaissance painting was hung low on the wall, at my
eye-level, and it looked softer, more human. Everywhere else
I went the paintings were raised high and I looked up at them
in more ways than one.)

I wanted to meet an Indian woman taxi-driver I'd heard
about the night before, so we phoned her firm.

'Why did you want to see me?' she said when she arrived.
'You need some help?' She was tiny, with kohl-black hair and
eyes, her lipstick a theatrical red, and she wore blue trousers
that should have made her look like a man. 'A dyke,' whispered
Juice, but she wasn't.

'I have a Scots boyfriend now,' she told me later in our
conversation, some time after I told her she was going to

drive through the pages of my book. 'I warn all the girls against Asian boys. They're no good; sex is what they want. Only sex.' Juice gasped with pleasure. 'You better believe me,' she said. 'An Indian boy will go to bed with you till his father snaps his fingers. Then he'll get married to the girl his family have fixed for him.' She had a powerful Punjabi-Scots accent, heavy and dramatic as if it had been created for her. 'It's okay for the Indian boy – when he tires of his wife he'll go looking for willing women again. What about the wife, huh? She can't go hunting, can she? There's only one thing for Asian girls to do: run away, fast.'

'Is that what you did?'

'Wait and listen. My family took me to Punjab when I was nineteen. I had grown up in London. But I fell in love in Punjab with an untouchable – I was a Jat, he was a Chamar – you know the caste system?'

'Yes.'

'My family found out. They were horrified that we might have already done something, so they found me a husband, a proper Jat.'

'Did you meet him before you accepted the proposal?'

'Why should I? It wouldn't have made a difference, I had to marry him anyway. Then I came back to London and I found he was illiterate. What could I do? I ran away. I didn't want to stay and teach him the alphabet. I went to Glasgow, I borrowed money and I set up a shop. But it failed. They said I could go bankrupt – I said, nothing doing: I'll pay my debts. I started driving a taxi. I paid back twe-lve thou-sand pounds. I did that.'

'Do you own this taxi now?'

'Yes, I came to Edinburgh and got this – now it's paid for.'

'What about your family? Are they pleased?'

She jerked around. 'Are you Indian or what? They hate me, they won't talk to me, not my parents, not my brother-sister.'

It was an enormous cost she had paid. I had once written: 'Families are like vitamins to us – without them our souls grow thin and emaciated.'

185

'How do people treat you here? Is it difficult being a woman and an Asian?'

The back of her black head bobbed. 'Oh yes, I get these customers who try to act smart – the other day I asked someone where he wanted to go and he said Pakistan. I asked him to repeat that and he said Princes Street! And one night I had this man who said he didn't have cash on him, he'd go upstairs and get it. So I told him, "You leave your shirt in my taxi before you get out." He said, "You can't take the shirt off a man's back." But I wouldn't let him go. So he took off his shirt and went out. That's the last I saw of him.' She turned and laughed.

I clicked the shutter in my head; there are some faces I don't want to forget. When we got off at the Botanic Gardens, she wouldn't take the fare. And for one brief moment I was looking over my shoulder, missing the country I had left behind.

Later that evening we went to the Caledonian Hotel for dinner. Juice was always showing off about how, on her other visits to Britain, she had only eaten at places like these. We decided to swank it at the Pompadour restaurant, and I loved the civility with which we were turned away. 'You don't want to go in there,' said the man outside. 'It's terribly stuffy, people in jackets and all that.' So we went to another restaurant in the hotel and I ordered haggis. When it arrived I wanted to wheel myself under the table. I took a mouthful and heard a rustle above me. 'If you don't like it,' said the waitress, 'you don't have to eat it.' I nodded and she took away my fifteen pounds of haggis. It was invisible on the bill I got at the end of the evening – 'You don't have to pay for what you don't eat,' said the Italian steward, a dashing figure with a black moustache like a Picasso brush-stroke.

We woke up late the next morning and dashed about from church to church trying to find a service that hadn't started. We ended up at one where the minister was the Moderator of the Church of Scotland. I expected it to be stark, somewhere John Knox might have preached, something like Antonia Fraser had described in *Mary, Queen of Scots*.

The sermon that day was based on the Gospel of St Mark. 'In it we find the human qualities of Our Lord – he is called the carpenter, and not the carpenter's son, which is what others call Him for fear of making Him seem undignified.' The minister had launched his text from the stained-glass images of the Apostles behind him. The church was not quite John Knox's thing, though the stained glass, I knew, was all right. Someone had once asked a minister of the Church of Scotland how he could sanction the decoration and colour of stained glass. 'But we can see through it,' he had answered. Besides the stained glass there was only the laminated wood of the lectern with a white glove painted on it. The glove was bleeding and the blood had coalesced into a shiny rose.

We were invited to coffee after the service by a large woman in a dress printed with small flowers. When she introduced us to the minister, I found out that he wasn't the Moderator after all; the Moderator was on holiday. The minister was surprised when he found out that we were Parsees, not Presbyterians. He couldn't believe that we had come all the way from India to find ourselves in a church that wasn't quite ours. There was a blind man with a Julie Andrews kind of wife and a large Lassie sort of dog. 'Just like *Jane Eyre*,' said Juice, so that I had to pinch her calf, the only decent part of her I could reach when she was standing.

I saw someone smiling at us under his moustache. He came up to us and told us he was an Elder with the Church; he was responsible for the spiritual welfare of ten families as long as he lived. I wondered how that made him feel about his old age.

There was a little woman – I could almost look into her eyes sitting down – who had lived in Zimbabwe. No, she said, looking into the air above her head, she had never noticed the political situation; she was not that kind of animal. Few of us are, I wanted to say, when we are not in a cage.

There was a blond girl about to leave for Pakistan, to teach psychology in Lahore. 'I am not afraid,' she said.

'There is no reason to be,' I reassured her. 'White people are treasured in the subcontinent.'

'But what about the weather?' she said. 'The heat won't know I'm white.'

It didn't know we were brown either, so we had to slip into the coolness of the National Portrait Gallery after lunch. 'The perfect bedroom,' said Juice, as we let ourselves fall asleep on the fat sofas in the foyer. We emerged into the piazza only when the heat was lifting away. That is what makes British weather endurable – nothing lasts too long.

Outside, there was a commotion. A young man with black hair swept back and a black sweatshirt and tight black trousers was waving a Bible in the air and shouting.

'What does the Church care about except clothes and cars? Who is going to do Christ's work? Who is going to look after the drug-addicts?' He paced in a circle drawn around him by people like us and the sound of hissed smiles blended with the buzz of film moving in camera. The young man was repeating his message for the seventh time, his arms stretched out like an aeroplane's, when an old man, his dead-black baggy trousers almost falling off, entered the circle.

'You're not preaching the Gospel,' he quavered. 'You're preaching hate. Look at me – I can't treat drug-addicts, I can't help alcoholics, but I can save souls. So I come here every Sunday when the weather is fine – the sun shone on his beige bald head – 'and I preach the word of Christ. I bring belief to the unbeliever.'

'You can't ever bring belief to me,' shouted a punk standing next to me. An orange cock's-comb divided his shaved skull and he wore a shocking pink vest.

'Come to me,' said the old preacher, 'and let me whisper the Word in your ear.' And the punk went up to him and put his ear to the preacher's mouth. The Word – a condensed version – was divulged to him in three minutes. At the end of that the punk was kneeling, on the knees that showed through his jeans, before the preacher, who was saying, 'Tell these people what has happened to you.'

'Christ,' hoarsely whispered the punk, 'has entered my heart. I believe!'

'God bless you,' said the preacher, holding the cock's-comb

like a rabbit's ears. 'I now leave you in charge of my friend to guide you in God's ways.'

The friend, in crisp white cotton shirt and close-cropped gold hair, advanced on the punk with a Bible aimed like a small black pistol. The punk stood transfixed. Then a big-shouldered woman in a black bathing-suit crashed into the circle and threw herself between the punk and the gun.

'You fuck off!' she shouted over her shoulder. 'He's mine and no fucking fanatic's going to get him.' The Bible wilted in the fanatic's hand. 'You all right now?' said the protectress. The punk nodded sheepishly and she left. But in a moment, the fanatic had moved back in; this time he wasn't taking any risks. His one arm went around the punk as he led him away from the piazza, the Bible in his left hand pointing the way.

As if to fill the gap, two groups started singing hymns, stamping their feet to drown each other out. And across the piazza came an old gypsy, dancing, pointing her pink slippers, shaking her parrot-green-scarfed head to the music. A black-bearded man in a dark suit stood up and began ranting. 'The Pope is the Anti-Christ,' he declared, and there was a fierce murmur from his listeners.

'How dare you say that!' challenged a short man with a broken nose. 'I'm not a Catholic, I'm not even a believer, but you can't say something so unjust.'

'I can and I will – the Bible says it about Pontifax Maximus – '

'Pontifax Maximus was the high priest of pagan Rome.'

'He was the Pope in Rome.'

'There was no Pope in Rome when the Bible was written, there was no Pope till the time of Constantine – '

'Oh – who cares about your argument?' demanded the young man who had started it all. 'All that matters are the things you do – all the rest is rubbish,' and he dropped his Bible into a dustbin.

I grasped my brakes, ready to roll away from the now certain riot. I knew, from India, how the smallest provocation – music outside a mosque, a cow's head found next to a temple – ended in stabbings and burning, looting and rape, and, finally, the dull thud of police bullets meeting angry bodies. Here, in Edinburgh, someone laughed, someone else whispered ominously, 'Take care, you're breaking the law,' and the crowd shifted uneasily and unmade itself.

I pointed this out to Juice, and she said, 'What if we were in Belfast – it would have been worse than Bombay, and you wanted to take me there.'

That night I dreamt of Moti Dalal. She was my teacher from the time I had been a little boy right until my first year at university. For me, who did not attend school, she had been a woman in a magnifying glass. She brought the world to me – her simple version of it – but it was enough to send me out on my own. To her, poetry was *We are Seven*, but it took me to Tintern Abbey; history was Queen Victoria, but it brought me to Edward II and Marlowe. 'Why did I dream of her?' I said to Juice the next day. And then I remembered where I was. And what I had felt when I had read that last line: 'There was a Miss Jean Brodie, in her prime . . .'

TWELVE

Newcastle: a strange place for saints

Juice was talking to the old woman sitting opposite her on the train to Newcastle, and the woman was pretending that Juice was a bit of British Rail upholstery. Juice had a thing for old women – the evening before she had trapped one into conversation on the seafront at Leith while I looked at the Firth of Forth, which wasn't looking very firthy, what with the fog like battlesmoke obscuring Fife. Not that I minded; the cold sea with its waves glinting like swords in the water reminded me of Brighton, which I had never seen, and of a boy I had known as a boy who had drowned himself in a novel called *Battledore and Shuttlecock*. Barbara Goolden, who wrote it, was still living, at ninety, in a village in West Sussex. I wanted to surprise her, to visit without asking; then I thought if I did the book would be spoiled for ever – if you saw God it would be hard to believe in man – and I tore up her address.

But that was a long way from the railway carriage, where Juice was now being grinned at by a woman with a perfect set of teeth, which I automatically thought of as false because my mother had a set from the dentist. 'My mother is deaf,' said the woman. 'She is eighty-five – twenty years older than me.' In the seat across the aisle, I pretended to write a letter, making baby-scrawls across the blue paper.

'Are you taking her home?' asked Juice.

191

'From home, poor thing. She's lived in Edinburgh all her life and now she's too old – '

'Oh, terrible!'

' – to manage. We've just been getting rid of all her things, every little bit she collected over a lifetime.'

'Oh, unbearable!' said Juice. I looked up. The woman looked at me, and smiled. 'Is she coming to stay with you then?' asked Juice.

'Oh no,' she said. 'I've earned my bit of peace. It's my son who is taking her in – he's forty. And she wouldn't want to be with me.' The mother wore the far-away face I knew so well.

'Does your mother know sign-language?' I asked. 'Because I do. I have a sister who is deaf.'

'Oh – she doesn't – isn't that a pity! I think she's quite glad to be deaf right now, the way I talk. She's always said I could talk the tail off a donkey. Right?' She faced the mother and mouthed the words slowly.

'Quite right,' said the mother, her smiling voice surprisingly deep.

'That's what's kept me going,' said the daughter. 'I've had my tough times.'

'During the war?'

'Yes, I used to weave the wire which held down the mines in the sea – it was very hard work, twelve hours on my feet every day. That's how I lost my first baby – ' Juice was miming grief, shutting and opening her eyes while her mouth pouted with pain. 'Then I had two sons, and would you believe it? Twin sons after that. When I took them home I asked the older boys to choose one and ever since they've felt responsible for theirs. "How's my twin?" they'll phone and ask.'

'What do they do?' Trains made me curious quickly.

'Oh, they were both in the army and now one is a bus-driver and the other is lorry-driver, but one of them is bald, the other isn't. What do you do?' I told her, together with some of the stories I'd collected on the way. 'Oh!' She shook her head and said to Juice, 'He must be such a joy to live with.' Juice nodded, and I wished I had an earring in my left ear and it was still that innocent era when men with earrings meant something.

'Do you travel?' I asked quickly.

'I've been to Canada – I love it there. Though I can't bear the heat. Oh yes, it can get very hot. I had to stay in my room all day. I want to live there but not while she's alive.' How well I knew the convenience, and corruption, of being able to talk about someone in the room as if she wasn't there. One of those things that should never be – a bit like having a switch in your hand with which you can make someone disappear.

We talked about politics. 'Good!' she said, showing me the imaginary dentures. 'I'm a Conservative too, my husband is Labour, just as it was with my mother and her husband. My son is a Liberal – recently he stood for elections to our local council. I went campaigning for him. On election day I was his agent at a polling-station. People came up to me and said, "Are you from the Liberals?" and I said, "No!" "Then what are you?" they demanded. "Conservative," I said proudly. "Then why are you doing this?" And I answered them: "Taking care of my own," I said. "That is what being Conservative is about."'

But she took care of us as well when it was time to get down, offering to put our luggage out, after us. 'I can manage,' said Juice, quite honestly, while I was saying, 'Thanks, that would be very kind.' Perhaps it was a shield against all the help I was always taking from people, but I believed they were as lucky as I. Surely, to be the giver in some way made you bigger, more aware of other people and, perhaps, of yourself. Lifting my wheelchair or opening doors for me was a quick, not too difficult way of helping. For someone like me there was so little possibility of this spontaneous reaching out: I could not pop around to the corner store for an old neighbour or look after a friend's baby for an evening. With me the commitment had to be premeditated, larger and more ponderous. So that I had to do things like read to somebody blind or teach someone illiterate in order to fulfil the same part of myself.

There was no porter on the platform, and we were glad of

her help. 'I hope we meet again,' I said, my usual parting pains
pricking through me.

'And perhaps we shall,' she said. 'Surprising things happen
in the world.' I knew, and nodded. It felt good, for once, to
end a journey with someone there to wave goodbye.

Newcastle seemed to me like an ugly child that was always
trying to make you forget its looks with its winning ways.

The five-foot tall porter at the station said to us, 'You're
not to worry about a thing – tell me when you want to leave
the town and I'll go to the station supervisor and arrange
everything. You won't be able to get to him, there's stairs on the
way.' Outside, I blinked at the familiarity of the blobbish grey
buildings, the streets in disarray, the disregard for appearance;
Bombay was like that, unmindful of the way it looked so that
even while you shut your eyes in the face of such aesthetic
shamelessness, you felt drawn to it. As you would towards
someone who was so happy being themself they didn't ever
bother to put across an impression.

The taxi-driver who took us to the tourist centre said,
'Newcastle is the place to live, there is nowhere else as alive!'

'What about London?'

'Agh! About as alive as a drug-addict,' he said.

We landed up at the Swallow Hotel, which the driver said
was 'about as posh as you can go'.

A young man with a crew-cut in a blue jacket was waiting
for me. 'Lovely day, sir,' he said.

'A bit too lovely.' The heat was biting into me. Like a fool I
had fallen for the English modesty about their weather. (Wasn't
it Julian Barnes who said that the Deluge was not forty days and
forty nights of rain – that was just an English summer?) And I
was travelling with woollen trousers and woollen socks.

I had picked the Swallow because it was supposed to be
wheelchair-friendly. Just how much, I discovered only when
Juice tried pushing me into the bathroom, the door said no
and I fell forward with the impact of its refusal saved only by
my cowlick, with which Juice managed to retrieve me.

We asked if we could change rooms. Andrew, the young

man who had welcomed us, said he would show us another one on another floor. This one was more forthright; it said no at the entrance door, so that I returned sheepish and shaken. 'I'm sorry,' said Andrew. 'I'll do anything to make you more comfortable – I know how it is. I have a brother in a wheelchair.' Later in the evening, when we were leaving the hotel, he offered to roll me down the ramp that spiralled to the street. 'I could have used my van,' he said. 'But you probably prefer this.'

'I do – I hate the fuss of getting me in and folding the wheelchair – '

'Yes, I know.'

'What does your brother do?'

'He can't do anything.' I looked up at his face, against the sun, and I saw the same strange calm eyes that my family had when they were asked about me, as if they knew something they could not explain. 'He is spastic and severely retarded. My brothers and I do everything for him, we love him as much as we can. We all chip in, we'd never put him away.' The sun was beginning to make my eyes water. 'I'll leave you here,' he said. 'Have a pleasant evening.'

The descent to the Tyne was like the down-slide of the roller-coasters I had never been allowed to get into. Juice behind was making little animal cries of terror. A woman with sideburns stopped. 'Like a hand?' she asked.

'Thank you,' I said.

'Do you know of a launderette?' asked Juice. 'We can't afford to get our clothes done at the hotel.'

'The Swallow,' I said, so she would know we were down but not out.

'There are no laundrettes here,' she said. 'That's the mad thing about Newcastle. I've lived all over the kingdom – ' I wondered why we never said about India 'all over the republic'.

The quayside was deadly dull, with none of the vulgarity I had seen in Bristol. There were small ships in the river, and across it what I thought must be Gateshead. Gateshead, I had read somewhere, had made all the money on which Newcastle lived. Now the shipping industry had been put to sleep by Thatcher's efficiency drive and it was Gateshead that had suffered the death blow. I wanted to get away from here.

'Your Thatcherite guilt,' said Juice.

We took a taxi to Jesmond, where we were meeting some friends of a friend, Anne and Joseph.

We had been asked for eight in the evening, and I couldn't understand if that meant dinner or not.

'Not,' said Juice. 'Or they would have said it.'

'The unsaid always counts with the English – we might as well take some wine.'

Wine was new to me, my only acquaintance with it in Bombay having been helping my aunt make her own. She would soak the grapes and sugar in grey plastic buckets and I would crush them with my hands till the pads on my finger-tips shrivelled and reddened like little grapes themselves. We would always do this at night, because Prohibition was in force in Bombay. And when weeks later the wine was filtered and ready to drink, we would slip into the dark with the waste, my wheelchair an alibi, and fling it all into an open sewer. My only reward was the thrill, since I hated the tart flavour of wine. Here, in Britain, when I said I did not drink, people looked at me with broadminded sympathy, as they might at someone who said he worshipped idols in his room. So that I was always saying, 'This has nothing to do with being Indian.'

But I did take a bottle of wine with me whenever I went to dinner, and I never knew what to buy, all those names – Muscadet and Frascati and Chablis - as alien to me as Saturn's moons. All I would say was, 'I want something for about five pounds, something good,' then turn the hard, cold bottle over to warm, waiting hands.

Joseph, who welcomed us to his first-floor flat, had small pudgy hands and plump good looks, with large eyes and a big nose. He and Juice carried the chair up three flights, sweating and smiling all the way. Anne, his wife, was like one of those huge ancient shapeless stone figures of the mother goddess, her eyes half-shut under heavy lids. We soon discovered there was to be no dinner that evening; perhaps they had had their tea at seven.

It was now eight, and light as a monsoon morning, the Town Moor, huge and silent, lying on its back after a long day. 'Developers want to grab this lovely bit of land,' said Joseph. 'They haven't succeeded yet.' His home was beautiful, rich with books and records. 'It's an appalling statistic,' he said, 'that the average British home has three books. And of course since people like us have a few more' – I loved that – 'many people can have none at all.' His wife used to work in a book-shop, but she spoke very little, much like an Indian wife, until we began talking of Indian superstitions.

'We have a lot of that here, as well,' she said, 'especially among the working class, from which Joseph comes.' I drew in my breath – in India you would never refer to someone's lower-class origins in their presence; perhaps the impossibility of climbing classes made it rude, like talking about somebody's squint when you knew they could do nothing about it.

'They have very stubborn rituals related to weddings or the birth of a baby that you have to follow.' I wanted to ask what, but couldn't think how to without seeming nosy. That is the pity of learning a cultural language too well; its faults become part of you. So that later, when I was leaving London, I discovered myself incapable of telling an English friend how much I would miss him, something I would have found as easy, in India, as switching on a ceiling fan in summer.

Joseph was a director of the arts for the local council. There was a new trend now, he said, to spend money on the arts in the north because it helped to change the image of a place like Newcastle, and encouraged tourists to come over – and, of course, it was the best kind of education. After that, there was no way I could tell him what I thought of taxpayers' money going into the arts, so that somebody who couldn't stand opera was paying for a production of *Turandot*. Now if I were stopped at the point of a gun (and that is what the state's power comes down to, in the end) and told I had to pay for a rock concert because rock culture was good and deserved to survive, the injustice would be intolerable. I enjoyed Shakespeare and ballet and opera – but if I stopped to think who was paying for it – the taxi-driver and the shop assistant and the plumber, among many others – my stomach turned.

'What do you think of Newcastle?' said Joseph.

'Ugly,' I said, 'but a welcoming kind of ugliness, a bit like Bombay's.'

'Ugly!' said Joseph.

'You are serious?' said Anne.

'Well, you should have seen Barrow-in-Furness, where we were living,' said Joseph. 'It's a submarine base, no trees, no children. When we came to Newcastle, we knew we had found heaven.' I was always amused at the way so many educated Englishmen spoke – 'I could have died!' and 'It was absolutely enchanting!' – a kind of borderline camp. As a gay American friend said to me, 'With them you can never tell who is a boy-boy and who isn't.' ·

Days have a way of starting as they are going to go on. I woke to my copy of the *Daily Telegraph* – to read anything else in leftist Newcastle would have been cowardice for me – and read that Thatcher had pushed Geoffrey Howe out of the Foreign Office. Remembering his dismal performance after Tiananmen Square, I was irrationally pleased.

I was unused to television showing anything but propaganda and Hindi songs and dance, so Kate Adie's frontline reporting in Peking had blown my head off. When I saw a bullet turning a Chinese boy's face into a splotch of blood, I was weeping (this was at a party in Bayswater) and remembering an interview I had seen on television in Bombay with a visiting Chinese academic; everyone, beside me it seemed, believed China was now half-way down freedom road, and the smiling professor confirmed their optimism. 'Soon,' he said, 'soon we will have a general erection.'

So now, when a sobbing student said, 'Go and tell the world what it is like here,' I had thought, at least I have done that always; and how easy it would be now to say, I told you so; and as if that mattered – as if anything mattered, except that for a little while some people had known what life could be, and had seen their reaching arms turned into bleeding stumps.

What poor Geoffrey Howe's *congé* amounted to was that I went to my morning meeting with Joseph fiercely angry with the West and its guilty innocence, its desire to disbelieve everything from Buchenwald to Stalin's Gulag to the true nature of China after Mao. Behind it, I knew, lay at least two things: a horror of admitting that man could be so evil (after all, every human's deeds awaken us to our own possibilities); and the unearned guilt about its own well-being that the West, like a disabled child's sibling, always carries. So that it is imperative to believe that things for the others are not as bad as reported.

'Victorian values,' sniggered Joseph, pointing at the red-brick monstrosity that held Riverside, a music centre that had won a BBC award. Created by unemployed people who wanted to bring music to the community, Riverside had got only half of the quarter million pounds of assistance it had requested.

'The government wanted it to be a failure so it wouldn't have to assist other projects of the kind,' said Andy, the slim, bald, bespectacled man who ran the place as manager. 'The workers argued too much to be able to take decisions, so they decided to hire me.' Riverside now almost supported itself, paying 93 per cent of its own cost, renting out space to a hairdresser who gave punk-cuts.

'Isn't that wonderful?' I said. 'That might never have happened if it had got all the money it asked for.'

'Yes, but it might not have survived – and that would have meant many other co-operative ventures never seeing the light of day.'

The building smelled of pipes and perspiration – 'We give new groups a chance, twin them with well-known ones so they get an audience,' said Andy, ushering us into a back yard that looked like a junk yard, with broken cars and bottles strewn around the table where we sat drinking tea.

'The difference between the north and south,' said Joseph, 'is that the idea of money has not entered the north.'

'Which is why it never has enough – cultures which don't respect money don't make it. I should know, I come from one.'

'But it's the community that's important here, doesn't that

count? People live in the same street all their lives, they care for
each other. The new economics is ruining all that. The men have
to move south to make money, and they don't make enough to
send home – lives are destroyed.'

'Yes,' said Andy, 'firms come in here from the south, make
money, take it back and that's the end. No contribution to the
community.'

'Surely employment is a contribution.'

'We hear a great deal about the work ethic,' he said. 'But
what do these employment training schemes amount to? People
work five days a week for just ten pounds more than the dole.
It's tragic how people's expectations have fallen. Five years ago
they would have resisted, they would have rather remained
unemployed.'

'Don't you think it's worth learning a skill, worth getting
into the habit of working? There are so many people who
live on the dole, cheat it and go to pubs, travel abroad at the
taxpayer's expense.'

'That's rubbish!' he exploded. 'I don't know of a single
person who does that. My parents never smoked or drank, but
without the welfare state I would never have had an education,
I would never have got anywhere in life. And now there are
third-generation unemployed people – and for business they
are just an opportunity for exploitation.'

'How can a job-offer be exploitation? It's an opportunity.'

'Look,' said Joseph. 'Don't you agree that multinationals are
exploiting cheap labour in countries like India?'

'Countries like India are poor because they don't allow
investment. Do you know how well multinationals treat their
employees, how many benefits they offer, how much better
they pay because they're big and can afford to? Indians long
for jobs with multinationals, they are the best jobs!'

'Don't you think what happened in Bhopal, thousands dying,
was an atrocity committed by a multinational?'

'Like an aircrash is an atrocity – does that mean you stop
flying planes? Isn't it funny how people in the West are enjoying
everything capitalism brings them but are always telling the
Third World that it's better off without the multinationals and

the business investment and the economic success?' I had made my speech and I was red and hot – so much for my grasp of cultural language.

We turned to the weather, we smiled. 'I hope this has been useful,' said Andy.

'Very useful,' I said, absolutely sincere.

When we got to Pontyland – 'a little place where disabled people live and work together' – I thought a miracle must have transformed the inhabitants. They walked confidently through the gardens, some bent over to pick vegetables from healthy plots, others carried huge parcels and stomped from house to house. I went to the little office and said I would like to have a look around. 'Sue will show you the way,' said the woman there.

Sue was gently retarded – she spoke slowly, laughed too easily and her eyes looked at you and saw something else. I understood where I had come and I was glad. Only too often had I dismissed minds that didn't work as nothing to do with me. A kind of snobbery that had its silly little feet planted in muddy fear. As a boy, in Bombay, everyone who met me thought I was retarded. There, the borders of disability were blurred – if I had a strange, small body it must follow that my mind looked the same – and I was determined to draw the divide, as it were, with the dark blue ink of my intelligence.

Now, things had changed: I no longer needed to prove my mind. It was there, between the covers of the novel I had written, and I was ripe for learning.

The fact that the inmates of the place ran a carpentry shop, a laundry, a market garden, did not surprise me. I knew from my life how much more I could do than people ever dreamt I could – from writing books to washing my own socks. And how each small deed – a table cleaned, my wheelchair polished – was like a fibre of muscle making me more capable and ready for that next event.

I went to one of the houses where the inmates lived, and it felt good that sometimes I could not tell the retarded from those taking care of them. When they went into the village, unescorted, their behaviour was impeccable, I was told – it had to be; they were judged more harshly than the rest of us.

There was a man of about my age who kept smiling. When he heard I was a writer he told me he wrote poetry.

'Shall I show it to you?'

The poems were about Ireland and they did not work.

'Are you a volunteer here?' I asked him.

'No, it's a job like any other job.'

'And you enjoy it?'

'Oh, yes – I'm pretty religious,' he added by way of explanation. 'How old do you think I am?'

'Same as me, probably, twenty-nine, thirty?'

He shook his head. 'I'm twenty,' he said.

'Then you've done a lot of growing.'

He nodded. 'I've known some tough times,' he said.

I told him people were always getting confused about my age. Because I was small there were people who thought I was still a teenager. On a visit to the elegant Ménage à Trois restaurant at the top of the Taj Mahal Hotel in Bombay, the *maître de* very politely told my friend, 'Sorry, no children allowed.' On the other hand, I once visited a friend whose seventy-five-year-old father had just died. Another visitor turned to me and said, 'You are his brother, aren't you – I just want to say how sorry I am,' while I sat there, speechless and twenty-five.

Juice was making conversation with a boy whose hair was shaven; I wondered why. 'I'm from India,' she told him.

'You . . . been . . . bombed?' He spoke as if his words lay scattered in a heap on the floor of his mind and he had to pick out the right ones.

'No – never,' said Juice. 'No bombing.'

'No . . . planes,' he said, holding up the Ladybird book on planes he had been reading. 'To . . . bombs . . . for . . . me . . . I . . . been . . . a . . . good . . . boy . . .'

When we were leaving, I said goodbye to him, thinking what a long journey I had made to shake his cold, uncertain hand.

'Something is wrong with your voice,' said Juice. 'I can hardly hear you, most of the time.'

She was right, except that my larynx was in tip-top condition. Britain is a quiet country – there are no street-singers or temple-bells to outshout – and slowly my voice was drifting lower and lower. At a dinner party in London, I had found myself trying to out-whisper the very civilised guests – an editor, a television producer, a writer.

But I missed my voice, not least because it was a very special voice; the same genetic fault that made my bones brittle let my voice stretch across octaves, so that I had a boyish soprano that could dip into a baritone.

As the colour began to fade from my voice, I began to miss the dirt-eating colours of home, the earth-reds and shouting-yellows of India. Somehow the Metro Centre in Gateshead brought it all back. Ever since I had arrived, every person I met – including the most anti-commercial socialists – had told me to pay a visit. The man who had built the mammoth shopping-precinct was a hero in his city, never mind that he was a Tory.

I liked the excess, the shops vulgar with names like Monte Carlo, the huge basket-balloons with teddy-bears bigger than me inside, the *faux* antique villages with a water-wheel and bridge you could not cross, the fake Mediterranean town with balconies pouting above blue- and green-painted doors. I was back in that bit of Bombay I was so familiar with. There were no shopping-precincts there, but the bourgeoisie thronged to the big hotels to share the air-conditioning and the unaffordable glimpses of gold in the shopping arcade, and the just-affordable cup of coffee at the all-night restaurants where you could gawk at Italians in shirts that cost more than your month's salary even as you sipped a drink on which you had spent as much as your servant's weekly wages.

But on our way back to the hotel our taxi-driver did not approve. About the same age as Thatcher, he wanted to see her dead. 'It's a terrible thing to say about anybody,' he growled, 'but I'd be glad if someone put a bullet into her.'

I looked at my hands and wondered what I might have done if I had bigger fists.

'All this tinsel she's made – won't last long. No real jobs, no factories. I've got three sons, two unemployed and me driving a taxi, don't consider that a proper job. Not that it matters – around here we don't leave money to our children. We finish what we have and we go.'

That evening we had dinner at the hotel's rooftop restaurant. Newcastle at this level was as fantastic as it was in its life at street-level. Here the sky was stretched thin so that you could see pale gold where it frayed against the sun, the colour of royal Duncan's blood.

They come in pairs, I thought, listening to the taxi-driver the following morning, like matter and anti-matter.

'People don't want to work – that's why there are so many of them in the dole queues. I know plenty who work quietly on the side – '

'And cheat the dole!' said Juice.

'Yes, you've met those have you?'

'Oh yes! A man told us he wanted to be on the dole for a few months to get back everything he had paid in taxes – and he was also making money on the side.'

'Yes, while I'm working since five last evening – I'm sending my son to a private school. I didn't get a chance but I'm going to give him one.'

'What about your other children?' asked Juice, thinking about the five children the average Indian woman had.

'He's the only one – that's the way you can change things in your family.'

At moments like these I felt absurdly hopeful for Britain; it was something I wanted to feel very much.

Simon, the man who ran the DENE centre for the disabled in Jesmond, used to be a Conservative Party agent. His candidate had won again and again but each time their overdraft had got bigger and bigger, until the candidate couldn't afford an agent any more. By this time Simon was an expert fund-raiser, and he had put his skills to use for the DENE centre so that it now managed to get £100,000 every year from private sources, and that was almost two-thirds of its budget. Simon had also been on the committee that planned the Newcastle metro.

'You must travel on it,' he said. 'It's a marvel for people in wheelchairs.'

'I don't know how you manage in London,' said a woman with a huge limp who was passing the door. 'I go crazy every time I go there – all those torrents of stairs.'

There was a young man, Bob, thin as his skeleton, with curling brown hair and curved nose and green eyes. Juice looked at me and nodded knowingly. I told her she looked like a procuress.

Bob showed me around the wheelchairs, and I was like a pianist in a studio of Steinways. There was a really tiny one that weighed only fifteen pounds, a sports-chair with a low-cut back over which I could toss a basketball, and big sleek ones heavy with the promise of a motor. 'Would you like to try any of these?'

'All,' I murmured, 'all.'

The lightweight sent Juice zooming. 'Ooh!' she shrieked, running away with me. 'I could take you up the Eiffel Tower in this.'

'They have lifts there, you know,' said Bob.

Walking can't be as wonderful as this, I thought, gliding around in a sleek black motorised chair. There was an amazing fluency about it, the same feeling I got when I read something by Philip Roth: under the easy movement, an unfolding, the release of a new prospect I could not have imagined. With one of these, life would rub against me with a different stroke; I could see myself browsing at Foyle's as long as I liked without worrying about whoever was with me getting bored, chugging up Primrose Hill whenever I felt in need of the view.

There was also a modern flat which had a kitchen with everything at wheelchair level, and I thought, this is how a child feels when it grows tall, this sense of reach and control.

We had an appointment with Joseph, but I said I would return afterwards – the centre was like a disabled heaven. When we returned in the evening Bob showed us around the other wonders of the place: a bed that went up and down when you pumped a switch, a bath-tub seat that rose to the level of my chair so I could slide in.

Bob was amazed when I told him there was no access for
the disabled anywhere in Bombay. 'How can it be? How do
you live?'

Looking at the things around me, I was beginning to wonder
too.

'I try to make people aware,' he said. 'Very often groups of
schoolchildren come to visit us, and before taking them around
I ask them how they would feel if they were on a planet where
everything was twice their size.'

He didn't stop working when he left the centre at five every
evening. He was a marriage counsellor with an organization
called Relate. 'Some people think I work too hard – one of
these days I'll disappear,' and he shrugged his thin shoulders
and laughed.

'I think you're just fine,' I said. 'What about gay life in
Newcastle?'

'I think it's difficult – not like London or Edinburgh. Most
people keep quiet about the way they are.'

I knew what he meant. It was the easiest thing in the world
to buy a copy of *Gay Times* in London, but in Newcastle when
I'd gone into a newsagent's something about the other people
there – a bluntness, an innocence – had pulled me back like a
strap against my chair, not letting me ask.

Bob didn't like the idea of a north-south divide. 'I don't
know why people keep trying to separate themselves from
each other,' he said. 'We're different enough anyway.'

It was time to leave. I told him how much I hated leaving people I met on this journey, knowing I'd never see them again.

'I just think how much worse it would be if I hadn't met the
people I have, someone like you. And isn't it a good feeling to
know that they are going on, somewhere?'

'I don't think you quite understand,' I said. 'Many Indians
believe that the objects around them have a life of their own,
so that they can relate to them.' I hated saying things like that –
they sounded so incredible.

'You mean someone in Bombay might feel this table can
talk to them?' I knew Joseph was being funny.

'Not talk – but if he happened to bump into it a couple of times he would say that the table didn't like him, and it wouldn't be just a manner of speaking.'

'Oh – English people make jokes like that.'

'That's just the point – it wouldn't be a joke. Objects have very real presences for so many of us. A saree bought can attract many more gifts of sarees. My own family believes that whenever they cook goat's trotters my uncle is transferred to a job out of Bombay. It's laughable, but we always find connections – any connections but the actual ones; cause and effect are too unforgiving to bear in a world where causes are so out of your control.'

I had had a reminder of that, if I needed any, that very morning, when we had watched the television screen in our room, denying the horror of what we were seeing. Bombay was drowned in a cyclone, the pictures were there for us to see, hundreds had died.

'Oh! My mummy-daddy,' cried Juice. 'They must be definitely dead – we live so close to the sea.'

'All of us in Bombay do – it's an island.'

But Juice was dialling Bombay, not getting anywhere with her frightened fingers.

'Let me try,' I said. I got the international operator and I could hear her talk to someone in New Delhi: 'Call for Bombay.'

'Impossible,' I heard the wavy Indian voice reply. 'In Bombay there is water or something everywhere.'

I put down the receiver and told Juice the lines would be up the next day, we could phone before leaving for Durham. 'Don't worry,' I said, 'it's only the people who live on the streets who die . . .' I had heard that kind of thing said all my life, but only now did I hear the obscenity of it. Sure enough, the next day we heard our families had survived what was, for them, just a big storm playing outside the strong windows of their cosy flats.

'I think Peggy will be waiting for us,' said Joseph. 'She's a very busy lady.' We had been having lunch in the cafeteria of the arts centre where he worked. With us was Sue, whose job was trying to get people to read. She was trying to tempt them into reaching Byron and Wilde by using the theme of Scandal for her programme. It was working well, and her next web was going to be woven around Romance, with the Brontës thrown in.

Peggy, whom we were going to visit, was achieving something completely different. She lived on a poverty-eaten estate called Stonygate.

'People shouldn't be asked to live the way they do there,' Joseph said, and I knew what he meant. There was scarcely a house in Bombay that did not have a view of slums – tattered cloth, straw and splintered board held together by desperation, so that a third of Bombay's nine million people lived in these primitive villages, in the belly of a city that was the New York of India.

But when we reached Stonygate I saw neat little gardens sunning themselves and houses with curtains dividing the windows. And I knew what relative poverty was.

Peggy was short and sinewy, with pale grey hair, and when I left her the only thing about her face I could remember was her smile. She was surrounded by about forty children whom she shooed away. 'I have a meeting and I don't want to be disturbed,' she said, leading us into a house with a dark, quiet parlour. 'Looks peaceful, doesn't it, without the children?' She laughed. 'We look after two hundred and forty, and all ages too.'

I asked her about the centre she ran. 'This is it. My house is next door, that's where it started. You've heard about Stonygate? What it was like? Four or five years ago it was the roughest neighbourhood in the area, and me and my husband, we wanted to move out, and then we said, "Oh no, we can't, this is where we've always lived," and I thought maybe we could do something to make things better.'

'Why did you choose children?'

'I saw what they were doing – you couldn't leave the washing out but they would steal it, if you left your home they'd get in and wreck it, they broke the street-lamps and your windows, they had nothing else to do. The parents were at home because they were unemployed and they wanted to be left alone.'

'And did anyone help you when you started?'

'Very quickly, yes. I began to take the children in, get them to play or do things, and then some of the women up the street began to help, and I have my daughters.'

'How did you manage to get this centre?'

'The local council saw what we were doing – things were changing, children were now painting and making garden gnomes to sell instead of wrecking. And there was the Inner City Project, so we got this vacant house. Now we have a television and a computer and a little kitchen. I make them chips when they are hungry, potatoes don't cost much.'

Stonygate looks very pleasant to me – have things changed since you started?'

'Sure they have, but with the children busy the adults have stopped having fights, all the violence is gone – maybe they always started fighting over the children, I don't know. But Stonygate is a new place now. Even the council knows that. Used to be a time when they didn't bother about maintaining the place – if they replaced a window it was smashed the next day. Now, they're here within twenty-four hours.'

'You won the OBE – what did you feel about that?'

'I almost passed away when I got the news. I was thrilled.'

'Do you feel you've been well rewarded for what you've done?'

'My, I've enjoyed it so much, I ought not to have been given the OBE at all!'

'Perhaps that is why you've been so successful.'

'I don't know – but I haven't done it for the money, that's for sure. The council keeps offering me a salary, but I refuse. I don't want to be tied down – I'm doing this for the pleasure.'

'What about the children?' I said. 'You must be meeting so many different kinds of families.'

'Oh yes, and some of them are lovely, but so many are sad. There's this boy David, he comes in one hot summer's day with long trousers and a thick jumper, and I make him take it off and what do I see? Bruises. All over his little body, red bruises, and he says his brother beat him. Then I find out his mother had her five children taken away from her, but when

209

she came to live here she got them back, what with the play centre and all. I go straight to her and tell her she can't do this but she denies it flat. Then another neighbour records a confession from her youngest one – the child talks about how her mother hits her elder brother on the head so that no one can see the marks. I take the tape to the police and they say a child's word is worth nothing – what can you do?'

'There is a huge amount of poverty here – how well do people cope?'

'They are always running out – there's a family down the road, and the woman, she always comes to me for a loan, and I give her money because it's for the children's grub. And she pays it back as soon as she gets her Giro. But the other day I meet her husband and he says to me, "Thank you, Peggy, now I can go to the pub and have a pint," and I say, "You ought to be ashamed of yourself; that money was for the children's grub." "Oh, they're fine," he says, "they've had some beans on toast," and off he goes.'

'They're unusual, I suppose,' said Joseph.

'Not as much as you think – there's another family, the parents are off for a holiday to Spain or Greece every year – '

'How can they afford that?'

'They take a loan from the bank – and they pay it back, or they won't get a loan the next year. They pay it out of what they claim and I'm sure the children starve.'

Before we left Peggy we met her daughter. She was about to have a baby. 'The pains have begun, Ma,' she said. 'I'm taking the metro to the hospital.'

'You'll be all right,' said Peggy with her smile. 'I'll call you at about nine to ask you how you are.'

'Not Mother Teresa of Calcutta, but certainly Saint Peggy of Stonygate,' said Joseph. And I thought yes, certainly. And how saints sometimes make strange mothers.

But there was nothing strange about the mother I saw at the hotel restaurant, that evening. They were a family with two sons and the older son was paralysed, but he could talk and joke and the family was in splits. I thought, someone who hasn't been there might suspect their laughter. But I was watching the mother spoon food into her son's mouth between gales of merriment and I knew the joy was as genuine as the courage. I watched them and I knew how lucky I was. I wasn't sentimentalising my brittle bones (it would have been hard to do that with all the trouble they had given me), but I had known something, I had seen a grace in my family, for which I felt I should be grateful. Only there was no one to be grateful to, and thanking my DNA seemed taking it a bit far.

THIRTEEN

Durham: from Blyton to Byron

'Admit it, sir,' whispered the waitress to me the next day at breakfast.

'I'm so sorry, I can't – I mean, I'm not.'

'But you look like him, your voice is his – I've taken a bet with that waiter and I'll lose. Just say it, just say you are that actor who's been on television.' I began to laugh. 'I know what!' she said, hitting her palms on her apron. 'You are acting as if you're not him – and it's easy for you.'

But later her conviction weakened. 'Your accent is different and your skin – oh, I'm sorry, sir, I shouldn't have insisted.'

'I'll forgive you if you remember his name – '

'I just can't, it's a funny name, he does these theatre workshops on television – he's marvellous.'

This had happened to me before in Britain, but I found out who my *doppelgänger* was only six months later, in Bombay, when I was flipping through the Cathay Pacific in-flight magazine. I saw a face so like mine, I knew I had found him, and his name was Nabil Shaban. I wondered if this would ever change. If one day people would say to him, 'You look just like that writer, the one with the funny name.'

The taxi-driver who took us to the station was someone who had driven us before, at the beginning of our visit to Newcastle. 'So how did you like it?' he asked.

'It's the first place I'd come back to, given a chance.'

212

'That's not how you felt three days ago, is it?'

'No,' I said. Newcastle had been a family joke. I had an aunt with airs who had lived in England, which was a kind of tautology for Parsees of my class. My father had once given her a bottle of Chivas Regal. She'd taken one look at it and said, 'I don't need this – it's like taking coals to Newcastle,' and my poor father had stood there, the smuggler-priced bottle humble in his hands.

'Did you try the metro?'

'Oh yes, it was wonderful, wheelchair lifts and ramps everywhere.' Later I ventured into the tube in London, and saw hundreds of stairs everywhere. As an American I knew said, 'It's your environment that's disabled, na-at you.'

When I got on the train to Durham I found that British Rail had made a slot for my chair by removing a seat. Then a BR man came up to me and said, 'Sorry, sir, we'll have to take you off this train – there's another gentleman who needs that space.' I was curious why he should have it rather than I, but there was a seat across the aisle into which I could move easily, and I did. An old woman wheeled a man with little bits of white tape sticking to his left ear into the space I'd surrendered. They were going home to Cardiff.

'We come to Newcastle every week to see a Chinese doctor – he's a specialist in acupuncture, he managed to get out after the Tiananmen massacre,' said the woman to me when we got talking. 'He hasn't improved yet, but we have hope.'

'I know about that,' I said. In India, hope wore the strangest faces – godmen who pulled wristwatches out of the air, or a fish that wriggled its way down your gullet. As a child I had had powdered pearls mixed into my milk and that was considered hardly strange.

We talked about travelling. 'I'm terrified of being separated from my friend,' I said. 'Sometimes she gets off to look for a porter and I keep thinking the train will take me away.'

'Oh, I know about that,' said the woman, nodding her small

head. 'There's a trick I use – always leave your carriage door open. The train won't move till all the doors are shut. Not that we travel these days – except to his doctor. I don't know how I'd manage with the wheelchair.'

'People are extremely helpful, though,' I said. 'You'd never really be left on your own.'

'Yes,' she said, 'isn't that funny? I never knew what a good place the world was till the wheelchair came into our lives.'

The world didn't seem such a good place in Durham, though.

'We can't put a chair into the bath,' said the young man at the hotel there. 'It might scratch the floor.'

He wore the Parkinson-rigid face that Englishmen put on when they are unbearably embarrassed. And to my amazement, I lost my temper and shouted, 'Then why did you tell us at the tourist centre that you could take a wheelchair? I've been travelling all over and I've had a chair in the bath everywhere. If you can't manage, we'll just look for something else.'

He murmured, 'I'll do my best, sir,' and I felt rotten. Here I was trying to bully my way through precisely because I knew how guilty English people felt about someone in a wheelchair. I was using his decency against him. In India, I would have put on my stoic suit and wheeled away quietly. How quickly I had learned to take consideration for granted.

When I got to my room (there was a shiny plastic chair in the bath) I was so exhausted I fell asleep. When I woke, the evening was cold and drizzly. Outside, the Wear had grey clouds floating on its surface and smug sunflowers on its banks, as if they were holding all the light of summer that they had saved up for a day like this.

Durham seemed a peculiar place – stunningly beautiful, yet full of menace. The taxi-drivers we had were surly, they grumbled or sulked. 'Can't stand the Bishop,' growled one, talking about the controversial David Jenkins. I was reading a book he had written in which he argued that God existed, only he couldn't make miracles; if he could and didn't at Belsen, that would mean he was a devil. The circle of unreason was complete. But I wanted to meet him and I telephoned his office and explained what I was doing in Durham. 'Sorry, young man,' said a plummy voice, 'but you've got the opposition. This is the Roman Catholic Bishop's office.' As it happened, David Jenkins was away on holiday. Not that I should have cared; according to the taxi-driver, 'The Bishop's done nothing but sell Church lands and shoot his mouth off.'

'Are you going to be here tomorrow night?' asked a tough-looking driver, hirsute as an orang-utan. 'You are? Just remember this is the roughest place in all of England on a Friday night. You know what they do? Shave the bristles off toothbrushes and melt blades into the plastic. Then they ride around on motorbikes slashing people. I once saw a group of roughs tossing a man into the Wear. And another time, I saw a man being stomped on – can you see that? On a dark night, and they damaged his brain. He turned blind, then he died.'

In the streets I met two mad people. One, a man, came up to me and asked for petrol. 'You've got plenty stored up there,' he said, pointing to my legs.

'Very little, I'm afraid,' I said, and he turned up his palms and walked away.

The woman I met was carrying a huge and invisible cake. Every now and then she would shut her eyes, puff her cheeks and blow out the candles. She stopped by me and said, 'I wish they wouldn't go on spluttering.'

'Stubborn ones you've got there,' I said, and she smiled and nodded. It must have been a relief, for once, to be believed.

Next to us at lunch had been two women, one deaf, wizened, clutching a black sling bag in her grey lap, the other tall, with a great white crown of hair. The tall one had been recently widowed and was having a problem with her grief. 'This is the best lamb I've ever had,' she said loudly; the other one smiled, then undid her smile when she heard, 'I could cry every minute of the day.' But this was followed by, 'As far as I am concerned, this is toppers.' The deaf woman gave up – from now on she used her mouth only to chew. 'John died of thickening of the arteries.' Then, 'I'm going to have two cups of coffee.

'It breaks my heart when I have to buy one lamb chop instead of three.

'But this last year we went to Edinburgh and London and Jersey.

'He left all that money to his son – no wonder he's in Switzerland now.

'Should I have the crêpes or the caramel? The crêpes sound smarter.'

The other one looked up from her chicken and said, 'I know how it is.'

The vicar giggled and said, 'I'm new here, you know. I think Mrs Snowdon has the keys.'

'I'm sorry to have bothered you,' I said.

'Oh, that's all right – all sorts of women have been ringing me up.'

I wondered what he meant; I wasn't surprised though. In Bombay, the receptionist at my barber's shop had asked me over the phone why, being a lady, I was asking for a gentleman's haircut.

Mrs Snowdon (who I quite irrationally thought would look like Princess Margaret) I did not get to see; our bright young taxi-driver went into the farmhouse and got the keys for us. We were on our way to St Mary's, Seaham, the church where Annabella Milbanke would have married Lord Byron except that she was posh and got married at her own house, nearby.

Gary, the driver, wore a three-stranded gold necklace and an earring; his hedgehog hair was gold as well. He had always lived in Durham with his parents and elder sister. He liked the way his sister doted on him – I knew about that, I had two. He was making good money driving the taxi, but he wanted to do better and was looking for a job on an oil-rig – he had done a course and got his qualifications. Besides, he was officially unemployed.

'Now why would you do that?' I asked.

'Thirty quid a week extra – good for a night on the town,' and he laughed; he was always laughing.

'Do you know anyone else who gets away with it?'

'Plenty of chaps – I have a friend who is a landscape gardener – nobody knows he's working. And there's another chap who paints houses. It's good, you know, especially for divorced men. If they're unemployed they don't have to pay maintenance.'

'Aren't you afraid you'll get caught?'

'I'm very, very, very careful,' he said. 'I've told the taxi firm to say I work just one day in the week. That way if I'm ever caught it's my one day.'

'What if they do find out?'

'They almost did. I had a girlfriend who knew I drove this car. When I went to take the dole, I found out she worked there. We had a huge row; she kept trying to convince me I was wrong, I'd have to pay back about three thousand pounds if I were caught. Finally, the tension got too bad and we broke off.'

Mrs Snowdon's keys took a long time to get the lock on the church door to say yes; vandals had made it cautious. Inside, defended by the wooden rafters and stone walls, was a shy silence. I wanted to stay there, between the windows set in niches and the dark choir stalls and the stone font. When we spoke, our voices broke the silence into a roaring resonance, so that I had to say the Lord's Prayer – I could imagine how marvellous it would be to be a clergyman, to hear your voice sound like the voice of God in a Hollywood movie.

Juice spotted a faded document dormant in glass: the marriage certificate of Lord Byron and the Princess of Parallelograms, as she was known for her sharp, mathematical mind. Byron was married in a room at Seaham Hall, the Milbanke mansion and our next stop. When we got there, we were greeted by four dying women, only one of whom managed to smile. The others were propped up in chairs. One was drooling, and above her was a portrait of the dashing Lord looking into the air above the artist's head. Seaham Hall was now a posh and private nursing-home, and the room where the ill-fated wedding ('I have married you,' said Byron to his bride, 'and that is reason enough to make me hate you') took place was now a geriatric parlour with its high ceiling and tall, sun-stealing windows. On the wall was a framed and ironic letter to Caroline Lamb telling her that ladies should not talk since it stops them from thinking. The marriage certificate I had seen in the church had the signature of John Hobhouse as witness – one of Byron's strange jokes. Hobhouse was homosexual, and with him Byron had many gay adventures in Europe, writing home slyly that he was 'conjugating the verb to love in both Hellenic as well as Romaic'. But he was not always frivolous in his passion. At Cambridge, he had loved a choirboy, John Edleston, deeply, and had written some of his finest short poems, including 'Thyrza', to him. When Edleston died, Byron wrote, 'I heard of a death the other day . . . of one whom I loved more than I ever loved a living thing . . .' In Bombay, years before, I had read a book called *Byron and Greek Love: Homophobia in Nineteenth Century England*; in it were descriptions of gay men put into pillories, pelted with rotten vegetables and killed. For the first time I had understood fully what it meant to belong to a persecuted minority; if I had been as I was only a hundred and fifty years ago . . .

We stopped at the sea, which was wide and clear of people. 'Did you ever read someone called Enid Blyton?' asked Gary. 'She wrote stuff about adventures by the seaside.' I grinned and said yes, and wasn't it wonderful how much children all over the world loved her writing, and because of it shared their childhood with each other. Of course, Blyton was very unpopular with the liberal Left. 'I never gave her books to my children,' Hororia Gaskell said to me, and later I heard how Noddy was being cleaned up to get rid of racist and sexist notions. And I thought, surely the Victorians must have felt as righteous when they bowdlerised Shakespeare and straightened out Plato.

'You must see the Beamish Museum,' said Gary. 'They have re-created a whole mining village of the last century.'

218

But on our way there, his car broke down.

'Give it a drink,' he said. 'See if that works.' He went to the nearest house and got a pail of water. I was surprised how easily the woman inside agreed to help a strange young man. Timothy Mo and I were always talking about how suspicious growing up in the East had made us. In that stratified world, guile was a legitimate ladder, a way of getting somewhere the stairs would never allow, and you learnt to be wary – of strangers, of generous offers and sudden kindness. Placing an advertisement in the *Guardian*, I was shocked to know that they were going to publish it before I had paid, and wondered if there was a catch somewhere, a method of charging interest on my bill or something even more dastardly that I couldn't think of, before it sank in that things worked on trust, and most of the time quite well.

Gary's car needed something stronger than water: it wouldn't start, and his radio wouldn't work. It was a very pleasing sensation, sitting there safe in an English country lane and at the same time knowing how dangerous this would be in a desert, with no radio contact, no water. About half an hour later, Gary got through and a taxi rushed over to pick us up. I was sorry to see Gary go. 'I'm punished,' he grinned. 'I have to sit with the corpse till they tow us away.'

The new driver had been a coalminer; he had a large moustache and I could see him lying dead and being washed like the miner in Lawrence's *The Odour of Chrysanthemums*. He said he used to work in a twenty-four-inch hole, leaning sideways, unable to move for hours. 'Running a taxi firm is a considerably better job,' he said.

He dropped us at a boat-station and we took a cruise up the Wear. The boat was swarming with children and I resigned myself to an hour of howling and scolding. But as the boat dipped into the green and brown water, all you could hear were bird-cries rising from the river banks and the slosh of branches reaching out from the shore. The children were not unnatural; they played and leaned over the railings, but they talked in whispers, and laughed and chased each other silently across the deck.

Later, I went to the cathedral, which I'd seen from the river
in one of those funny reversals. I had a picture post-card of
it, and I thought, yes, it's right, just like the photograph. It
was a grey evening, but faint particles of light floated through
seven panels of stained glass. I sat there and watched, and
thought of myself and where I'd arrived, and, mixing my
metaphors and my echoes as usual, I said, 'It was my prime,
my *belle époque*.' That was from *The Swimming Pool Library*,
but England was England to me; I couldn't divide it into bits
of literary experience, nor would I want to for a long time.

It was India that was in the mind of the woman in the wheelchair
who met me in the lobby of the hotel that evening. 'My parents
lived there,' she said. 'Oh! Here is my mother.' Who was
beautiful in a soft, twilit way. 'We were in India, in Quetta,'
she said.

'Pakistan, you mean.'

'Yes, it was all the same then, wasn't it?'

I nodded. My mother felt like that, and she'd always wince
when I drew the map of India for my geography lessons in
school. 'We used to draw all this,' she'd say, rubbing her
fingers wistfully over the North-West Frontier.

When we got talking, the woman in the wheelchair, forty
and as beautiful as her mother must have been, said, 'Let me
show off a bit.' And she shifted from her chair to a sofa so that
she could detach the wheels. 'I do this and fling the rest of the
chair over my shoulder into the back seat of the car! It's a new
kind of chair – weighs just about fifteen pounds. Expensive.
But it makes me free.'

I was enchanted; I wanted to find out more about her life –
she had talked about a daughter who was singing at a concert
in Durham. But a waitress came to tell us there was a table
free for dinner, and that embarrassed her.

'I've kept you from your food,' she said. 'Please don't wait a
moment longer,' and she wheeled off, her Englishness lending
speed to her chair.

FOURTEEN

Bradford burning

'Blue film in Bradford. That could be the name of a chapter,' said Juice, enthusiastically watching a Red Indian squaw reaching orgasm.

'If nothing worse happens to us before the night is out,' I said, and quite unbelievably, that's when the fire-alarm went off.

I had arrived in Bradford thoroughly shaken. At Leeds, the black porter had placed me in the doorway of the train, saying, 'It's just a ten-minute ride.' But it had taken half an hour and had seemed much longer. If I put on my brakes I rocked from side to side like Mr To-and-Fro in Enid Blyton's *Tales from Toyland*; if I let them go the chair whirled and raced between the doors like a tiresome child. Finally, I stayed put and had Juice hold my shoulders for stability, while the sentimental English smiled at our urgent display of affection.

Bradford gave us an Indian welcome – it was July, the monsoon month, and Bradford was awash in rain. We had a black porter who told us to go ahead, he would get our bags to the taxi-rank. But remembering the other black man that morning, I felt he was not to be trusted, and I kept looking back to see if he was there until I realised what I was doing, how easily I had wheeled across the borders of racist territory.

The handsome taxi-driver was from Karachi. 'Not so far from where you live, is it?' he said. I told him about the cousins in Pakistan I had never met. He said he was leaving the next day for a six-week holiday back home. And I tipped him as much as the fare again. I wanted him to enjoy his holiday, and somewhere, that meant, I was homesick. 'Are you sure about the money?' he shouted, and I couldn't turn because Juice was holding my handles.

When they saw me at the Norfolk Gardens Hotel they brought out a huge wooden ramp and threw it across the steps. 'This is going to stay here,' said a long-faced man with a dividing moustache, 'as long as you do, sir.' That set the tone: the doors were right and the bath had a chair waiting. I fell asleep with relief.

When we stepped out in the evening, I was surprised. Bradford did not look like a satanic mill-town, or even like little India. It had a prosperous Victorian air, wide roads and stately buildings, though at a street corner I saw an astonishingly un-Victorian sight, something I had not seen even in the streets of Soho: tired of waiting for a taxi, two men in dark jackets held each other in a long kiss that ended when a cab stopped for them.

'Exhibitionists,' snorted Juice, which described her perfectly an hour later. We were at the Museum of Photography, wandering around the fancy gadgets and cameras with which you could make and cut and mix film images. Everywhere the children had taken over from their admiring and too embarrassed parents, who stood like obsolete animals unable to cope. There was a little boy who was leaping about on a table covered with a rug. The thing was called a magic carpet, and on the screen above the boy was transformed into an enchanted child flying over deserts, skimming the flames of hell.

Soon he tired of watching himself and jumped off the magic carpet. Before I could threaten her with something dreadful, Juice had climbed on and was prancing in her peach Marks and Sparks dress on the carpet, which now floated serenely above a tropical jungle. From there she was beckoning, asking me to go with her; I was bent over, pretending to examine my tyres for punctures, when I felt a tap on my shoulders. 'I think,' said a lady in a lilac hat, 'your wife wants you to join her in her travels.'

222

After that, all I wanted was dinner. At the hotel, the musta-chioed man told me that 'two packages of tourists had arrived' and they were going mad. Which meant that dinner took a bit longer than necessary – but there was the blue film to look forward to. In Bombay, they were difficult to get, and, since most young people lived with their parents, almost impossible to watch.

The one we saw that evening at Bradford was quite insane, involving magic, murder and not a glimpse of male nudity. 'Where are the men?' shouted Juice through clenched teeth, and for once I could sympathise with her.

'They make these for straight men,' I said. 'I'm going to bed – you're wasting your time.'

'We've paid five pounds to watch this,' she said, 'and it's not that bad.'

When I heard the fire-alarm, I thought of the tapes on which I'd been keeping my notes. 'Pick up that bag,' I said to Juice calmly. 'There's a fire in the hotel.'

'In your dreams,' she said.

'There's a fire,' I shouted. 'Can't you hear the alarm?'

'Ssh,' she whispered. 'It's part of the film – it shows the squaw is getting there.'

That's when the thumping began, closer and closer until it was on our door. 'Fire! Wake up!'

'The tapes,' I screamed, and started putting on my shoes.

'You can't walk,' said Juice. 'What's the point?' She hooked the bag on my chair and we were in the corridor. Ashen-faced stewards were trying to find the emergency exits while people ran up and down just for the sake of doing something. They saw me and they stopped. 'We'll get you down, don't worry,' said someone.

'There's a wheelchair,' said an old lady in a pink dressing-gown with a black purse under her arm. 'Make way for the wheelchair.'

A loud sigh swept the corridor as the emergency exit fell open. 'Can I use the lift?' I asked one of the white-faced staff.

'No, sir, no one's allowed to.'

And to my amazement I began to tremble, and I only knew because I could feel my Parsee undershirt of muslin shiver against my skin. 'I'll help you,' said a voice straight out of a shipwreck and a place on the lifeboat. I began to descend, my chair tilted back for safety; now I could see him, a man in a red pullover, about sixty, overweight and grey-haired. I smiled, someone else smiled at me. 'You go ahead,' he said.

'Oh yes, don't crowd the wheelchair.'

Every time we found a landing someone would catch up with me and say, 'Are you all right?' And all I could think was, if this happened in India I would have been dead. Not because Indians were unkind, but because someone like me didn't matter as much as other people, and there was so little discipline or straight thinking that there would have been a stampede down the stairs; and the next day I would have been found somewhere, buried under my chair – though that might have happened to me at Hillsborough as well.

When we were almost at the bottom I looked up and saw my saviour, scarlet and sweating. 'Will someone please take over?' I shouted. 'This gentleman is exhausted.'

'Oh no', he gasped. 'I'm not tired.'

But someone from the hotel had taken over, and all I could do was turn my head and say, 'Thank you, three floors – I don't know what – thank you.' And, of course, I never found out his name; and I never saw him again in the confusion below.

We had to stand outside the hotel. That's when Juice realised she had her hair up in curlers like a little black flower-pot, and that she was barefoot, though she could walk, while I, in my white *sudrah*, wondered what the English must be thinking of this peculiar, see-through, sleeveless nightshirt. And the comic part was that I never, in my life, had slept in it. This one night I had run out of clean pyjama tops and had decided to make do. On my wheelchair I discovered two jumpers that I had taken off before getting into bed. It was cold now, midnight, and the rain had given way to wind. I tied a jumper around my waist; I am so small, it reached my ankles. The other one I wore over my *sudrah*. Warmer, I could look around, but before that someone had stepped out on to the pavement and was saying, 'It's probably a false alarm.'

We were let into a little lobby, Juice and I with a pink lady and her friend in green. 'It was I who woke my friend,' she said.

'What a scare it has been!' said Juice.

'Fun as well, I think,' said the pink woman. 'So much like the war – we should have a sing-song here.'

'What I feel we should have is a cup of tea.'

'You seemed to have enjoyed it all,' said the green one to me.

'Well, most of it – I kept imagining columns of flame climbing the stairs.'

'Oooh! Don't say that.'

Behind us was a larger lobby, and the long-faced man with a moustache who had welcomed us was managing things. Suddenly he was buttonholed by a large man in a white suit.

'Just you wait!' the attacker roared, 'I'll get you. Wasn't good enough to get in, was I? What time do you go out of here? Tell me, if you dare.' And poor long-face, standing very straight, said, 'Four a.m.,' while no one moved to help him. But the drunk was satisfied and lurched past us and out.

'Who do you think that was?' quavered Pinkie, clutching her black bag tight.

'A troublemaker, of course, what else?' her friend replied. 'What were you doing, dear,' she asked Juice, 'when the alarm sounded?'

'Uh-ah-' – and Juice shifted from foot to bare foot while the two women blushed and looked away.

Like the vanquished in ancient Rome, we had to parade in all our absurdity down the street to the front entrance and the waiting lifts. Juice remembered my camera in the tapes-bag, and I began clicking the firemen, so comforting in their uniforms, the young men without their shirts, the hotel staff, now coloured an English pink once again. It was one big party to celebrate our recovery. Someone tapped me on the shoulder and said, 'You wouldn't be doing that now if this were real.'

Outside my room, I waited to get a shot of the happy faces

returning home. The old women saw me and shrieked, 'Oh! He's got us in our dressing-gowns.' Back inside, the squaw was at it again. 'Oh good! They've just started, I can see how it ends,' said Juice. I wanted to smother her with the generous hotel pillows, but I had to laugh when the film ended in a huge raging fire.

I wheeled to the window to seal a crack in the curtains. When I saw what was outside, I threw them open. Like exquisitely crafted crystal, a silver, green and gold-lit clock tower climbed into the ebony sky; it called out the time, its voice soft and deep and singing. And all I could think was, if the fire had been real, I might have missed this.

'I am becoming a prince in Pakistan,' said the taxi-driver to me on our way to Sunday service.

'How does one do that?'

'Simple. Make money here, take it there – it becomes big. I can buy anything in Pakistan, my son can go to top school – '

'But he won't have as many opportunities.'

'That's okay. He'll have status, he'll be a rich man's son.'

'Yes,' I said, 'and that is all you can hope to be in our countries.'

'Exactly – here I have built up capital. I own my house and extra house where I keep lodgers. Here we are at your church.'

This was Roman Catholic, rich and splendid; the stained glass made the singing more lovely, the altar-boys lent their innocence to the priest, the old crosses gave weight to his words, the incense sent me back to my childhood. In the evening, when the lights came on, we burned incense, bowing before the glowing embers in the censor while the smoke sent the mosquitoes to flight. So we were reminded each day of the light inside, the brightest part of ourselves which we had to keep burning into the night. Or at least, I saw it that way; and whenever days went dark, when I fractured my bones, I would think of my future as a fire that was keeping me warm from far away.

When I grew up and entered that future, the meanings began

to change. I knew I came from a community that reached back to the captivity of the Jews in Babylon, from which a Parsee emperor had set them free; to the battle of Thermopylae that Byron had celebrated (he was not on our side). But now the Parsees were dying quicker than they were being born. In two hundred years they would have vanished, like the dodos and the dinosaurs, but to my mind so much more beautiful.

Afterwards, I met the priest who had celebrated the mass.

'Where do you come from?' he asked, and I told him about the book. 'In which of India's many native languages is it to be?' he said, folding his forearms over his tummy. 'The only one I'm literate in,' I answered, and he nodded.

He had come from Durham, where he had studied.

'Oh yes!' I said brightly. 'You have that magnificent cathedral there.'

He shook his head in sorrow. 'That is the Protestant cathedral, my son.'

Back in the taxi, our princely driver said, 'I knows the Brown Tees very well – they lives in Haworth.' But he lost his way. 'What shall we do?' he asked, his young face suddenly miserable.

'Ask for the parsonage,' I suggested.

He brightened, and waited for a young woman to catch up with his car. 'Excuse me,' he shouted, 'where is the parson?'

'On holiday, I think.'

'She is incapable of understanding,' he said. 'Many English are like that – upper storey empty,' and he tapped his forehead.

The next time, I asked, and then we were there. The Brown Tees had obviously never used wheelchairs, but I didn't mind. Every time someone helped me over stairs I told them it was all part of the adventure, the book I was writing. They would be large-eyed with amazement, ask if I'd written anything else, and I'd promptly make a pitch for my novel.

Of course, Charlotte and Emily and Anne could never do that, what with all those male pseudonyms behind which they hid their talent. There, wheeling through their house, I was surprised at how light and ordinary it was. Everything had told me to expect small, dark, haunted rooms with frosted windows; and here I saw the rain-washed garden outside, as if one wall were painted with delicately chosen colours for flowers and a more robust and rampant green. That was the view Emily must have seen as she died on the small black sofa pushed against a wall. Every person who entered the room – the Brontës' dining-room – exclaimed in the many native accents of England, 'This is where Emily died – right here on the sofa.' And sometimes more riveting things like, 'The wallpaper is Laura Ashley, isn't it, dear?' I sat there, in that room, because I couldn't go upstairs and there wasn't much else to see below, except the Parson's study – in that austere room you could see that the Brontës were not rich – and the kitchen with brass weighing scales and a big black stove for the winter evenings. Much later, when I returned to Bombay, I discovered that *Wuthering Heights* had lost its power, had turned into a fantasy in the smiling mouth of a woman living in a large, happy household. So it was always, for me, on this journey around Britain, sudden and unexpected losses that I carried back with me. And with that, strange pieces of understanding, like jagged bits of a jigsaw brought to a room far away from where the puzzle was laid out on a table. What the parsonage told me was how ordered and secure Victorian life had been, and how cruel and oppressive – Charlotte was not allowed, by her father, to marry till she was forty, and then only to die in childbirth.

In one of the village shops, I found Shrewsbury biscuits straight out of my childhood. An Englishwoman had brought the recipe to Poona, where she started a bakery, and every childhood holiday was, for me, sweet with Shrewsbury. My parents would buy me boxes on the day we left, so that back in Bombay I could imagine that the holidays were not yet over.

My attempt at being Heathcliff wandering over the moors was sabotaged by the turnstiles that had no time for wheelchairs, but our taxi-driver was only too happy to take us over and across. As we climbed higher and higher, leaving behind the fields drawn carefully as rectangles in a geometry class, he turned to me and said, 'We only have the God with us now.'

And watching the world fall away, I could shake my head from side to side in an Indian yes.

'Ships!' he said. 'Look at the ships!' but there was no sea in sight.

'Where?' I asked, squinting at the horizon.

'Where are you looking?' He laughed. 'Here on your side – can't you see the ships eating grass?'

'Yes,' I said, covering my mouth, surprise my excuse.

'And kettles.'

'Electric or whistling?' said Juice from behind, but I was watching the sleek, fat cows, so different from India's scrawny but sacred flocks. 'Are you surprised to see so many kettles in the field?' he asked.

'No,' I said. 'In Bombay there are cows on the streets and you have to wait patiently for them to move – they are holy; we often have riots between people who want to eat them and those who want to ban cow-slaughter.'

'Oh yes, I forget,' he said. 'You are Hindu majority.'

The moors were soaring into greater loveliness, with purple heather smudged into the dove-grey stone and trees clutching the hillsides with their old gnarled hands; it was like being on the roof of the world. In the distance was a railway line discreetly folded between steep hills, just like the place in *A Fairly Honourable Defeat* where Peter tells his aunt that he is in love with her; Iris Murdoch would not, I knew, have dreamt that scene in Yorkshire.

We passed a barge drawn by a horse, and I was taken back to the Severn and that unnamed book which had been for me an anaesthetic sent from the English world. But as we left the moors behind, I could think only of an old friend in Bombay who had never been out of the country. 'There are three things to see in England,' she had said to me when I left. 'The Yorkshire moors, Stratford and Madame Tussaud's – all the rest you can miss.'

I frowned at the four Asian men sitting next to me on a bench in Manningham Park. I could see that they were having a ferocious conversation, hands thrusting at each other's chins, noses wrinkling, teeth sucking, and I couldn't understand a word. Perhaps, I thought, they might switch to one of the three Indian languages I understood. Instead, they glared back and walked away, their heavy black shoes flattening the grass.

An oval-faced woman in a pink Punjabi suit smiled, but I couldn't tell if she was smiling at me or her son and daughter who were playing in front of her. I wheeled over and greeted her husband.

'Wisitor?' he said. He had plump dark cheeks and long-lashed eyes pushing their way out.

'Yes, first time in Bradford,' I said.

'Meeting wife and kids – British-born, these are.'

'Oh, really, then you must have lived here a long time.'

'Since my boyness – she only came here on marriage to me. You from London.'

'Oh, no, from India.'

His lashes tickled his cheeks. 'Then how come such good English?'

'School,' I said. 'Your children must have always gone to school here,' I said to his wife.

She rolled her eyes skywards. 'She doesn't speak English,' he said. 'How much I've been telling her learn, learn, she won't listen, she'll only sit and think about her willage.'

'Then I'll talk to her in Hindi,' I said in Hindi.

And as if, after a long and cruel deafness, some doctor had restored her hearing: her eyes switched on, her shoulders came alive, and then her voice emerged, tentative with surprise; this is how my sister might look, I thought, if ever she started to hear.

'You must be from Punjab,' she said. 'Do you know the priest at the *gurudwara*?'

I shook my head, but I knew exactly what she meant . . . some of my older aunts were like that. If they were out of town and met someone who came from Bombay, they would ask him if he bought his medicine from the same corner store as they did. They could not imagine strangeness, too big a gap between their own lives and someone else's. It was, without being cruel, a provincialism of the heart, born of the need to keep everything small enough to fit their hands.

'I'm so unhappy here,' she said. 'No one to talk to, he goes to work, they watch television – '

'Have you been to Haworth?' said Juice, so proud of her idea.

'I'm telling you, she knows nothing about this country,' said her husband.

'Would you like to go back?' I asked her.

She looked at him. 'How can we?' he said.

'Why should we?' asked the daughter, who was about ten.

'We can only farm there,' said the woman. 'And how much money is there in that? You know. And we have relatives – '

'Thousands of pounds flowing, flowing, from here to there – '

'What can we do? Brothers, sisters get married, we have to give televisions, fridge, gold ornaments . . . Still' – she leant forward, her palm upturned in my face – 'they want more.'

'What have you given us, they say,' he said. 'They think we have money growing like grass – ' and he pointed at the lush lawns. 'But we have our home responsibilities. I am working in textiles but I am waiting for him' – he ruffled his son's hair – 'to grow up, then he can help me with a business, shop or something.'

'What about me?' said the daughter, her small hands at her waist. 'I'm going to be in the business too.'

'Look at her,' he said. 'How different – if she were in Punjab would she be talking like this? So much confidence for a girl.'

'And free schools,' said his wife. 'In Punjab, how could we ever have afforded a proper education for them?'

'And here I drive a taxi extra,' he said. 'In Punjab if you are a farmer you are a farmer. You can't be two-three things.'

'I think we will be old here,' said his wife. 'It is not a happy life, but where is it better?'

'My daughter is also disabled,' said the Italian woman on the next bench, when we moved over to her.

'Really? In a wheelchair?'

'Much, much worse – she is disabled in the head.'

'Oh yes, does she go to school?'

'She cannot – she only bangs her head like this,' and she twisted around and hit her forehead against the back of the bench. 'That's all she does. So I leave her and I come here' – by now tears had turned her plump cheeks into waxed apples – 'and sit in the park, and I cry and cry and cry and . . .'

'Cry,' said Juice helpfully, while I thought of my mother and what Carl Bode had said about parents who wonder 'which is worse, God's displeasure in this world or the next'.

Khalid was handsome, his carved Pakistani nose matching the fashionable curve of his haircut. 'I'm not afraid of life here,' he said. 'Not like the others. I can't get a job, so I drive a taxi. Make a hundred quid a week, not bad?' He turned and grimaced. 'When I apply for a job I know they chuck my form into the wastepaper basket – because of my name, you see. Khan, they know an Asian name when they see one.'

'Doesn't that make you furious?'

'Why should it? If I had a business, I would have Muslim boys working for me. They are only looking after their own.'

He took us to the Pakistani community centre. 'I'll wait as long as you need to be inside,' he said.

The man who greeted us was suspicious. 'Why do you want to see our place?' he demanded, impatiently rubbing a fat black moustache. 'Are you doing research or something?'

'Oh no!' said I, wide-eyed. 'I was feeling so homesick, so far away from India, and then one taxi-driver told us about your place. We are like long-lost brothers, Pakistanis and Indians.'

He nodded heavily.

'Tell me,' I said, 'about our people here – '

'We got money to start this from government four years ago – since then we have been doing so much, mainly teaching. You know, for children every day after school, one and a half hours of religion and Urdu – our children are growing up with Muslim culture.'

'Are they quite happy to attend these classes? After school?'

'You know, funny thing – there used to be some reluctance,

then Salman Rushdie wrote that book and everybody got so angry they all came back to religion.'

'So you mean something good actually came out of the Rushdie affair?'

'Strangely, the answer is yes.'

'Did you read the book?'

'No-no, I would never, it would be too painful, we have been hurt too much, our people, by this writing.'

'What do you think should be done about *The Satanic Verses?*'

'Accommodation.'

'What is that?'

'Compromise.'

'What kind of compromise?'

'I cannot say.'

'Do you mean the book should be banned?'

'That could not happen.'

'What could happen?'

'Accommodation.'

I gathered he wanted to change the subject. 'Can I meet some people here?' I asked.

'Only women are around just now – '

'That's fine.'

'They won't see you. They like being left alone, you see. Men make them self-conscious. They are having classes; they like being by themselves.'

I was familiar with this; keeping women in *purdah*, away not just from men but from life. And always the justification for oppression – that this was how the subjugated wanted it. In India, I knew people who said women liked being beaten – they felt it was a mark of their husbands' affection, the proof that men cared enough to do this to them.

'There is one woman,' he said, 'training here, whom you can meet. Firdaus!'

'Yes,' I said, at the same time as a soft voice behind me.

'You have the same name,' he said.

Firdaus was very friendly, willing to talk. Her accent was a surprise – it bore no sound of Pakistan, not the hard d's and t's, nor the rolling vowels. 'I was doing a teacher's training,'

she said, slinging her long black plait over her shoulder. She
was beautiful, with the rose-cream complexion and translucent
hazel eyes of the Punjab. 'Then – I got engaged – '

'A love marriage!' exclaimed Juice, who had stoutly refused
to get arranged into one.

'No, of course not,' said Firdaus. 'An arranged marriage –
to my own cousin.'

'So you must have known him.'

'Yes,' she said. 'I am the most luckiest girl in the world.
Usually girls get married to men they don't know. Not only
have I known him always, but we can meet and talk now that
we are engaged.'

'Do you go out together?'

'Of course not! We meet in the presence of elders. Also, Amir
is very highly educated – that is something wonderful.'

'Really – what has he studied?'

'I don't know – I cannot ask him.'

'Will you work after you are married?'

'That's another great thing – my fiancé and his parents have
agreed that I continue my teacher's training after marriage.
Who would agree to so much?'

And seeing her joy, the small liberation which seemed so
amazing to her, I could only smile and nod. I knew how
tiny triumphs could be and how much they would mean, not
as an achievement but as a signpost to a half-dreamt future.
Firdaus's fiancé, whom we met at a multiracial community
centre, was a humble man working quietly at a typewriter.
He was from Azad Kashmir, he said, Free Kashmir, that part
of the kingdom which Pakistan had within its control and
which in India was called Occupied Kashmir. He had been
there recently and wanted to make a life in Mirpur, the town
he had visited. 'Life is so peaceful there,' he said. 'No worry,
no hurry.'

I was worried for Firdaus. 'Wouldn't you hate it there after
some time, wouldn't you find it small, suffocating?'

He shook his head. 'I find this life suffocating,' he said.
'Rushing all day trying to make money.'

He introduced us to some of the people who worked at

the centre. There was Zaheer Ali, tall, silver-haired, a bit like Cecil Parkinson. He too was from Pakistan, but in his pale blue pin-striped shirt and his suit he might have been English. He was interested in the Parsees, though he didn't know very much about them (neither did I). But it gave me a chance to find out how he felt about being a post-Rushdie Muslim in Bradford.

'It's very clear,' he said. 'We enjoy the benefits of British law and we must take the bad with the good. Rushdie must not be killed in Britain.'

'Do you feel he deserves to be – have you read the book?'

'I have read excerpts in papers – there was a bit about our Prophet's wives being prostitutes. I was nauseated.'

'Most of us read things which make us feel ill – I feel that way when I hear someone praising communism after everything that has happened in this century. But I wouldn't dream of demanding that things like that be banned.'

'But why publish this book? Why write it?'

'I'm sure you can understand that a writer can only write the books inside him, he doesn't choose to write them, in that sense.'

I saw him straightening, as if he knew I was testing his refinement. 'Oh, I understand the meaning of writing,' he said, 'which is why I say that we who enjoy the benefits of life here must keep the law. But, and it is an important but, Rushdie is an apostate, and the Koran says that the punishment for apostasy is death. Now, if Rushdie steps into a country where the laws of the Koran are kept, he must be killed. He will be killed. That is just.'

How clearly he had said it: British laws and Western values were an imposition, a price to be paid for the luxury of living in a capitalist economy. But there was no attachment, no belief in tolerance, for freedom was only an expedient. And how civilised and moderate he sounded asserting only the equivalence of values – in some societies it is all right to kill a man for writing a book, in others it is not. After all, decades of leftism had legitimised the view that values were ethnocentric. The savage had as much right to savagery as Western society to civilisation. And who, the Left had said, had the right to assert their moral superiority? Under that blanket of equivocation, the individual man and woman lay smothered, under sentence of death.

When Mr Chowdhury, round, brown, bespectacled, came into the room I asked Zaheer Ali how Hindus got on with Muslims in Bradford. In India, with its huge Muslim minority, communal riots were almost as common as the Troubles in Ulster, the rage fed by the memories of the Partition of the Empire when millions were killed on both sides. Said Zaheer Ali, 'We are like brothers here – there are no borders in Bradford.'

But no sooner was he out of the room than Mr Chowdhury's voice dropped, his tones turned conspiratorial. 'I'll tell you a secret,' he said. 'I am tired of these Muslims – you can't criticise anything they do, because they pounce on you and call you communal. Me? Communal? Do you know, my father was Hindu but he stayed back in East Pakistan after Partition because he would not leave his patients behind.'

'Why would you want to criticise them?'

'I'll tell you – Asians have contributed so much to the culture of Bradford and now it is very sad to see seventy per cent unemployment among them.' He rolled his eyes, directing my gaze at a young man arranging some files in a corner; he lifted a dozen and walked out.

'I have to be very careful,' said Mr Chowdhury. 'That man there was a Muslim. I'll tell you a secret – all this unemployment is only amongst them. We Hindus have almost zero unemployment. Why? Because we are hardworking and they are backward-looking. If you see their houses, their wives – like servants in torn slippers, with a veil covering their faces, uneducated, no conversation. And children, children – I have one daughter and I won't have any more; my wife is a part-time teacher. We also care about our community – we are importing an idol of Goddess Durga to preserve our tradition. But these people are absurd – all this book-burning nonsense.'

For me, it was difficult to tell how much of this was objective and how much part of the visceral hatred that poisons the subcontinent. After all, Mr Chowdhury had told me that more than two decades after his father's brave decision to stay on, Pakistani troops had tried to kill him as part of their campaign to murder intellectuals and leave destitute the new state of Bangladesh. Such violence was a stranger to my life in Bombay; I knew it existed outside and I knew it travelled only too well.

'Why,' said old Abdul, a Muslim in traditional long beard and loose trousers, 'why should I ever go back to Pakistan? I have land there, but there is killing everywhere, the people say it is their nature. But it isn't, it is only learning from their fathers who have learnt it from theirs. People follow patterns in Pakistan – that is why I am in Bradford. Here our children will make their own patterns.'

I was surprised to hear him talk like this, finding myself guilty as the people he talked about of following patterns I had made in my mind. Something in this old man must have turned his sight away from the old land.

'My daughter,' he said to me, 'has been to France alone.'

And I thought, he is offering me the most shining piece of his thinking, his courage that allows him to send his daughter unescorted into a foreign land. And he wants confirmation, someone to see the price he has paid to be different.

'Please come and spend the night in my house,' he said. 'Why stay in a hotel when you have a friend?' I told him I had paid the hotel to stay that night. 'Next time?' he said. 'You will come back to Bradford, won't you?'

'Yes,' I said. 'Though I never thought I'd want to . . .'

'Live and learn,' said Juice. 'I always do.'

FIFTEEN

Lord Mayor of Leicester

'Plan biscuits, please,' said the man sitting next to me. He had a strange face, with a thick black beard like a battlement and heavy-framed spectacles defending his vulnerable eyes. 'It's strange, here,' he said. 'Pipple can't understand what I say. Now I asked for plan biscuits and she looked as if I had asked for something bad.' He shifted in his seat; I looked at the scenery rushing past like something from a Hollywood studio. 'And it is not as if I am uneducated – I have a degree from Lahore University, Pakistan.' I smiled and nodded. 'You are a-also from that region?'

'Yes,' I said. 'Bombay.'

'Muslim?'

'No, Parsee.'

'I know Parsees – prosperous in Pakistan – one of them manages the Halton Hotel. You must have heard of this – Halton Hotels are placed all over the world.'

'Oh, yes, yes – are you living in England?'

'I got married to a girl here, Muslim of course.'

I remembered a taxi-driver I once had in London. A woman friend had helped me into the car, and as soon as we were off he said to me, 'You think your friend might like to go out with me?' I looked at him to see if he was laughing, but his small, sculpted face was impassive.

'I don't think so,' I said.

'Why not? We could have some fun. Do you know any other girls I could go out with?'

'But you are a Muslim, aren't you? Wouldn't you want a Muslim bride?'

'Only Muslim – but I'm not talking brides now, I'm talking pleasure.' I sat there speechless, abashed by my naïveté.

But the man in the train was asking me about religion. 'Can you eat pork? How many times in a day do you have to pray?'

'I don't pray, I'm an atheist.'

He moved his head sideways as if I had slapped him. 'Why?' he said.

'Because I don't think there is a god.'

'I think you are making big mistake,' he said, blinking his eyes. But later, when I was writing a letter, he looked over my shoulder and said, 'Such wonderful handwriting – I wish I could write like that.' Watching my scrawl, which sends my typist screaming to her optician, I wondered what he meant. Then he said, 'I wish I had your English – you can get on in two worlds. That is a doubling of life.'

At Leicester Station there was an old woman with the most dreadful limp walking alongside my chair; every time she put her right foot forward it wiggled uncertainly from the ankle before flopping down. 'Can I use the lift, please?' she asked, pointing at the sign which said 'For Disabled Passengers Only'. When we reached the street she began to walk smartly away from the station, looking back once to wink at me.

The taxi-driver was white – a surprise after Bradford – and fat. When I asked him about the Asians who make up almost a fourth of Leicester's population he said, 'Do you want the truth or a lot of rubbish?'

'Or I wouldn't have asked.'

'Too many,' he said. 'Just too many of – look, I don't mean any offence. Individually they are as nice as you or the lady in the back, but put together they are taking away jobs, making money and sending it home – '

'It is their money, they have made it – '

'That's not the point. You live in a community, you give

239

back to the community; these people, they'll do anything to
save a bit of money – a dozen of them will live in one house,
if they have a car they'll pack it till it bursts.'

'What do you think should be done about this?'

'Stop them. Just stop them in their tracks wherever they
are, Pakistan, India. You can't talk like this to people, they
say it's racist – what do they know about living with Asians?
You know, there are places in the south where they never see
a black face. It's easy for them to talk, isn't it. And Labour –
Labour is in power here in Leicester – they give in to every
demand from the Asians.'

'Why don't people vote in the Conservatives?'

'They're no good,' he said. 'They crush all the little people –
black or white.'

The next day I went to see the ex-Mayor, Gordon Palmer –
that is what people called him. He was of Indian origin and
his name was actually Giordhan Parmar. He lived in what the
novels I used to read in Bombay would have described as a neat
row of terraced houses. When we went in, we found he wasn't
at home. But his wife was, and I heard her speaking Gujarati
to an old woman sitting in front of a silent television set.

'I speak Gujarati too,' I said to her, and after that we didn't
stop talking. She was a beautiful woman in a red and white
chiffon saree, with glossy black hair coiled in a bun. She was
from Kenya, she had married her husband when he was in
Tanzania. Then they had moved to Britain.

'From the very start, I worked,' she said. 'And we earned
every penny we spent. Not a pound from the state, we bought
our own house, brought up our children, got so many relatives
over and helped them to make a start – that's my sister.'

A plainer version of herself had walked into the room. She
smiled in surprise when I said I was from India. 'We have just
been there,' she said. 'For a long holiday – it was so beautiful
except – ' Her sister laughed and nodded. 'Except the toilets,'
she said. 'We couldn't live with the toilets.'

'Frankly,' said Mrs Parmar, 'nor could I – they were so
filthy.'

I nodded, but I knew how difficult it was to be clean

240

when you didn't have even a change of clothes or water to wash in.

'We were there,' she said, 'to visit the Mayor of Rajkot, in Gujarat – that's my husband's original home town. The Mayor was a very strange man, he would only take us to visit rich people. Sometimes we got away and met ordinary people, poor people.' I like the way she put the simple equation of Indian life.

'Is it difficult, as an Indian woman, to work here?'

'No, you can get jobs – I work in a school with parents and teachers. We, Indian women, especially from East Africa, are doing very well – it's the Pakistani women who still don't go out to work.'

Giordhan Parmar, when he came in, was alight with charm, smiling, moving his small frame easily. He had a moustache, and bright black eyes.

'Oh yes, I remember every bit of my childhood in India,' he said, 'though we left for Tanzania when I was ten.'

'And why did you leave Tanzania?'

'The political climate was not good.'

I thought of Nyerere and his socialism that had ruined the once prosperous country. 'You mean economic failure?'

'Oh, no, no.'

'Then what was it?'

'Just generally – I had to leave.' And I thought, he cannot condemn socialism even when it does not work. 'I came here and I became a bus conductor and I joined the Transport and General Workers' Union – and I was always with the Labour Party. I became a county councillor and then a city councillor. Then they wanted me to become Mayor, but I refused. I felt I wasn't ready; so I became High Bailiff and I'd be with the Mayor most of the time.'

'Then,' said his wife, smiling and raising her eyebrows, 'he became Lord Mayor of Leicester – let me get the photographs.' I smiled; this was just like my parents, who were always getting the photo albums out for strangers to see.

'See that chain I'm wearing,' she said, 'full of gold and diamonds.' A little while before she had told me about the jewellery shops that sparkled down the main street where they lived. Jewels and precious metals are an old Indian obsession – substance, unshakable in its value, solid amidst a history of invasion and communal strife. How often I had heard my neighbours in Bombay talk about how they fled to India after Partition with nothing but little packets of diamonds sewn into their clothes, the only wealth they had been able to rescue from a life of fine houses and rich lands and thriving trade.

'What I was very proud of,' said Giordhan Parmar, 'was that white people supported me so well when I was Mayor. I was not just the Asian candidate.' He pointed at a picture of a gleeful little boy. 'I met him on a visit to a hospital and I promised him a drive in the Lord Mayor's car if he got well. When he got home he phoned me and I kept my promise.'

'And the endoscopy – ' said the wife.

'Yes, I raised an appeal for a hundred thousand pounds to start an endoscopy unit – and it overshot its target.'

'So they've named it after him.'

Their happiness was infectious, but I had to move to less pleasant things. 'What do you think of the state of the Labour Party today?'

'We are going to form the next government.' And he nodded and stamped his smile on his words.

'What about the hard Left?'

'Those policies are not what the electorate want.'

'But they represent a pure socialism – if Labour moves away from that it moves away from its ideals.'

'But what is the purpose of offering policies nobody wants? And anyway, I don't consider the hard Left a separate group; we're all part of the Labour Party.'

'But once you're elected, will you go back to the policies the people don't want but Labour wants?'

'Certainly not.'

'In that case, won't the hard Left make trouble – or do you feel they'll keep quiet because they have nowhere to go?'

'They can always form a separate party and become irrelevant like the SDP.'

I asked him about racism.

'The situation was very bad when I first came here – if you were Asian the only jobs you could get were clerical jobs. But after the Labour government passed the Race Relations Act in 1968 things began to change. And in Leicester we have an equal opportunities policy which private firms promise to follow – I don't know how many of them do.'

'And in the last ten years?'

'Thatcher encouraged racism, she came to power in seventy-nine because of that speech she gave about people feeling swamped – '

'I thought she won that election because Labour had done such a bad job.'

'Certainly not – it was her racist remarks that made her popular.'

I wondered if he believed this or if it was the Party line, a collective self-delusion to make defeat, the long loss of power, bearable.

He walked us to the main street. 'I'm going to have a beer,' he said. And I felt curiously happy to see how comfortable he was in this way of life, how different from so many others like him, for whom Britain was a place of loss.

I could have seen the street I was wheeling through in Bombay, I thought to myself, though it would not be as prosperous or clean. But there were the jewellery shops and the saree-clad mannequins in the display windows, their plastic hair moulded into elaborate coils, dark eyes elongated with kohl. When I was a boy, keeping my secret of bad eyesight, I had once entered a shop in my father's arms and said a loud hello to the woman waiting with hands folded in greeting, only to be met by her unblinking stare while my father laughed at what he thought was my sense of fun.

We went to the Sharmilee sweetmeat shop, and though the name means Shy the music playing there was not. It was an old song from a Hindi film and the singer, with a leer in his voice, sang:

You are the queen of my heart
You are the princess of my body.

So that the words, familiar from the festivals of my childhood, loud from the bazaars, informing my little life of another and tawdry world, made me ache for the home I had never made my own.

SIXTEEN

Our Lady of Grantham

'Going to worship at the shrine,' growled Liz Calder when she saw that I had included Grantham in my itinerary. There was that, of course – a trip around Britain had to include the birthplace of the woman who had helped to shape the culture I had come to, at the tail-end of the eighties. But the real purpose of my visit was to see and perhaps understand what Margaret Thatcher came out of, and that, I believed, would tell me more about her than all the books I could read.

When we got to Grantham and its clean little station there was someone to help us – a pale, handsome man with the stern lips of a Puritan from my Ladybird book on Oliver Cromwell. I asked him the inevitable question, to which he replied with a snort. But then, as we were crossing the railway tracks, he said, 'She is no good – for Grantham or anywhere else. And nobody likes her, nobody.'

But the taxi-driver outside did. He was like a pink rabbit, with translucent ears and protruding teeth. 'You can't believe how proud people feel that she comes from here. I don't think we've had a prime minister like her since I was born.'

At the Shirley Croft hotel where we were staying the beds weren't ready, so we sat in the dark little bar munching ham sandwiches and talking to a couple surrounded by children. 'That's her little boy,' said the man, Bob, 'and my daughters.

We have to look after them, so we thought we'd have an outing.'

He was envious that we were from India. 'You can live there for three months on five hundred pounds,' he said.

'If you make five hundred pounds,' I said.

'Yes – I'm talking of travellers. I'm going very soon. Things are going well here – jobs, money, aren't difficult like they used to be. And the dole queues don't come down – you know why?'

Juice nodded wearily.

'Cheating,' he said. 'Signing on and staying there.'

When we went to the tourist office asking about Mrs Thatcher's school and birthplace, the woman there said, 'Of course, you're not from Britain. It's funny, we get admirers from everywhere, Germany, America, even India. But almost never from Britain.'

You could interpret that in two ways, I thought: some would say that only people who lived through the Thatcher years could know the full horror; others that no patient likes a doctor who makes him live in a whole new way – and anyway, even if they liked her, Britons were hardly the type to go looking for her birthplace.

There was an interview with Thatcher on video at the tourist office. She was talking about her childhood, so determined by rectitude and reason: 'How one longed for something that was not serviceable!' There was an unintended gaffe. She had been brought up, she said, to believe that cleanliness was next to godliness. And a little later, talking about buying furnishing material, she said she wouldn't pick the pretty one – 'The dirt will show.' Did that mean dirt was all right so long as it didn't?

But perhaps I was quibbling – what came through, what surprised me, used as I was to politicians who never believed a word of what they said, was that not only did she speak with conviction, but that her beliefs had been thought about and argued through.

And then there were the tears when she quoted her father, who had been Mayor and Alderman and had been turned out by a Labour council: 'In honour I put on this gown, in honour I set it down.' I remembered those words on that amazing November morning, more than a year later, when I woke to the words, 'She is standing down!'

That day in Grantham, seeing the order of the little town, not a leaf out of place, the weight of school and church, I grasped for the first time the antipathy to Margaret Thatcher that rippled through Britain. There was the upbringing, disciplined, solid, carefully aimed towards a future – quite unlike that of the mass of people in Britain, tangled in divorce and unbelief. And this was Thatcher's vision, the strong and hard as polished wood vision that she pointed at again and again: this, she said, is what your lives must become, what you must be.

I could see the value of that vision, having known both the folly of an unthinking culture and the stability, the inner balance, that a middle-class upbringing had granted me, and which stood me in such good stead even when I wandered away from it. But Britons have a different picture of themselves; their hand-held mirrors show someone decent and kind, but not very stubborn on convictions, giving way to make life easier for everyone, rejecting ideas as the mainstay of a future or of success. Reality being what it is, ideas and a coherent philosophy proved their power when they were done away with in a consensus that considered them divisive, and slowly, inexorably, dragged Britain into bankruptcy.

When Thatcher came, she came with a philosophy, and when she won election after election, perhaps she mistook those victories for an acceptance of her ideas. There was very little of that. Her philosophy was humbug for most people; it did not go with what they saw in those mirrors; it did not go with British civilisation as it had evolved, a gentler Western version of Japanese compromise and social control. They voted for Thatcher because they needed someone to make life better, to make the world, as it were, work again. They wanted her for what she could do and not for what she believed. That there was a crucial connection between the two – that without both philosophy and determination Margaret Thatcher could not have corrected the chronic leftward scoliosis of the

British spine – was not something Britons, at large, could ever accept.

The bitter demonology that surrounded Thatcher emerged from outrage at her perceived failures and, more accurately, out of the change that the new, undeniably better, life which Thatcherism brought to so many demanded from them. It was the most dangerous change to demand from anybody – a change in self-image. Britons were being asked to admit that they wanted more money, that risk, competition and even failure are part of success, that being decent is not a substitute for working hard, that welfare benefits come not from a mythical state but from the pockets of those who work for their money.

It was a dangerous enterprise that Margaret Thatcher undertook, and in a fundamental sense she seems to have failed. Money, in Britain, remains a dirty word, an unpleasant necessity; and the idea that everything the state provides is paid for by somebody has yet to percolate into most minds. On the other hand, the natural human reaching for a better life, has, for the first time, received not only recognition but legitimacy from government, so that greed, if that is what the impulse to live in houses instead of huts is called, is good at last. And there, perhaps, lies the best hope for Britain's long-term success. People who reject Thatcher's philosophy remember the psychological possibilities it has opened up to them – wanting something and knowing that they can have it if they earn and save in an economy where earning and saving is becoming easier. And that might lead them back to the ideas which made the huge leap in British standards of living so real in the eighties.

But that could only be in another time. On that morning of Mrs Thatcher's resignation, thinking of my own country and how much it needed someone like her to break the obsolete machines of statism, I could feel only bitterness. And if it is a truism that people get the leaders they deserve, I could not help thinking that they also lose the leaders they have done nothing to earn.

'Knew Margaret Roberts, I did,' said the woman we met in Dysart Park that day.

'How did that happen?'

'Her father and mine trained for grocery together.'

'And what did you think of her?'

She snorted. 'Liked her sister better – that's all I'll say.'

The old man looking after the car park was willing to say something more. 'I'd like to see her in hell – and I'll give up a year's wages to pay her way there.'

'That won't be enough – Margaret Thatcher is a long way from hell.'

'If you think so, I pity you.'

'What about Asians?' I said, ashamed at having abandoned my neutrality. 'Do you think they are making Britain a better place?'

'Worse – and pardon me for saying that to you. They are eating up the country, jobs, everything. And now they want to let the Chinks in – the ones from Hong Kong. What for? I know we had an empire and all that, but we taught them things, didn't we?'

That was an unusual, or at least unspoken, view in Britain. At meeting after meeting, breast-beating Britons would apologise to me for what they had done in India – 'taken away your freedom, ruined your country'. How much, I would wonder, and sometimes ask, did they know of Indian history? Of the feudal tyrannies, the anarchy, the pillage and war that prevailed there when the East India Company began to stretch its hungry fingers into the land.

Later that evening Juice and I had dinner in the house where Margaret Thatcher was born. The shop in front had been kept as it was, with brown boxes of tea and sugar and tin of McVitie's biscuits.

'I never discuss politics,' said the tall man with the blond moustache who owned what was now the Première Restaurant. I had asked him if he was a Thatcherite. 'I discovered very early that it was no good talking about that to my clients.' He was in a hurry that day – the cook had had a fall and he was managing alone. But when the food arrived, I said, 'Everyone who reads *Heaven on Wheels* has to know this is the best place I have eaten at.' There was a raspberry sorbet with melon drowned in Drambuie, followed by duck in peach and honey, and to finish a crème brûlée with warm cream and a cold lemon sorbet inside.

And in my silly, sentimental way it pleased me to think of the excellence I found in the place where Our Lady of Grantham was born.

SEVENTEEN

Cambridge: an inspiration beyond cliché

Cambridge was my metaphor for England, and it was strange that when I left it it had become altogether something else, because I had met Stephen Hawking there.

Strangely, though, when I went there I was thinking not of him but of another best-selling writer, Jeffrey Archer, who lived in Rupert Brooke's house in the Old Vicarage, Grantchester. When we went there we saw the gardener laying out chairs on the lawns for the one-man play on Rupert Brooke that was to be staged there that afternoon. So we wandered off to see the church clock, which had been freed from its captivity at ten to three; perhaps someone had read the Muriel Spark novel where the heroine feels sickened by the soggy nostalgia of the arthritic church clock.

When we got back to the Vicarage we discovered that the gardener was Jeffrey Archer and were reminded of the un-Indian fact that a squire can carry chairs. And squire he was that day, smiling and teasing the women who were queuing up to buy tickets. 'Where did you find that, dear?' pointing at a funnel of a hat. 'Where do you come from? Arizona? Who has ever heard of a place like that?'

Later, I had a word with him. 'Why,' I said, 'are the Conservatives unable to put across a message that is moral as well as pragmatic?'

'I'm trying to do something about that – I'm going round

the country lecturing at universities.' I hope he missed the size to which my eyes had grown. 'I'm trying to sell my wife's book,' he said, holding up a copy of Mary Archer's book on their house. 'Five pounds,' he shouted, 'only five pounds.' I began to wonder if my Thatcherism was dissolving before this sight. 'Well,' he said, 'I've talked to you, now I must make money. That's what being Conservative is about, isn't it.' I nodded and, perhaps because I was snubbed, I thought how strangely unreal, he seemed, two-dimensional – much like his novels . . .

The sun poured redundant gold on the blond head of the actor who was playing Rupert Brooke. Together, he and the house in the background recreated all the confusion of love and talent and self-disgust that makes Brooke's photograph almost as powerful as his poetry. For me, there was also the longing, the dry nights in India when I had read:

Ah God! to see the branches stir
Across the moon at Grantchester!

More powerful, and fake, than that was the sonnet that was actually being spoken; the words were torn from my life, even if my head knew it wasn't true, it wasn't true. But this is what I would say even now, at the end of my time in Britain:

If I should die, think only this of me:
That there's some corner of a foreign field
That is for ever England.

I was weeping and laughing at the thought of how un-English I was being when I looked out of the corner of my eye at the woman sitting next to me. She was straight-backed, her face serene, while from her eyes the tears marched quietly, with dignity. And then she turned to me and smiled, and we nodded at each other.

It was on a walking tour through Cambridge that the guide mentioned Stephen Hawking, 'poor man, who is quite disabled now, though he is a worthy successor to Issac Newton, whose chair he has at the university.'

And I started, because I had quite forgotten that this most brilliant and completely paralysed astrophysicist, the author of *A Brief History of Time*, one of the biggest best-sellers ever, lived here. But there wasn't much time to think. It was a peculiar kind of walking tour where we were ambushed at irregular intervals by disorienting figures like a bow-legged Henry VIII ('But he had a fine leg,' I wanted to say, as usual showing off) and an ersatz Elizabeth I who asked me to be one of her courtiers because she liked my bright eye, while I wondered how one bowed from a wheelchair.

When the tour was done, I rushed to a phone booth and, almost tearing the cord so it could reach me outside, phoned Stephen Hawking's house. There was his assistant on the line and I told him I had come in a wheelchair from India (perhaps he thought I had propelled myself all the way) to write about my travels in Britain. I had to see Professor Hawking – even ten minutes would do. 'Half an hour,' he said. 'From three-thirty to four.'

And suddenly I felt weak all over. Growing up disabled, you get fed up with people asking you to be brave, as if you have a courage account on which you are too lazy to draw a cheque. The only thing that makes you stronger is seeing somebody like you, achieving something huge. Then you know how much is possible and you reach out further than you ever thought you could.

'I haven't been brave,' said his disembodied computer-voice, the next afternoon. 'I've had no choice.'

Surely, I wanted to say, living creatively with the reality of his disintegrating body was a choice? But I kept quiet, because I felt guilty every time I spoke to him, forcing him to respond. There he was, tapping at the little switch in his hand, trying to find the words on his computer with the only bit of movement left to him, his long, pale fingers. Every so often his eyes would shut in frustrated exhaustion. And sitting opposite him I could feel his anguish, the mind buoyant with thoughts that came out in frozen phrases and sentences stiff as corpses.

'A lot of people seem to think that disabled people are chronically unhappy,' I said. 'I know that's not true myself. Are you often laughing inside?'

About three minutes later, he responded, 'I find it amusing when people patronise me.'

'And do you find it annoying when someone like me comes and disturbs you in your work?'

The answer flashed. 'Yes.' Then he smiled his one-way smile and I knew, without being sentimental or silly, that I was looking at one of the most beautiful men in the world.

A first glimpse of him is shocking, because he is like a still photograph – as if all those pictures of him in magazines and newspapers have turned three-dimensional.

Then you see the head twisted sideways into a slump, the torso shrunk inside the pale blue shirt, the wasted legs; you look at his eyes which can speak, still, and they are saying something huge and urgent – it is hard to tell what. But you are shaken because you have seen something you never thought could be seen.

Before you, like a lantern whose walls are worn so thin you glimpse only the light inside, is the incandescence of a man. The body, almost irrelevant, exists only like a case made of shadows. So that I, no believer in eternal souls, know that this is what each of us is; everything else an accessory.

'What do you think is the best thing about being disabled?' I had asked him earlier.

'I don't think there is anything good about being disabled.'

'I think,' I said, 'you do discover how much kindness there is in the world.'

'Yes,' he said; it was a disadvantage of his voice synthesiser that it could convey no inflection, no shades or tone. And I could not tell how enthusiastically he agreed with me.

Every time I shifted in my chair or turned my wrist to watch the time – I wanted to make every one of our thirty minutes count – I felt a huge relief and exhilaration in the possibilities of my body. How little it mattered then that I would never walk, or even stand.

I told him how he had been an inspiration beyond cliché for me, and, surely, for others – did that thought help him?

'No,' he said; and I thought how foolish I was to ask. When your body is a claustrophobic room and the walls are growing narrower day by day, it doesn't do much good to know that there are people outside smiling with admiration to see you breathing still.

'Is there any advice you can give disabled people, something that might help make life better?'

'They should concentrate on what they are good at; I think things like the Disabled Olympics are a waste of time.'

'I know what you mean.' I remembered the years I'd spent trying to play a Spanish guitar considerably larger than I was; and how gleefully I had unstringed it one night.

The half-hour was up. 'I think I've annoyed you enough,' I said, grinning. 'Thank you for . . .'

'Stay.' I waited. 'Have some tea. I can show you the garden.'

The garden was as big as a park, but Stephen Hawking covered every inch, rumbling along in his motorised wheelchair while I dodged to keep out of the way. We couldn't talk very much; the sun made him silent, the letters on his screen disappearing in the glare.

An hour later, we were ready to leave. I didn't know what to do. I could not kiss him or cry. I touched his shoulder and wheeled out into the summer evening. I looked back; and I knew he was waving, though he wasn't. Watching him, an embodiment of my bravest self, the one I was moving towards, the one I had believed in for so many years, alone, I knew that my journey was over. For now.

A NOTE ON THE AUTHOR

Firdaus Kanga was born in Bombay where he lives and works as a writer and journalist.